**Whitestein Series in Software Agent Technologies and Autonomic Computing**

Series Editors:
Marius Walliser
Stefan Brantschen
Monique Calisti
Stefan Schinkinger

This series reports new developments in agent-based software technologies and agent-oriented software engineering methodologies, with particular emphasis on applications in the area of autonomic computing and communications.

The spectrum of the series includes research monographs, high quality notes resulting from research and industrial projects, outstanding Ph.D. theses, and the proceedings of carefully selected conferences. The series is targeted at promoting advanced research and facilitating know-how transfer to industrial use.

**About Whitestein Technologies**

Whitestein Technologies is a leading innovator in the area of software agent technologies and autonomic computing and communications. Whitestein Technologies' offering includes advanced products, solutions, and services for various applications and industries, as well as a comprehensive middleware for the development and operation of autonomous, self-managing, and self-organizing systems and networks.
Whitestein Technologies' customers and partners include innovative global enterprises, service providers, and system integrators, as well as universities, technology labs, and other research institutions.

www.whitestein.com

# Emerging Web Services Technology

Cesare Pautasso
Christoph Bussler
Editors

Editors:

Cesare Pautasso
IBM Research GmbH
Zurich Research Laboratory
Saeumerstrasse 4
CH-8803 Rueschlikon
Switzerland
c.pautasso@ieee.org

Christoph Bussler
BEA Systems, Inc.
475 Sansome Street
San Francisco, CA 94111
USA
chris.bussler@oracle.com

2000 Mathematical Subject Classification: 68U35, 68N17, 68T05, 68T27

Library of Congress Control Number: 2007929515

Bibliographic information published by Die Deutsche Bibliothek
Die Deutsche Bibliothek lists this publication in the Deutsche Nationalbibliografie;
detailed bibliographic data is available in the Internet at <http://dnb.ddb.de>.

ISBN 978-3-7643-8447-0 Birkhäuser Verlag AG, Basel – Boston – Berlin

© 2007 Birkhäuser Verlag, P.O. Box 133, CH-4010 Basel, Switzerland
Part of Springer Science+Business Media
Printed on acid-free paper produced from chlorine-free pulp. TCF ∞
Printed in Germany

# Contents

## I. Opening Keynote

## II. Service Management

## III. Model Driven Engineering for Web Service Composition and Discovery

## IV. Mobile Services

## V. Web Service Technology Challenges

# Preface

The Workshop on Emerging Web Services Technology (WEWST06) took place in conjunction with the 4th European Conference on Web Services (ECOWS'06) on 4th December 2006, in Zurich, Switzerland.

Acting as the natural extension to the main ECOWS conference, the main goal of the WEWST workshop is serving as a forum for providing early exposure and much needed feedback to grow and establish original and emerging ideas within the Web Services community. The wide variety of tools, novel techniques and emerging technological solutions presented in WEWST share one common feature: they advance the current Web services research in new directions by introducing new and sometimes controversial ideas into the field.

WEWST focuses on research contributions advancing the state of the art in Web services technologies in the following areas: Model Driven Engineering for SOA, Mobility and Services, Streaming Services and Event Driven Architectures, Dynamic Web Service Discovery and Composition, Lightweight Orchestration Engines, SLA Creation and Service Delivery, Semantic Web, Managing Change and Service Evolution, Business Driven Development, Service-Oriented Grid Computing Middleware, Business Process Management for Web Services, Software and Service Engineering. WEWST covers the whole spectrum which makes it a very important part of ECOWS.

We would like to thank the authors of the papers for their submissions and for their contribution to the timely preparation of these proceedings, as well as for their high quality presentations and lively discussions during the workshop. In particular, we would like to thank Jürgen Angele for accepting to present a well received keynote on the topic: 'Ontoprise: Semantic Web Technologies at Business' showcasing a very important example of an emerging Web services technology. We would also like to thank Monique Calisti and Whitestein Technologies AG, for the invaluable support in finding a suitable venue for publishing the workshop proceedings and Stefan Schinkinger from Birkhauser Publishing Ltd. for fast tracking the WEWST proceedings through the publication process. And, last but not least, we would like to thank the ECOWS conference organizers (Thomas Gschwind, Abraham Bernstein, and Wolf Zimmermann) for their trust and availability to make this workshop a success.

*Cesare Pautasso, Christoph Bussler*
Program Chairs WEWST06

Rüschlikon - San Jose
April 2007

# Organization

## Program Chairs

Cesare Pautasso, IBM Research, Switzerland
Christoph Bussler, BEA Systems, San Francisco, USA

## Program Committee

Farhad Arbab, CWI, The Netherlands
Luciano Baresi, Politecnico di Milano, Italy
Steven Battle, Hewlett-Packard Labs
Boualem Benatallah, University of New South Wales, Australia
Abraham Bernstein, University of Zurich, Switzerland
Walter Binder, EPFL, Switzerland
David Breitgand, IBM Research, Israel
Geoffrey Coulson, Lancaster University, UK
Theo Dimitrakos, BT, UK
Jürgen Dunkel, FH Hannover, Germany
Schahram Dustdar, TU Wien, Austria
David Eyers, University of Cambridge, UK
Dieter Fensel, University of Innsbruck and DERI, Austria
Ioannis Fikouras, Ericsson, Germany
Bogdan Franczyk, Leipzig University, Germany
Christian Geuer-Pollmann, Microsoft, Germany
Chris Giblin, IBM Zurich Research Lab, Switzerland
Paul Grefen, Eindhoven University of Technology, The Netherlands
John Grundy, University of Auckland, New Zealand
Thomas Gschwind, IBM Zurich Research Lab, Switzerland
Manfred Hauswirth, Digital Enterprise Research Institute, Galway
Reiko Heckel, University of Leicester, UK
Martin Henkel, Stockholm University, Sweden
Alexander Keller, IBM Research, USA
Christoph Kiefer, Universität Zürich, Switzerland
Nik Klever, University of Applied Sciences, Germany
Birgitta Koenig-Ries, University of Jena, Germany
Ernö Kovacs, NEC Europe Network Labs, Germany
Jochen Küster, IBM Research, Switzerland
Frank Leymann, University of Stuttgart, Germany
Welf Löwe, Växjö Universitet, Sweden
Ronald Maier, Universität Halle, Germany
Ingo Melzer, DaimlerChrysler Research, Germany
Jean-Philippe Martin-Flatin, NetExpert, Switzerland
Rainer Neumann, PTV, Germany

# Introduction

No single event could completely capture the current flurry of research and development activities related to Service Oriented Architecture and Web Services. These proceedings of the first Workshop of Emerging Web Services Technology 2006 attempt to gather outstanding research achievements cutting across a wide, but representative set of emerging technologies: semantic Web services, service management, model-driven engineering for service composition and discovery, mobile services, and challenges such as change management and successful standardization. Accordingly, the proceedings have been organized into five different parts, one for each topic of the workshop contributions.

Part I opens the proceedings with the keynote given by Jürgen Angele, discussing the challenges that emerging semantic Web technologies are facing during their transition from academic prototypes into industrial products.

Part II covers several aspects of service management. It begins with a paper by Thilina Gunarathne, Dinesh Premalal, Tharanga Wijethilake, Indika Kumara and Anushka Kumar presenting a lightweight approach to the design of service composition engines. Whereas most existing BPEL (Business Process Execution Language) engines are complex platforms with heavy weight deployment requirements, the authors have shown how to radically simplify such an engine so that it becomes embeddable, delivers better performance and becomes much easier to manage. Performance optimization in service delivery is also the topic of the second paper, by Nicolas Repp, Rainer Berbner, Oliver Heckmann and Ralf Steinmetz. This position paper advocates a holistic approach to Web service performance monitoring. The authors show how to diagnose performance problems by taking a snapshot of key indicators across the entire communication stack so that more detailed information can be fed, e.g., into the planning component of a service orchestration engine. Service Level Agreements (SLAs) are also a very important aspect of Service Management. In the third paper, Halina Kaminski and Mark Perry propose to use intelligent agents to automatically create such agreements. As an alternative between the reuse of fixed boilerplate agreements and the costly manual negotiation of customized SLAs, the authors propose to automatically create SLAs using agent-based negotiation starting from a set of Service Level Objectives. Giving a good definition to Quality of Service is of paramount importance for properly managing Web services in production. Christian Schröpfer, Marten Schönherr, Philipp Offermann and Maximilian Ahrens attack the problem of defining non-functional properties for semantic Web services. In their paper, OWL-S (the Web Ontology Language for Services) is extended to support modeling of service lifecycle information and Quality of Service guarantees.

Part III is devoted to model-driven engineering applied to service composition and discovery. With the goal of raising the level of abstraction of current languages and tools, the first paper by Ricardo Quintero, Victoria Torres and

Vicente Pelechano argues that both structural (static) and behavioral (dynamic) aspects need to be combined. In particular, the paper extends the Object-Oriented Web Solutions methodology to drive the generation of BPEL code from high level conceptual models. The same methodology is also extended in the second paper, where Marta Ruiz and Vicente Pelechano deal with the design of Web service interfaces. The authors present a comprehensive solution to obtain well-designed Web services. Taking into account the requirements of model-driven service composition, the third paper is about service discovery, also a fundamental challenge of Service Oriented Architectures. In this paper, Adina Sîrbu, Ioan Toma and Dumitru Roman present a logic-based, formal discovery model based on capability matching that is meant to be integrated with service composition.

Part IV focuses on services and mobility. The first paper by Elena Sánchez-Nielsen, Sandra Martín-Ruiz and Jorge Rodríguez-Pedrianes addresses the problem of consuming Web services from resource-limited, mobile client devices. The authors present and evaluate the design of a concrete prototype based on dynamic proxies. The second paper introduces a set of software metrics for observing mobile service-oriented systems and effectively measuring their runtime efficiency. The authors (Pablo Rossi and Zahir Tari) show how such metrics can be used to perform service migration decisions.

Part V concludes the proceedings with two different technology challenges. The first is about dealing with changes of Web service interfaces through dynamic client adaptation. In this context, Mehdi Ben Hmida, Céline Boutrous Saab, Serge Haddad, Valérie Monfort and Ricardo Tomaz Ferraz apply Aspect Oriented Programming techiques to modify BPEL service compositions at run-time. The second challenge is related to current Web service standardization trends. The paper of Tosca Lahiri and Mark Woodman takes a critical look at the progress and the quality of current Web service standardization efforts.

Whitestein Series in Software Agent Technologies, 1–2

# Ontoprise:
# Semantic Web Technologies at Business

Jürgen Angele

In former days Tim Berners-Lee proposed a soon breakthrough of the Semantic Web. As a breakthrough he considered every second web page to be connected to an ontology. In the mean time we have seen a lot of applications of semantic technologies, like semantic web services, semantic information integration, and ontology based search for documents. However it seems also clear that the forecast of TBL did not (yet) arrive. While in the last years there has always been great academic interest in Semantic Web and in semantic technologies and even first industrial products appeared, we did not see the industrial breakthrough of Semantic Web technologies. On the other hand there was a strong increasing interest in other trends like SOA architectures, Web 2.0 etc. which ruled out Semantic Web in publicity and in connected activities like new product developments, foundations of new companies, and money involved. The question arises what are the reasons for that and which of these newer trends could have an influence on the further development of semantic technologies. While so far the Semantic Web was driven to a large extent from the academic side, its future acceptance and relevance to the industrial world heavily depends on whether the future development of Semantic Web technologies is influenced by industry needs rather than pure academic ones. This becomes essential and will decide whether semantic technologies are considered as relevant technology and will be used in future industrial applications and products. In actual industry applications, it was proved that the combination of trendy topics like SOA and Web 2.0 with intelligent features of semantic technologies generates large impact for the industrial and business world and thereof - the breakthrough of the Corporate Semantic Web. The keynote illustrated present work, proposals and requirements which will lead us to the next wave of semantic technology impact.

Prof. Dr. Jürgen Angele is currently CEO, CTO and shareholder of Ontoprise GmbH, a provider of semantic technologies. Ontoprise has been co-founded by him in 1999. In 1994 he became a full professor in applied computer science at the University of Applied Sciences, Braunschweig, Germany. From 1989 to 1994 he was a research and teaching assistant at the University of Karlsruhe, Institute AIFB. He did research on the execution of the knowledge acquisition and representation language KARL, which led to a Ph.D. (Dr. rer. pol.) from the University of Karlsruhe in 1993. From 1985 to 1989 he worked for the companies AEG, Konstanz, Germany, and SEMA GROUP, Ulm, Germany. He received the diploma degree in computer science in 1985 from the University of Karlsruhe. He published around 90 papers as books and journal, book, conference, and workshop contributions. Topics were about semantic web, semantic technologies, knowledge representation, and their practical applications. He is leading several research and commercial projects. He gave more than 55 courses at Berufsakademien, Fachhochschulen and Universities. Topics were about: Expert Systems, Software Engineering, World Wide Web, Database Systems, Digital Image Analysis, Computer Graphics, Mathematics. He supervised around 30 master and Ph.D. theses.

Jürgen Angele
ontoprise GmbH
Amalienbadstr. 36
D-76227 Karlsruhe
e-mail: angele@ontoprise.de

Whitestein Series in Software Agent Technologies, 3–20

# BPEL-Mora: Lightweight Embeddable Extensible BPEL Engine

Thilina Gunarathne, Dinesh Premalal, Tharanga Wijethilake, Indika Kumara, Anushka Kumar

**Abstract.** Web Services have become the de-facto standard for architecting and implementing business collaborations within and across organization boundaries. Web service composition refers to the creation of new (Web) services by combining the functionalities provided by existing ones. A process-oriented language for service composition has been proposed as BPEL4WS. BPEL4WS specification defines an XML based formal language and provides a general overview of the framework. However no design and implementation issues are described in it. Most of the available BPEL4WS compliant process engines are heavy weight, complex and not extensible. This paper describes the design and implementation of an embeddable, scalable and extensible BPEL4WS compliant process engine. This paper highlights the concepts and strategies that were followed during the design and implementation. Primary contribution of this paper is the design of stateless process model and the design of run time core engine using a multi-processor scheduler.

**Keywords.** Web service composition, lightweight, BPEL4WS, Axis2.

## 1. Introduction

Service Oriented Architecture (SOA) together with web services have become the de-facto standard for architecting and implementing business collaborations within and across organization boundaries. SOA takes a "software as a service" approach by exposing the functionality of software components as services. These isolated and opaque service components need to be able to collaborate in order to realize more complex functionality. There exist several web service based workflow models such as Business Processing Execution Language for Web Services (BPEL4WS) [1] in order to cater the above requirement.

BPEL4WS is an XML based language that is intended to facilitate the building of more portable business processes based on Web Service Description Language (WSDL)[2]. BPEL4WS defines how multiple services can be composed together to create new services by combining the functionalities provided by those existing services in a coordinated way. Architecture of a workflow based application typically consists of two programming model abstraction layers denoted by the process model and the individual components. Web services architecture naturally provides the component layer abstraction while BPEL4WS provides the process model. Almost all the available BPEL4WS compliant process engines are found to be complex and heavy weigh, while very few are extensible. Objective of BPEL-Mora was to design and implement a lightweight embeddable, extensible BPEL4WS compliant engine. BPEL-Mora engine was designed to facilitate service composition, service orchestration, non service orchestrations as well as execution of client side workflows based on BPEL4WS model. BPEL-Mora engine is designed to be embeddable in Apache Axis2 [3].

BPEL-Mora consists of four major modules. (1) Process Model (2) Kernel (3) Information model (4) Web service layer. Process Model is used to represent the business process inside the engine. Process model tree for a business process can be created either programmatically or by deploying a BPEL4WS document. In order to maintain low memory foot prints we separated out the process model (Meta data about process) and run time state data of process instances. An Information model consisting of a context hierarchy was introduced to store the run time state data of the process instances. Scalability of the engine was achieved by introducing a kernel based on a multi processor, single queue, non pre-emptive, priority based scheduler to execute the activities given in a process model. BPEL-Mora kernel was designed to minimize the resource requirement per process instance by avoiding thread proliferation. BPEL-Mora empowers user with the ability to write and add custom activities to the engine. This can be achieved very easily by using the provided abstract classes for activities and complex activities. BPEL-Mora is integrated with the Apache Axis2 web services engines through an abstraction layer. Each and every process in BPEL-Mora is registered and exposed as a service through the web services engine. An interface similar to that of WSIF [4] is used for dynamic invocations based on WSDL bindings, with plans to migrate to WSIF later.

The rest of the paper is structured as follows. Section 2 and 3 review the background and related work for the subject of this paper. Section 4 motivates and defines our new approach. Section 5 and 6 present the information and process model of BPEL-mora. Section 7 introduces the design of the BPEL-Mora kernel and Section 8 discusses its architecture more in depth with respect to the four major architectural modules. Sections 9 and 10 conclude the discussion with evaluation, conclusion and future work.

## 2. Background

### 2.1. BPEL4WS

The Business Processing Execution Language for Web services (BPEL4WS or BPEL for short) is a Turing complete XML based programming language that is intended to build more portable business processes based on WSDL. BPEL was created by merging two existing workflow languages, Microsoft's XLANG[5] and IBM's WSFL (Web Services Flow Language)[6]. Architecture of workflow based applications typically consists of two layers of programming model abstractions denoted by the process model (also called orchestration layer) and by the individual components. Web services architecture natively provides an abstraction layer which separates out the implementations from the service definitions. This abstraction can be considered as the component layer of the workflow based applications. BPEL fits to the web services architecture as the orchestration layer or the process model for web services. BPEL was originally created by BEA, IBM, and Microsoft. Now it is undergoing standardization process at the OASIS consortium.

BPEL can be used to define two kinds of processes, namely executable processes and abstract processes. Abstract process is a protocol which specifies message exchange between different parties without revealing the internal behavior of them. Executable process specifies execution order of number of activities.

The building block or each element of a process is known as an activity. An activity can either be a primitive activity or a structured activity. Examples for primitive activities defined in BPEL are Invoke, Receive, Wait, Assign, etc. Structured activities are defined in BPEL in order to enable the presentation of complex structures by composing the primitive activities. Sequence, Switch, While, Flow are examples for structured activities.

### 2.2. Apache Axis2

Apache Axis2 [3] is a complete re-design and a re-write of the widely used Apache Axis SOAP stack. Apache Axis2 is more efficient, more modular and more XML-oriented than the older version. Apache Axis2 is compliant with most of the new versions of core web services specifications and provides WS-* support through its sub projects.

Apache Axis2 supports SOAP 1.1 [7] and SOAP 1.2 [8] and has integrated support for the REST style of Web services too. Hence, the same business logic implementation can offer both a WS-* style interface as well as a REST style interface simultaneously. Axis2 engine is based on a one way message processing model where the engine either perform send or receive functions with respect to a particular SOAP message. Apache Axis2 has the ability to support any Message Exchange Pattern. Axis2 has complete asynchronous messaging support ranging from API level asynchronous support to transport level asynchronous support.

Apache Axis2 is built on Apache Axiom, a new high performing, pull-based XML object model, which provides a simple API for SOAP and XML info-set. Axis2 engine contains a context hierarchy accessible to all services and handlers.

All the run time state data are kept in this information model. Apache Axis2 further improves the popular handler architecture introduced by Axis 1.x by adding the concept of phases. In addition Axis2 introduces a concept called Message Receiver [9] which represent a service inside Axis2 and designated as the ultimate recipient of a particular SOAP message from the architecture point of view of the Axis2 engine.

Apache Axis2 is carefully designed to support the easy addition of plug-in "modules" that extend its functionality for features such as security and reliability. Apache Axis2 has a more improved versatile deployment model with support for hot deployment. This deployment model introduces a service archive format and a module archive format for easy deployment of services and modules.

## 3. Related Work

In this section we look at some of the other commercial and open source BPEL implementations along with some research literature.

The ActiveBPEL [10] engine is a widely used open source BPEL engine. It is designed to be deployed as a servlet in a standard servlet container such as Apache Tomcat. Apache Axis1.x [11] Web service engine is embedded internally in ActiveBPEL. ActiveBPEL is designed around the visitor pattern [12]. Active BPEL does not claim to provide a way to add custom activities in addition to BPEL activities.

An interesting study about the scalability of ActiveBPEL engine has been presented earlier [13]. According to that ActiveBPEL engine requires two OS threads for the creation of a new BPEL process instance. This shows that when the number of process instances increases in ActiveBPEL, the number of threads may go well beyond what most systems can handle, eventually making the work-flow to be aborted. Also users may run into deadlocks if they try to limit the size of the thread pool of the servlet container [13]. The above study concludes by deciding that the scalability of ActiveBPEL is limited only by the limited hardware resources, which will not be acceptable for an embeddable engine.

PXE is another open source BPEL engine. It has many features such as microkernel architecture, pluggable persistency module, JMX-based administration, etc. [15].

IBM WebSphere Process Server (Version 6 as of 2006) is a proprietary BPEL engine running on top of the WebSphere Application Server. WebSphere Process Server is a part of huge software with a wide range of functionality. WebSphere Process Server needs a minimum 1.3 GB (1350 MB) available disk space for installation, installer also requires approximately 600 MB of temporary space during installation and minimum 1 GB physical memory in Linux or Windows platforms [14] as the minimal system requirement.

There are many other open source and proprietary products like Microsoft BizTalk, Oracle's Business Process Manager, etc. which support BPEL.

## 4. Motivation and Our Approach

People tend to think about BPEL complaint business process engines as heavy weight, complex, resource hungry, expensive server side components which are meant to be used by high profile users. On par with the above mind set, almost all the available BPEL engines are found to be complex and heavy weight. But when having a closer look at most existing BPEL engines, we can see that most of them are tightly coupled with business process design modules and business process management modules making them heavy weight and complex. Some of them were built on top of older workflow models making it much worse.

In our opinion the above perception conceal some of the interesting use cases in which BPEL can be used. These use cases can range from service-enabling a device by embedding a BPEL compatible engine to running client side business processes along with custom activities. Our effort is to design and implement a lightweight, embeddable, easy to use BPEL compliant engine as oppose to the above perception. Almost all the existing implementations embed web service engines inside the BPEL engine. As oppose to that we thought of developing a BPEL-Mora as a plug-in to an existing web service engine. Following are some of the use cases for such an engine.

Let's consider a simple BPEL use case where a user wants to expose a new web service by combining the functionalities provided by couple of simple web services in a coordinated way. With the currently available tools the user needs to have a bulky BPEL compliant engine installed in his server for this requirement. Our objective is to provide a simple yet powerful BPEL compliant engine as an add-on to a web service engine. Then the user will be able to perform his service composition inside his web service engine with the same simplicity and ease of deploying a web service, with no extra cost or effort. Also if we consider a scenario where a user needs to invoke several web services, then depending on the result he needs to invoke two other services and needs to get the a combined result. In simple words the user needs to do a mash-up. A lightweight BPEL library with a programming API is ideal for such a use case.

A client side application might have a requirement to interact with several web services to produce a result or to execute a workflow. This requirement can be easily & flexibly fulfilled by using a light weight BPEL runtime which can be embedded to the client application. This runtime will be more useful if the developers are given an option to create the process model programmatically using a simple API. Also the developers will become more creative and empowered if they can add custom activities to that run time. One example is a custom activity to take user input in a client side process by showing a dialog box. Another use case is that users need to do non-web service orchestrations at the server side by extending BPEL functionality. One such example would be to send e-mails as part of a business process.

## 4.1. Design principles

This section articulates some of the principles that have guided our efforts to design a BPEL engine that is light weight and embeddable.

**Low Memory footprint.** The BPEL-Mora engine should have a very low memory foot print in order to be embeddable. BPEL-Mora engine has deployed processes and instances of those processes running. A single deployed process can have several process instances of itself running. It can even be hundreds of instances per process. Reducing the increase of memory usage per new process instance is one of our main concerns. We achieve this by separating out the run time state data of the process instances and the metadata about the process. Process model representation represents only the process. Once the process is deployed its process model remains unchanged during the run time. All the run time state data are separated out to the context hierarchy which we call as the information model.

**Scalability.** A deployed business process may contain several numbers of parallel paths. BPEL does not impose any restriction for number of parallel paths a process can have. At the same time, there can be several instances of a process running at a given moment. If we take a given moment, there can be $l$ number of processes deployed, there can be on average $m$ number of parallel paths per deployed process and there can be on average $n$ number of process instances per process running in the engine. $l * m * n$ gives the total number of parallel paths of execution at that given moment. This $l*m*n$ number can easily go up to hundreds. In a typical production environment it might well go up to thousands. This might give rise to thousands of threads if the OS or language threading libraries are used to create separate threads for each and every parallel path. As a solution to this we came up with a software emulated engine using a multi processor scheduler to execute the activities in process instances.

**Extensibility.** Our objective is to make BPEL-Mora an extensible workflow based service orchestration and composition engine with complete support for BPEL and with the ability to support many more. To make BPEL-Mora extensible BPEL-Mora should provide users with the ability to write and include their own activities. Visitor pattern [16] is popularly used in many BPEL engines to provide this extensibility. With the use of visitor pattern all the execution logic goes to one visitor class, making that class huge and unmanageable. Users need to be given access to modify this visitor class in order to add new activities and the user will be directly modifying the most important class of the engine.

Because of those defects, we wanted to avoid the visitor pattern to come up with much more modular, pluggable, component architecture. BPEL-Mora provides two abstract classes, one for simple activities and another one for complex activities, for the users to extend when writing their own custom activities. Users can use their custom written activities in process model by having the newly written activity classes in the class path. Users will be able to share these custom activities with other users.

## 4.2. High level architecture

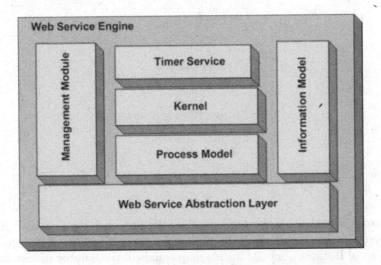

FIGURE 1. High Level Architecture of BPEL-Mora

**Process Model** is used to represent workflows inside the engine. Any workflow that needs to be executed in the BPEL-Mora engine needs to be represented using an instance of an object model. Process model acts as the execution model of the workflow. Process model for a workflow can be created either programmatically or by deploying a BPEL document.

**Information model** consists of the context hierarchy, which stores the runtime state of the engine and processes in various levels.

**Kernel** with a multi processor scheduler is introduced to ensure the engine scale without proliferation of threads.

**Web service layer** consists mainly of BPEL Receive and Invoke activity implementations. BPEL-Mora is built on top of Apache Axis2 web services engine.

**Management module** provides the functionality to deploy BPEL processes and to do simple management tasks.

**Timer service** is used by the Wait and Pick BPEL activities and for deciding time outs in several queues like in the message buffer of Receive activity.

## 5. Information Model

Information model is designed to store the run time state of the engine. Four contexts have been introduced to store state data at various levels.

**Engine Context** holds the run time state data of the engine. This is the top element of the context hierarchy. Engine Context contains a map of all the deployed Process Contexts.

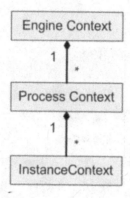

FIGURE 2. Context Hierarchy

**Process Context** holds the run time state data of a deployed process. A ProcessContext contains a map of all the top level InstanceContexts of that process. The number of InstanceContexts in this map equals to the number of instances of this process running in the engine.

**Instance Context** holds the run time state data of a single path of execution. It also holds a pointer called current activity which points to the activity being executed now or to the activity to be executed next. Each process instance running in the engine has a top level InstanceContext which represents that process instance. There can be a tree of InstanceContexts per process instance depending on the number of parallel paths in the process. When encountered a BPEL Flow activity BPELMora engine creates new InstanceContexts per each parallel path defined. Flow activity completes execution when all of its parallel paths are completed. On completion of the parallel paths, the original parent InstanceContext continues in the remaining execution path. This parent InstanceContext is used to store the state of links of the respective Flow activity while it's waiting for the completion of the parallel paths. More about handling links is discussed in the section 6.

**Scope Context** is used to store the data belonging to BPEL Scopes such as values of variables and correlations. InstanceContext always maintains a reference to the scope context of its current scope. BPEL uses lexical scoping. A new ScopeContext object is created whenever a ScopeActivity is encountered in an execution. This newly created ScopeContext is made a child of the existing ScopeContext giving rise to a ScopeContext hierarchy as shown in figure 3. BPEL-Mora uses this hierarchy as a search tree for variable and correlation values and fault handlers. A recursive look up of the ScopeContext hierarchy happens when a variable, correlation or a fault handler is referenced by an activity. BPEL-Mora first checks whether it is defined in the current scope, if so looks up for that in the current ScopeContext. If it is not defined or found in that context, then the engine looks up for that in the hierarchy until the value is found. This scoping context hierarchy provides lexical scoping with the price of a performance penalty due to the recursive lookups. But we can ignore this performance penalty as negligible since scope hierarchies are shallow and simple in most of the BPEL documents.

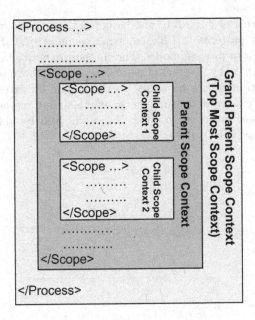

FIGURE 3. Lexical Scoping System

## 6. Process Model

Purpose of the process model is to provide an object model representation of a deployed process capturing the meta-data from the BPEL document. We can also call the BPEL-Mora run time process model tree as an execution model. Objects in process model are designed to be run time stateless. Process model tree contains information about the process, but not about the process instances. Process model contains implementation classes corresponding to each and every activity specified in the BPEL specification. There are two main categories of activities specified in the BPEL specification namely simple activities and structured activities. As shown in figure 4, process model contains abstract classes to capture the common functionality needed for the above two activity categories.

Each and every class corresponding to an Activity contains an execute() method which contains the execution logic for that activity. This method takes in an InstanceContext object as the parameter. This InstanceContext object is used to store and retrieve all the state date regarding the process instance. According to the BPEL-Mora architecture implementations of execute() method needs to be re-entrant. On other words, the values of the local variables of that Activity object cannot be changed within this method. This gives the ability to share a copy of an activity object among different process instances without worrying about concurrency issues.

A need for return of control to the parent activity arises when implementing several workflow patterns [17] like *sequence, parallel split* (BPEL Flow) and *while* using BPEL-Mora process model. The method `executeParent()` has been introduced to the `Activity` abstract class to cater to the above requirement. New powerful custom activities can be added to the engine by extending one of the above two abstract classes and using the `executeParent` method to return the control back to parent whenever needed. Users will also be able to share their custom written classes with other BPEL-Mora users.

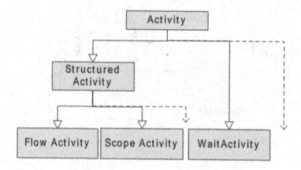

FIGURE 4.  Class hierarchy of the Process Model

Process model tree is created using a linked list approach. Child activity objects of a structured activity maintain parent-to-child, child-to-parent doubly linked relationship in first and last child with the parent activity object. A single child-to-parent link relationship is maintained in other children. All the siblings maintain a link to the next sibling connecting all the children of a structured activity.

### 6.1. Handling Links

A BPEL flow activity executes its immediate child activities concurrently giving rise to several parallel paths of execution. Flow activity enables expression of synchronization dependencies between activities that are running on different parallel paths. The link construct is used to express these synchronization dependencies. Links of a flow activity are separately defined inside the flow activity. Exactly one activity can declare to be the source and another activity can declare to be the target of a link. We say X has a synchronization dependency on Y, if activity X is the target of a link that has activity Y as the source.

As discussed in section 4 when met with a flow BPEL activity, BPEL-Mora creates new child instance contexts for each parallel path, while the parent instance

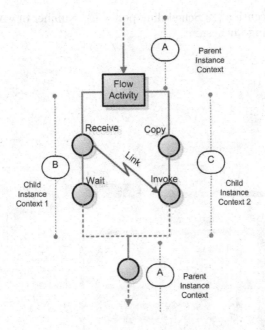

FIGURE 5. Links

context waits till execution is complete in all the parallel paths. BPEL-Mora uses this parent instance context to store a list of Link objects whenever a Flow activity with defined links is executed. These Link objects can be in true state, false state or not evaluated state depending on the state of the source activity of that link. When the Link object status is not evaluated target activity has to wait till the Link state is evaluated. In BPEL-Mora implementation an Instance Context executing in a parallel path target Activity can register with a Link object in not evaluated state to be notified when the link is evaluated.

## 7. Kernel

A kernel with a multiprocessor scheduler is introduced to BPEL-Mora in order to ensure the engine scale without proliferation of threads. Following sections discuss about the scheduling of process instances and the life cycle of process instances.

### 7.1. Scheduling BPEL activities

A multi processor scheduler with a configurable number of processors is implemented in the BPEL-Mora kernel. In here normal java Threads in a thread pool were used to emulate the processors. Each worker thread in the thread pool simulates one processor. The decisions that we had to take with regards to the scheduler were (1) Unit of execution (2) Scheduling policy (3) Number of worker threads (4) Number of scheduling queues.

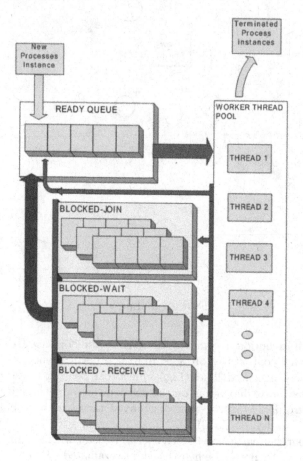

FIGURE 6. BPEL-Mora Kernel

As shown in Fig. 6, a worker thread picks an Instance Context object (represents a process instance) from the head of the scheduler queue and executes the current activity of the process instance. Then, depending on the resulting state the process instance is put into the relevant queue.

A single activity in a process model is chosen as the unit of execution for simplicity and clarity. All the currently supported activities including all the BPEL activities were designed to have a limited number of instructions per execution. All the current activities were carefully designed not to block the worker threads during the execution. Examples for this behavior are Receive, Invoke and Wait activity implementations. When a Receive or a Wait activity is executed, the Instance Context object belonging to the execution will be put into the appropriate waiting queue freeing the worker thread. A call back object is used to store the Instance Context object in the case of Invoke activity.

With the above design an assumption can be made that a BPEL-Mora activity will be executed in a predictable small bounded time period. With this assumption, a non-pre-emptive priority based scheduling policy is used in the BPEL-Mora scheduler. BPEL-Mora run time does not enforce any time constraint for the duration of execution of an activity. Priority for a process can be specified at the deployment time. Above assumption invalidates if users add custom activities that take longer times to execute.

Number of worker threads in the scheduler thread pool is made configurable to cater for the various underlying resource requirements. As an example, a server with parallel processors can gain advantage by increasing the number of threads while a single processor pc can harness the best by having a small number of threads like 5 threads.

Currently, BPEL-Mora scheduler uses a single scheduler queue assuming the context switch time is very small relative to the time taken for a unit of execution. Another option is to have a scheduler queue for each and every worker thread. An implementation like that can reduce the context switching time. On the other hand it will unnecessarily increase the complexity of the scheduler due to the need to perform queue load balancing. The scheduler queue implementation needs to be blocking and thread safe. Hence, we have chosen a PriorityBlockingQueue [18] as our scheduling queue implementation.

### 7.2. Process instance life cycle

Process instances are created with the reception of a designated `startable` invocation message and are destroyed when the last activity of the process instance completes execution. Between those two we can define several more states with regards to the scheduler. Process instances may have parallel execution paths. These parallel execution paths can be in different states at a given time. Because of this it makes more sense to discuss about process instance life cycles with regard to a single execution path, which will be referred to as "single path of execution" here after. These single paths of execution are represented inside the engine by the instance context objects.

Four major states can be identified in a single path of execution of a process instance. They are (1) ready (2) running (3) blocked (4) terminated. All the paths of execution in the `ready` state are waiting in the scheduler's queue. New process instance entering the engine are initially in the `ready` state. A process instance is in the `running` state when it is executing inside the engine. A single path of execution terminates either when the process instance terminates or when it finishes executing the last activity in its execution path. A single path of execution represented by an instance context enters into the blocked state in 3 ways.

1. A single path of execution represented by an instance context enters into `Blocked-Join` state when it is waiting for a `link` to be evaluated. Instance

context waits till the link gets evaluated. An instance context in `Blocked-Join` state moves to the `Ready` state upon successful evaluation of the `link`.

2. A single path of execution represented by an instance context enters into a `Blocked-Wait` state when a `wait` BPEL activity is executed. An instance context in `Blocked-Wait` state moves to the `Ready` state upon reaching of the given deadline or upon expiration of the specified time period.

3. A single path of execution represented by an instance context enters into a `Blocked-Receive` state when a `receive` BPEL activity is executed as well as a synchronous Invoke activity is executed. An instance context in `Blocked-Receive` state moves to the `Ready` state upon receiving the expected message.

## 8. Interfacing with web service engine

BPEL-Mora is built on top of Apache Axis2. By the use of Axis2 BPEL-Mora takes a lot of features for granted such as performance, ability to invoke RESTful Web services, asynchronous support, WS-* capabilities through Axis2 modules, and so on. Interfacing with web service layer is done through the implementations of invoke and receive BPEL activities.

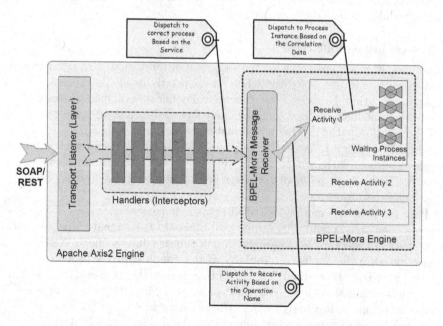

FIGURE 7. Apache Axis2 integration with the receive activity

### 8.1. Providing web service operations

Each and every process in BPEL-Mora is registered as a service with the web service engine. Hence, we expect the web service engine to route the messages to the correct service, which in BPEL-Mora scenario is to route the message to the correct process. Web service layer in BPEL-Mora consists of a MessageReceiver implementation. MessageReceiver is an interface provided by Axis2, to use per service basis. Axis2 delivers the incoming messages to particular service to the specified MessageReceiver [9] implementation. BPEL-Mora MessageReceiver of a deployed process maintains a map of references to receive activity objects in a process against their operation names. BPEL-Mora uses this table to route messages to the correct receive activity object within the deployed process based on their operation name. Each and every Receive Activity object maintains a queue of InstanceContext objects (process instances) blocked by waiting at that activity. Following sequence is followed when a message is received to a receive activity.

1. If the message receive activity object is designated as *startable*, then it will create a new instance of the process.
2. Otherwise the message is routed to the correct process instance in the queue based on the correlation data [1] in the message.
3. If a matching instance is not found in the queue, the message is buffered in a separate queue for a certain time period waiting for a matching process instance.

### 8.2. Invoking web service operations

Invoking of external web services is done through an interface similar to WSIF [4]. This interface supports the creation of dynamic clients based on the WSDL binding. The web service invocation interface is an implementation of Adapter Design pattern [19]. The invocation model wraps Axis2 [3] client programming API and provides a Dynamic Invocation Interface (DII). BPEL-Mora web service invocation supports DII with or with out the WSDL. It is mandatory to provide the end point reference of the target service, in the case where the WSDL is not available.

Invoke Activity implementation handles all the request-response type invocations through the Axis2 client side non-blocking invocation mechanism. A special callback handler object containing the InstanceContext object corresponding to the process instance is used to receive the response.

## 9. Evaluation

Two tests were done to measure the performance of BPEL-Mora.

First test focuses on measuring the scalability of BPEL-Mora kernel and the scheduler. We used an embedded BPEL-Mora engine inside a test case and programmatically created and deployed the process. The process contained a flow activity inside a sequence activity. A custom activity which simply prints out its number and the execution count with a small time consuming logic was used as the children of the flow activity. This process was triggered programmatically.

| Number of children for the Flow activity | Time taken to execute (ms) | Avg. Time per 100 children (ms) |
|---|---|---|
| 100 | 745 | 745 |
| 500 | 2064 | 412.8 |
| 1000 | 3443 | 344.3 |
| 2000 | 7130 | 356.5 |
| 5000 | 15701 | 314.12 |
| 10000 | 29642 | 296.42 |
| 15000 | 41578 | 277.18 |

TABLE 1. Scalability of the scheduler (figures are the average of 5 runs)

These tests shows scalability of the engine and the fact that number of parallel paths and the overhead of creating InstanceContext object per each path do not affect the performance.

A second test was focused on the memory foot print of the engine. BPEL-Mora was deployed inside Apache Axis2 1.1 running inside Apache Tomcat 5.0.28 with jdk 1.4.2. A 25 kb BPEL document was deployed in BPEL-Mora. This process was designed to go into Blocked-WAIT state as soon as the process instance was created.

BPEL-Mora implementation followed a minimalist approach from day one. As a result of that the size of BPEL-Mora library remains less than 130kB. BPEL-Mora depends only on the Axis2 and its dependent libraries. Due to that adding BPEL capability to an existing Axis2 server can be done with the mere addition of 130 KB BPEL-Mora library. To embed BPEL-Mora in an application or to run it standalone requires the addition of Axis2 and dependent libraries, which are of size 2.8 MB.

## 10. Conclusion and future work

BPEL-Mora is a lightweight embeddable extensible BPEL compliant process engine. BPEL-Mora can be embedded into the web service engine to execute server

| Process Instances | 1 | 100 | 200 | 300 | 400 | 500 | 600 | 700 |
|---|---|---|---|---|---|---|---|---|
| BPEL-Mora Mem. usage | 2.4 | 10.4 | 25 | 33 | 41.5 | 48.4 | 61.4 | 66 |
| ActiveBPEL Mem. Usage | 2.6 | 37.3 | Reached a Thread limitation | | | | | |

TABLE 2. Memory usage Vs No. of process instances

side processes. BPEL-Mora has the capability to serve as a process run time to execute client side processes. In this paper, we presented the motivation behind our effort, discussed the architecture of BPEL-Mora engine and major design decisions we took in implementing BPEL-Mora. Affect of issues related to scalability, extensibility and memory foot print, to the embeddability of the engine was also addressed in this paper. Information model captures the run time state data of the process instances and manages the lexical scoping of variables. Architecture of the stateless object model was discussed focusing on extensibility and memory foot print. Architecture of the Runtime engine with its scheduler was discussed along with the various decisions we had to take during the implementation of the scheduler.

Providing full BPEL capability including fault handling and event based constructs together with improving the programming API to ease the programmatic creation of processes can be seen our immediate future objective. BPEL specification does not define how WS-Transactions [20, 21, 22] set of specifications can be used to provide transaction capability for BPEL processes. Adding transactions support for business processes using WS-Transactions family of specifications will be one of our future research goals.

## References

[1] T. Andrews, F. Curbera, H. Dholakia, Y. Goland, J. Klein, F. Leymann, K. Liu, D. Roller, D. Smith, S. Thatte, I. Trickovic, and S. Weerawarana. Business Process Execution Language for Web Services Version 1.1, May 2003. ftp://www6.software.ibm.com/software/developer/library/wsbpel.pdf.

[2] E. Christensen, F. Curbera, G. Meredith, and S. Weerawarana. Web Services Description Language (WSDL), Version 1.1, March 2000. http://www.w3.org/TR/wsdl.

[3] Web Services Apache Axis2 , June 2006, http://ws.apache.org/axis2.

[4] Web Services Web Services Invocation Frame work (WSIF), June 2006, http://ws.apache.org/wsif.

[5] Thatte, S. , XLANG: Web Services for Business Process Design,Technical report, Microsoft, 2001.

[6] Leymann, F. , Web Services Flow Language, Technical report, IBM, 2001.

[7] D. Box et al, Simple Object Access Protocol (SOAP)1.1, May 2000. http://www.w3.org/TR/SOAP.

[8] M. Gudwin et al, Simple Object Access Protocol (SOAP)1.2, May 2000. http://www.w3.org/TR/soap12-part1/

[9] Apache Axis2, Architecture Guide. http://ws.apache.org/axis2/1_1/Axis2ArchitectureGuide.html

[10] Active BPEL, June 2006, http://www.activebpel.org

[11] Web Services Apache Axis1.x , June 2006, http://ws.apache.org/axis.

[12] ActiveBPEL Engine Architecture, July 2006, http://www.activebpel.org/docs/architecture.html

[13] Wolfgang Emmerich, Ben Butchart, Liang Chen and Bruno Wassermann, Grid Service Orchestration using the Business Process Execution Language (BPEL), October 2005. (pp. 28-30), http://sse.cs.ucl.ac.uk/omii-bpel/publications/bpel.pdf

[14] WebSphere Process Server Version 6.0 System Requirements, July 2006. http://www-306.ibm.com/software/integration/wps/sysreqs/

[15] FiveSight PXE, June 2006, http://pxe.fivesight.com/

[16] J. Palsberg and C. B. Jay. The Essence of the Visitor Pattern. In Proceedings of COMPSAC'98, 22nd Annual International Computer Software and Applications Conference, pages 9-15, Vienna, Austria, August 1998. http://www.cs.ucla.edu/~palsberg/paper/compsac98.pdf

[17] Workflow patterns, June 2006, http://is.tm.tue.nl/research/patterns/patterns.htm

[18] J2SE 5.0, Concurrency Utilities, June 2006, http://java.sun.com/j2se/1.5.0/docs/
relnotes/features.html\#concurrency

[19] E. Gamma, R. Helm, R. Johnson, and J. Vlissides.Design Patterns. Addison-Wesley Pub Co, January 1995. ISBN 0201633612.

[20] F. Curbera et al. Web Services Coordination (WS-Coordination),Version 1.0, August 2005.

[21] F. Curbera et al. Web Services Atomic Transaction (WS-AtomicTransaction),Version 1.0, August 2005.

[22] F. Curbera et al. Web Services Business Activity Framework (WS-Business Activity),Version1.0, August 2005.

**Acknowledgment**

Many thanks to our Project Supervisors Sanjiva Weerawarana and Sanath Jayasena for many insights and discussions. We thank our Project Coordinator Shantha Fernando and Vishaka Nanayakkara for their support throughout the project.

Thilina Gunarathne, Dinesh Premalal, Tharanga Wijethilake,
Indika Kumara, Anushka Kumar
Department of Computer Science and Engineering
University of Moratuwa
Sri Lanka
e-mail: thilina.gunarathne@cse.mrt.ac.lk, dinesh.premalal@cse.mrt.ac.lk,
tharanga.wijethilake@cse.mrt.ac.lk, indika.kumara@cse.mrt.ac.lk,
anushka.kumar@cse.mrt.ac.lk

Whitestein Series in Software Agent Technologies, 21–32
© 2007 Birkhäuser Verlag Basel/Switzerland

# A Cross-Layer Approach to Performance Monitoring of Web Services

Nicolas Repp, Rainer Berbner, Oliver Heckmann and Ralf Steinmetz

**Abstract.** An increasing amount of applications are currently built as Web Service compositions based on the TCP/IP+HTTP protocol stack. In case of any deviations from desired runtime-behavior, problematic Web Services have to be substituted and their execution plans have to be updated accordingly. One challenge is to detect deviations as early as possible allowing timely adaption of execution plans. We advocate a cross-layer approach to detect bad performance and service interruptions much earlier than by waiting for their propagation through the full protocol stack. This position paper describes an approach to gain detailed real-time information about Web Service behavior and performance based on a cross-layer analysis of the TCP/IP+HTTP protocols. In this paper we focus especially on TCP. The results are used to make decisions supporting service selection and replanning in service-oriented computing scenarios. Furthermore, generic architectural components are proposed implementing the functionality needed which can be used in different web-based scenarios.

**Keywords.** Web Services, Monitoring, Cross-Layer, Service-oriented Architectures.

## 1. Introduction

Almost every Internet user has encountered problems while using services in the Internet, e.g., browsing the World-Wide Web or using Email. Long to infinite response times due to congestion or connection outage, non-resolvable URLs, or simple file-not-found errors are some of the most common ones. Human users tend to be flexible in case of any service "misbehavior". Users wait and check back later or even select a different service if the originally requested service is not available. In contrast, computer systems as service consumers are not as flexible. Appropriate strategies to handle those runtime events have to be implemented during design time of the computer system.

Services are the key building block of service-oriented computing. A service is a self-describing encapsulation of business functionality (with varying granularity) according to [1]. Following the service-oriented computing paradigm, applications can be assembled out of several independent, distributed and loosely-coupled services [2]. Those services can be provided even by third parties. One option to implement services from a technical perspective is the use of Web Services. Web Services are based on different XML-based languages for data exchange and interface description, e.g., SOAP and the Web Service Description Language (WSDL). For the transport of data and the Web Service invocation mainly the Transmission

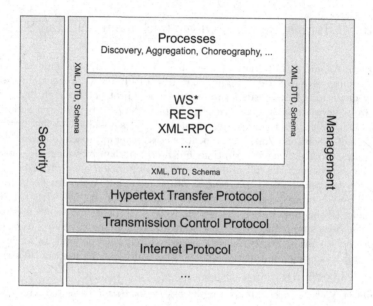

FIGURE 1. Modified W3C Web Services Architecture Stack [3]

Control Protocol (TCP) / Internet Protocol (IP) suite (e.g., RFC 793, [4], or [5]) as well as the Hypertext Transfer Protocol (HTTP - e.g., RFC 2616 or [6]) are used. Figure 1 shows the W3C Web Services Architecture Stack enhanced by alternative Web Service technologies and the communication protocols used. It will be the basis for our further considerations.

In order to build applications from different existing Web Services the following generic phases are needed [7]: First, suitable Web Services have to be selected according to the functional and non-functional requirements of the application. Second, the selected Web Services have to be composed to an execution plan. Hereto, a composition can be described, e.g., on basis of the Business Process Execution Language (BPEL) [8]. In the next step the execution plan can be processed. During the execution phase it is possible that parts of the composition do not act as expected with regard to the non-functional requirements. Reasons for misbehavior of Web Services are manyfold, e.g., server errors while processing a request, network congestion or network outages. Therefore, it is necessary to select alternative Web Services and to replan the Web Service execution [9]. Replanning is always a trade-off between the costs of creating new plans to fulfill the overall non-functional requirements and the costs of breaking the requirements [10]. Timely action is required to reduce the delay·in the execution of an application due to replanning and substitution of Web Services. Hence, we propose a proactive approach initiating countermeasures as soon as there is evidence that a deviation might occur in the near future with a certain probability $p$. To start replanning before the deviation happens allows replanning to be carried out in parallel to the service execution itself. The results of replanning have to be discarded with probability $1 - p$ as the alternative plans are not needed.

Furthermore, current approaches often lack detailed information about the status of a Web Service due to the information hiding implemented in the layer model of the TCP/IP+HTTP protocol stack underlying Web Services. For this, we advocate a cross-layer approach to detect bad performance and service interruptions. Cross-layer analysis allows decisions based on deeper knowledge of the current situation as well as decisions made much earlier than by waiting for information propagating through the full protocol stack.

The rest of this position paper is structured as follows. In the next section we describe Quality-of-Service (QoS) and its meaning for Web Services. We especially focus on performance as a part of Web Service QoS. Afterwards, the relation between TCP/IP+HTTP and Web Service performance is discussed. Our cross-layer approach to performance monitoring a performance anomaly detection of Web Services is introduced thereafter. The paper closes with a conclusion and an outlook on future work.

## 2. Quality-of-Service and Performance of Web Services

In this section we discuss QoS with regard to Web Services and Web Service compositions with a focus on Web Service performance.

### 2.1. Quality-of-Service with regard to Web Services

Similar to QoS requirements in traditional networks, there is a need to describe and manage QoS of Web Services and Web Service compositions. Generally, QoS defines non-functional requirements on services independent from the layer they are related to. QoS can be divided into measurable and non-measurable parameters. The most common measurable parameters are performance-related, e.g., throughput, response time, and latency. Additionally, parameters like availability, error-rate, as well as various non-measurable parameters like reputation and security are of importance for Web Services [10, 11]. The meaning of QoS requirements can differ between service providers and service requesters in a service-oriented computing environment [11]. From a service providers' perspective, providing enough capacity with the quality needed to fulfill Service Level Agreements (SLA) with different customers is a core issue. Service requesters are more focused on managing bundles of Web Services from different vendors in order to implement their business needs. Therefore, management of QoS requirements is done on aggregations of Web Services, to a lesser extend on single Web Services.

There is a variety of other definitions of Web Service QoS. A more extensive approach identifies the following requirements [12]: performance, reliability, scalability, capacity, robustness, exception handling, accuracy, integrity, accessibility, availability, interoperability, security, and network-related QoS requirements. Especially the last requirement is of further interest. As many requirements of Web Service QoS are directly related to the underlying network and its QoS, implementations of network QoS mechanisms, e.g., Differentiated Services (DiffServ) or the Resource Reservation Protocol (RSVP), are also covered by the definition as well.

## 2.2. Performance of Web Services

Performance of Web Services is not a singular concept. Rather, it consists of several concepts which themselves are connected to different metrics and parameters. Again, there are several definitions of Web Service performance. We will use the definition provided by the Web Services Architecture Working Group of the W3C as a foundation for our own defintion. According to the W3C, performance is defined in terms of throughput, response time, latency, execution time, and transaction time [12]. Both execution time and latency are sub-concepts of the W3Cs definition of response time. Transaction time describes the time needed to process a complete transaction, i.e., an interaction consisting of several requests and responses belonging together.

For this paper, we define performance in terms of throughput and response time. Response time is the time needed to process a query, from sending the request until receiving the response [13]. Response time can be further divided into task processing time, network processing time, i.e., time consumed while traversing the protocol stacks of source, destination, and intermediate systems, as well as network transport time itself. In case of an error during the processing of a request or a response, the response time measures the time from a request to the notification of an error. We define response time as follows:

$$t_{response}(ws) = t_{task}(ws) + t_{stack}(ws) + t_{transport}(ws)$$

A large fraction of a web service's response time is determined by the processing time for requests and their respective messages in both intermediate systems and end-points. For the measurement of the response time, the encapsulation of data into XML messages and vice versa, compression and decompression of data, as well as encryption and decryption of messages also have to be taken into account. Furthermore, time for connection setup, for the negotiation of the connections parameters as well as the amount of time used for authentication are part of the response time as well.

Throughput, measured in connections, requests or packets per second, describes the capability of a Web Service provider to process concurrent Web Service requests. Depending on the layer, different types of connections can be the basis for measurements, e.g. TCP connections, HTTP connections, or even SOAP interactions. We define the throughput of a Web Services as:

$$throughput(ws) = \frac{\#requests(ws)}{time}$$

Additionally, we have to define the concept of "performance anomaly" we will use later on. Performance anomalies describe deviations from the performance expected in a given situation. Performance anomalies do not have to be exceptions or even errors, e.g., a response time which exceeds the value defined in a SLA is also a performance anomaly with regard to business requirements. Furthermore, performance better than expectations is also an anomaly.

## 3. A Cross-layer Approach to Performance Monitoring and Anomaly Detection

In this section we describe an approach for performance monitoring and performance anomaly detection based on packet capturing and the application of simple heuristics. Therefore, we analyze IP, TCP, and HTTP data. The analysis of SOAP is not in scope of this paper, as we want to stay independent of a certain Web Service technology. Our approach can be applied to various alternative Web Service technologies as well, e.g., XML-Remote Procedure Call (XML-RPC) or Representational State Transfer (REST). Nevertheless, in our examples we use SOAP as it is the most common Web Service technology in use.

### 3.1. Protocol Parameters for Performance Monitoring

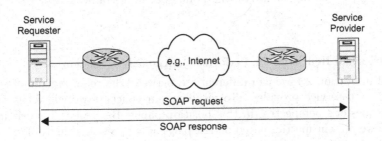

FIGURE 2. Simple Web Service interaction

Consider the simple Web Service invocation of a single Web Service as depicted in Figure 2. A service requester generates a SOAP request and sends the message using HTTP to the service provider for further processing. The message has to pass several intermediate systems on its way between the interaction's endpoints. The SOAP response message is again transported using HTTP.

During data transfer several problems can occur, which all have an impact on Web Service execution. Beginning with the network layer, we may face routing problems, e.g., hosts which are not reachable, congestion in Internet routers as well as traffic bursts. Additionally, on transport layer there are also potential pitfalls like the retransmission of packets due to packet loss or connection setup problems generating delays. Finally, there are also some potential problems on application layer with regard to Web Services for example in form of resources, which are not existing or not accessible for HTTP or problems in processing of SOAP messages due to incomplete or non-valid XML data.

Although, many of the above problems are solved in modern protocol stack implementations, we can use the knowledge about them to define measurement points for performance monitoring. Depending on the problems in scope different protocol parameters have to be used. Table 1 gives an overview of measurement points on different protocol layers. We will use the transport layer parameters as an example to derive metrics and heuristics for performance anomaly detection in the following section.

| Protocol | Measuring Point / Parameter |
|----------|-----------------------------|
| IP | ICMP messages |
| TCP | Size of advertising window |
| | Roundtrip time (RTT) |
| | Sequence numbers in use |
| | Flags used in packets |
| | Information about timers |
| HTTP | Header information |

TABLE 1. Measuring points per protocol layer

### 3.2. Metrics and Heuristics for Performance Anomaly Detection

As noted in Section 2.1 we can differentiate between the requirements of service requesters and service providers. To visualize our concepts we will focus on the service requester's perspective in this position paper. Before basic heuristics are proposed we present metrics based on the parameters presented in Table 1, which will be the foundation of our heuristics.

We propose several metrics based on parameters of the transport layer protocol:

- $M1$ - Average throughput in bytes per second (BPS).
- $M2$ - Throughput based on a moving average over window with size $n$ seconds in BPS.
- $M3$ - Throughput based on exponential smoothing (first degree) with $\alpha$ varying in BPS.

- $M4$ - Roundtrip time based on a moving average over window with size $n$ segments in seconds per segment.
- $M5$ - Number of gaps in sequence numbers based on a moving average over window with size $n$ seconds in number of gaps per second.

The aggregation of single metrics in combination with the usage of appropriate thresholds allows us to build heuristics in order to detect anomalies with performance impact. The following two simple heuristics show the idea how to design heuristics based on the metrics discussed. Both were derived from experimentations in our Web Service test environment.

- $H1_{Requester}$: $M1$ (or $M2$, $M3$) in aggregation with $M4$, i.e., throughput combined with RTT.
- $H2_{Requester}$: $M4$ in aggregation with $M5$, i.e., RTT combined with the amount of gaps in TCP sequence numbers.

Singular metrics are in some cases not sufficient for robust monitoring, e.g., $M5$ without any information about RTT does not offer useful information.

In addition to those transport layer based heuristics, further parameters from other protocol layers and the respective metrics can be combined in order to create different cross-layer heuristics. Nevertheless, it is important that metrics and the related heuristics have to be calculated in an efficient way in order to keep additional processing times of our approach low.

### 3.3. Exemplary Evaluation of Our Approach

To show the feasibility of our approach we set up an experiment. The test environment consists of a 1.4 GHz Centrino with 1.256 GByte RAM running Windows XP as service requester and a 1.42 GHz G4 with 1 GByte RAM running Mac OS X as service provider. Apache Tomcat 5.5.17 is used as an application server. Both systems use Java 1.5 and Axis 1.4 as SOAP implementation. They are connected by 100 MBit/s ethernet. For packet capturing windump v3.9.3 is used.

First, we measure the response time of a Web Service in our test environment. As payload we use SOAP messages of variable size. Table 2 shows the results of measuring 20 individual runs both with and without network outage for a payload of 20 MByte, a test scenario, which was already implemented in our test environment. Similar results can be observed with a payload of 150 KB. Network outages are equally distributed in the interval $[0;\max(t_{response}(ws)$ w/o outage$)]$. A network outage is modelled as a permanent 100% packet loss, i.e., without a restart of the connection. Other scenarios, e.g., varying or temporary packet loss,

| $t_{response}(ws)$ [ms] | minimum | maximum | average |
|---|---|---|---|
| w/o outage | 8,743 | 9,604 | 8,891 |
| w/ outage | 601,204 | 605,831 | 604,186 |

TABLE 2. SOAP response times

are not in focus of this position paper. As Table 2 shows, the response time of our Web Service varies between 8.9 seconds (without outage) and 10.07 minutes (with outage) for a 20 MByte payload.

| $rtt$ [ms] | minimum | maximum | average | |
|---|---|---|---|---|
| $H1_{Requester}$ | 0.22 | 0.41 | 0.31 | |

TABLE 3. Roundtrip times

In a next step, we apply $H1_{Requester}$ on our sample with network outages. Especially the roundtrip time extracted from TCP packets can be used as trend estimate for the overall response time in our scenario. Table 3 shows the average roundtrip times of all 20 runs. Using a moving average of the roundtrip times measured as a benchmark for the roundtrip time of the packet in transfer, a warning to the replanning system, e.g., if the estimated time (or a multiple) is exceeded twice or more in a row. Unfortunately, throughput was not as good as the RTT as an indicator for performance anomalies in the given scenario.

### 3.4. Identification of Required Architectural Components

In order to implement our ideas several architectural components are needed. The key building blocks are depicted in Figure 3.

The upper part of Figure 3 describes existing generic components used for planning and executing of Web Service compositions. The *Interface* allows deployment of workflows and configuration, the *(Re-)Planning Component* generates and adapts execution plans, which are thereafter executed by an *Orchestration Engine*. We propose the use of our Web Service Quality-of-Service Architectural Extension (WSQoSX) as implementation means for the functionality needed. WSQoSX already supports planning and replanning of compositions [7, 10].

The lower part of the figure describes the two core components of our approach in addition to the protocol stack. This enhanced architectural blueprint is named Web Service - Service Monitoring Extension (WS-SMX). The *Monitor* specifies a component capable of eavesdropping of the network traffic between service requester and provider. It also implements pre-filtering of the data passing by reducing it to the protocol data of interest. Its data is passed to a *Detector* component, which is responsible for the data analysis and therefore the performance anomaly detection. The *Detector* component will implement the heuristics discussed in Section 3.2. The *Orchestration Engine* initializes the *Detector*, which itself prepares the *Monitor*. The *Detector* analyses the data received by the *Monitor* and triggers the *(Re-)Planning Component* in case of any critical findings. Additionally, the *Detector* component can be configured using the *Interface*. Both *Monitor* and *Detector* are implemented in a first version in our test environment based on Java 1.5 in combination with libpcap for packet capturing.

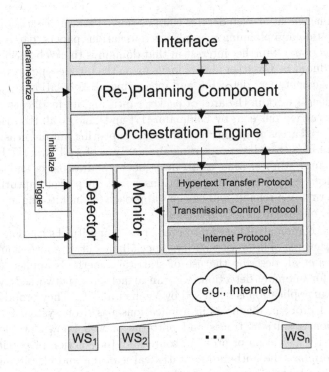

FIGURE 3. Proposed architectural components

## 4. Related Work

As our approach is based on research of various domains this section gives an overview of related work in those domains. Gschwind et al. [14] describe WebMon, a performance analysis system with focus on Web transactions, i.e. transactions between a Web browser and a Web server. Monitoring is done on basis of HTTP. Web Services as remote method invocations as well as a further processing of the results of the analysis are not in scope of their paper. Similar mechanisms as the ones proposed by us are implemented in the commercial software package Vital-Suite by Lucent, which is used for capacity planning and QoS management in large networks. VitalSuite can also analyze different protocol layers simultaneously. In contrast to the system we propose, VitalSuite's focus is on reporting for end-users instead of automated management. A more detailed view on performance management of Web Services is discussed by Schmietendorf et al. [15]. The Web Services Trust Center (WSTC) allows Web Services to be registered at and measured by an independent third party for SLA management. WSTC enables the monitoring of performance and availability of Web Services, but not under real-time requirements.

The management of Web Service compositions, their orchestration as well as their optimization and planning is emphasized in various papers, partly mentioned in the introduction. Of further interest in that domain is the Web Service Manager (WSM) introduced by Casati et al. [16] focusing on the business perspective of Web Service management, e.g., detecting and measuring SLA violations.

Fundamental work in the area of packet capturing, its justification and optimization was carried out e.g., by Feldmann [17] and Mao et al. [18]. Both do not focus on potential areas of application for packet capturing but on measurement itself. Feldmann uses cross-layer capturing and analysis of TCP and HTTP for later Web performance studies. Mao et al. describe both drawbacks and advantages of performance analysis of Web applications based on packet capturing mechanisms. Furthermore, a reliable and efficient approach for monitoring in distributed systems based on dispatching is discussed.

The idea of anomaly detection to predict certain critical situations is already used, e.g., in the area of network security, especially in network intrusion detection. Mainikopoulos et al. describe the use of statistical methods applied to network usage traces for anomaly detection, e.g., an attack on a networked system [19]. Another area of application is discussed by Yuan et al. [20]. They propose a system for automated problem diagnosis in applications based on system event traces. The correlation of current traces and patterns of well known problems allows an automatic identification of problem sources and prediction of possible system errors. Furthermore, the authors use statistical learning and classifying methods to dynamically adapt and improve their system.

## 5. Conclusion and Future Work

In this position paper we show that it can be beneficial to use information gathered on different protocol layers for decision support. We present an approach and several architectural components, which use hidden, low layer technical information for proactive replanning of Web Service compositions. As this is a position paper there are still some open issues we are researching. We are currently testing machine learning algorithms for anomaly detection. Furthermore, we are working on enhancements of existing optimization models for Web Service compositions to support replanning [10]. Additionally, we will test our approach from a service requester's perspective in real world scenarios, using Web Services available to the public, e.g., from Amazon or via Xmethods.

Using our approach for proactive replanning is not limited to SOAP Web Services. As we are collecting our data on lower layers, the type of Web Service can be exchanged, e.g., REST and XML-RPC based Web Services can also be supported. But we are not even limited to Web Services as an area of application. The approach can be of benefit, e.g., to enhance Web browsers to detect network problems in a faster way.

# References

[1] M.P. Papazoglou, *Service-oriented computing: Concepts, characteristics and directions*. In: Proceedings of the Fourth International Conference on Web Information Systems Engineering (WISE 2003). (December 2003) 3–12.

[2] M. Bichler, K.J. Lin, *Service-oriented computing*. IEEE Computer **39(3)** (March 2006) 99–101.

[3] D. Booth, H. Haas, F. McCabe, E. Newcomer, M. Champion, C. Ferris, D. Orchard, *Web services architecture*. (2004) http://www.w3.org/TR/ws-arch/, accessed: 2006/07/02.

[4] W.R. Stevens, *TCP/IP illustrated (vol. 1): the protocols*. Addison-Wesley Longman Publishing Co., Inc., Boston, MA, USA (1994).

[5] A.S. Tanenbaum, *Computer Networks*. Fourth Edition, Prentice Hall, Indianapolis, Indiana, USA (August 2002).

[6] J.C. Mogul, *Clarifying the fundamentals of http*. In: Proceedings of the 11th international conference on World Wide Web (WWW 2002). (May 2002) 25–36.

[7] R. Berbner, T. Grollius, N. Repp, O. Heckmann, E. Ortner, R. Steinmetz, *An approach for the management of service-oriented architecture based application systems*. In: Proceedings of the Workshop Enterprise Modelling and Information Systems Architectures (EMISA 2005). (October 2005) 208–221.

[8] F. Curbera, R. Khalaf, N. Mukhi, S. Tai, S. Weerawarana, *The next step in web services*. Commun. ACM **46(10)** (2003) 29–34.

[9] G. Canfora, M.D. Penta, R. Esposito, M.L. Villani, *Qos-aware replanning of composite web services*. In: Proceedings of the IEEE International Conference on Web Services (ICWS05). (July 2005) 121–129.

[10] R. Berbner, M. Spahn, N. Repp, O. Heckmann, R. Steinmetz, *An approach for replanning of web service workflows*. In: Proceedings of the 12th Americas Conference on Information Systems (AMCIS06). (August 2006).

[11] D.A. Menasce, *Qos issues in web services*. IEEE Internet Computing **6(6)** (2002) 72–75.

[12] K.C. Lee, J.H. Jeon, W.S. Lee, S.H. Jeong, S.W. Park, *Qos for web services: Requirements and possible approaches*. (2003) http://www.w3c.or.kr/kr-office/TR/2003/ws-qos/, accessed: 2006/07/03.

[13] R. Jain, *The art of computer systems performance analysis: techniques for experimental design, measurement, simulation, and modeling*. John Wiley & Sons, Inc., New York, NY, USA (1991).

[14] T. Gschwind, K. Eshghi, P.K. Garg, K. Wurster, *Webmon: A performance profiler for web transactions*. In: Proc. of the 4th IEEE Intl Workshop on Advanced Issues of E-Commerce and Web-Based Information Systems (WECWIS 2002). (June 2002) 171–176.

[15] A. Schmietendorf, R. Dumke, S. Stojanov, *Performance aspects in web service-based integration solutions*. In: Proc. of the 21st UK Performance Engineering Workshop (UKPEW2005). (July 2005) 137–152.

[16] F. Casati, E. Shan, U. Dayal, M.C. Shan, *Business-oriented management of web services*. Commun. ACM **46(10)** (2003) 55–60.

[17] A. Feldmann, *Blt: Bi-layer tracing of http and tcp/ip.* Comput. Networks **33(1-6)** (2000) 321–335.

[18] Y. Mao, K. Chen, D. Wang, W. Zheng, *Cluster-based online monitoring system of web traffic.* In: Proceedings of the 3rd international workshop on Web information and data management (WIDM 01). (November 2001) 47–53.

[19] C. Manikopoulos, S. Papavassiliou *Network intrusion and fault detection: a statistical anomaly approach.* IEEE Communications Magazine **40(10)** (October 2002) 76–82.

[20] C. Yuan, N. Lao, J.R. Wen, J. Li, Z. Zhang, Y.M. Wang, W.Y. Ma, *Automated known problem diagnosis with event traces.* In: Proceedings of EuroSys2006. (April 2006) 375–388.

**Acknowledgements**

This work is supported in part by E-Finance Lab e.V., Frankfurt am Main.

Nicolas Repp
Technische Universität Darmstadt
Multimedia Communications Lab (KOM)
Merckstrasse 25
64283 Darmstadt
Germany
e-mail: repp@kom.tu-darmstadt.de

Rainer Berbner
Technische Universität Darmstadt
Multimedia Communications Lab (KOM)
Merckstrasse 25
64283 Darmstadt
Germany
e-mail: berbner@kom.tu-darmstadt.de

Oliver Heckmann
Technische Universität Darmstadt
Multimedia Communications Lab (KOM)
Merckstrasse 25
64283 Darmstadt
Germany
e-mail: heckmann@kom.tu-darmstadt.de

Ralf Steinmetz
Technische Universität Darmstadt
Multimedia Communications Lab (KOM)
Merckstrasse 25
64283 Darmstadt
Germany
e-mail: steinmetz@kom.tu-darmstadt.de

Whitestein Series in Software Agent Technologies, 33–46
© 2007 Birkhäuser Verlag Basel/Switzerland

# Employing Intelligent Agents to Automate SLA Creation

Halina Kaminski and Mark Perry

**Abstract.** Service Level Agreements (SLAs) are commonly prepared and signed agreements that form the contracts between a service provider and its customers, defining the obligations and liabilities of the parties. Naturally, SLAs should reflect the business needs of both customer and supplier. SLAs are usually formed through either the adoption of a boilerplate agreement from the provider, or through a mediation/negotiation process between the parties. With the increasing adoption of software supply being implemented as a network service, such schemes are rigid or slow and costly, This paper proposes a system that the parties can use to facilitate both fast and flexible agreements. It proposes automation of SLA creation from a set of Service Level Objectives (SLOs), making use of software agents and adopting a social order function by incorporating it into the decision process.

**Keywords.** Service Level Agreements, Service Level Objectives, Web Service, Negotiation Manager, Software Agents, Software Service Provision.

## 1. Introduction

One of the many benefits offered by high speed and reliable large scale network services has been the opportunity for software vendors to move rapidly into providing web services, and treating software delivery as a service. This movement away from traditional packaged software requires a different type of agreement between the providers of such software and their customers, which was previously managed by simple licensing agreements, shrink wrap licenses and the like, or, for larger systems, by negotiated licenses. In the service provision environment, the relationship between the provider and customer is typically embodied in Service Level Agreements (SLAs). These are commonly prepared and signed contracts between a service provider and its customers, defining the obligations and liabilities of the parties. Depending on the nature of the agreement, it may take the form of adopting a boilerplate contract from the provider, or for larger scale agreements, a fully negotiated contract. Although the former may satisfy many aspects desired by the customer, it is likely that there are many issues that do not fully meet the customer's needs. Fully negotiated agreements will avoid the inclusion of such non-satisfactory terms, but will require the intervention of personnel who can bring technical, business needs and legal perspectives to the negotiations [1]. It is crucial for both parties to ensure that the terms of the agreement are realistic and meet their requirements, as the financial consequences of failure can be fatal to the business. For example, many service recipients do not require service availability to be guaranteed for 99.99% of the time, as this would be very expensive, and a provider guaranteeing a service that it cannot support may find itself subject to penalties.

This paper proposes the automation of SLA creation from a set of Service Level Objectives (SLOs), employing software agents and adopting a social order function by incorporating it into the decision process. By adopting this system, the service provider can form SLAs and satisfy the need for fast and flexible agreements. Earlier work in SLA management has focused on a bottom up approach, looking to capture managed SLA data [2]. However, the present study concentrates on automatic SLA creation that integrates an effective negotiation process, removing the need for the service provider to engage highly qualified personnel at the time of SLA adoption by the customer. One area in which companies are seeing increased cost is support personnel for their system offerings. Where a company's business is primarily (software) service provision, such costs are critical to contain. In such an environment there is a need to automate with the result of reducing support and management costs [3]. This environment makes it very desirable to automate the monitoring, selection, and decision making processes, leaving the service provider more resources to focus on the provision of better services. Generally, most of the business decisions are based on resource prioritization. In this paper by a *resource* we mean any service that is quantifiable, such as application, server, CPU usage, disk space, license etc. Such automation can be achieved by building a software system that embodies high level decisions and which possesses the properties of autonomy, social ability, reactivity and pro-activeness. Intelligent agents can provide this type of functionality, and an SLA real-time negotiation system that utilizes these features will prove to be a great asset to service provision enterprises.

## 2. Service Level Agreements

Most SLAs are formed by the provider of services, although it is possible that a customer may come up with a totally original SLA in extraordinary circumstance. Here, we focus on the provision of SLAs from the provider side, but this does not preclude the development of customer originating agreements. Naturally, the provider's perspective is for the SLA to reflect the business goals of the company. It is likely that this will also include the maximization of the customer satisfaction in addition to the limitation of provider liability for problems such as non-performance or failure to meet the quality goals. Rather than simply an end issue, the development of SLAs must be considered a vital step in the business process. Although static, preformed SLAs, which are basically monolithic agreements, may continue to have a role to play in the future, it is desirable to enable clients to select elements of an SLA, or the overall type of SLA, that can meet the requirements of their own situation. Our aim is to provide methods for dynamic, automated SLA creation. As well as benefiting the service provider with automation, such a flexible, dynamic system will allow customers to choose the type of SLA scheme that they want and, consequently, exercise control over the policies for which they have the most concern.

An SLA is not created in isolation, simply to meet the technical needs of the parties, although these need to be considered. The total business strategy of the service provider must be integral to the process. Generally, every SLA should include:

a) the specification and availability of the service to the customer,
b) the performance goals of various components of the customer's workloads,
c) the bounds of guaranteed performance and availability,
d) the measurement and reporting mechanisms,
e) the cost of the service,
f) priorities if service can not be delivered,
g) penalties if the customer exceeds the load,
h) penalties if the provider does not provide service as agreed,
i) schedules for follow-up meetings and interface [3].

SLAs become more complex when the provider offers multiple services such as networking, online databases and end user direct support [4]. Usually, the services provided by such businesses vary both in diversity and intricacy. Many organizations are now utilizing service level objectives (SLOs) as a means of expressing the aims of the company, and to establish parameters for the tracking of the effectiveness of their service infrastructure.

## 3. Service Level Objectives

A business in the highly competitive and growing online, on demand, service environment must have a clear business plan and define service levels that can be attained. Every resource that is offered to a customer should have an indication what its business levels are and what performance is acceptable to the end-user. These will include performance requirements for applications offered as services, and, in addition, more general business objectives that need to be attained by the system. It has been suggested [5] that SLOs must be realistic, quantifiable (measurable), clear and meaningful, manageable, cost effective and mutually acceptable. The target goals of SLOs have to reflect reality and should be attainable. They also should include the metric definition which contain how the values are measured and reported to the managing authority. Each SLO has to have a meaningful description of the service level such that it can be easily understood by a customer. For example, expressing service performance in packets dropped or server congestion may not be of significance to the end-user. Most importantly, SLOs have to be cost effective. There is a belief that the best SLOs are impractical because they are too expensive to be measured. Simply having the objectives by themselves is not sufficient to provide a high quality service.

A wide variety of service offerings poses another difficulty: to create the best possible SLA from a selection of SLOs from an option pool requires careful consideration and quantification of resource dependencies and the connections between resources wherever possible. As an example, by having two servers that are each capable of handling ten thousand transactions per second does not necessarily mean that we can provide a service of twenty thousand transactions per second to a customer. Both servers could be using a secondary resource that is limited to a lower capacity (a common router for example). Thus the overall performance of the entire business system is unlikely to be a simple summation of the resources available. Many objectives can be embodied in a single SLA, and within the parts of the SLA; for example, with a network service provision agreement there may be ones dealing with availability, network latency, packet delivery and even reporting. This will clearly differ between clients and so there will be a different, though similar, set of objectives associated with each client.

As an example, a partial SLO set for a resource (SellSolution application) is shown in Table 1.

| Application name = SellSolution | | | | ... |
|---|---|---|---|---|
| Service Level | Platinum | Gold | Silver | ... |
| Number of transactions | unlimited | 1000 | 500 | ... |
| Initial Response Time | 10 sec | 12 sec | 15 sec | ... |
| Transaction Processing Time | 2 $\mu s$ | 3 $\mu s$ | 5 $\mu s$ | ... |
| Monthly Availability | 98% | 97% | 95% | ... |
| Validity Time Start/End | To be filled at the SLA creation time | To be filled at the SLA creation time | To be filled at the SLA creation time | ... |
| Cost | $500.- | $ 150.00 | $ 80.00 | ... |

TABLE 1. SLOs for a specified resource

It is our goal to be able to set service levels for the resource (service) in such a way that they are not custom made, but predefined and reusable. Ideally there should be many levels for the same resource and the levels would differ in QoS and the cost for flexible offerings. Levels of service can be predefined for the resources of the same type, and the same level of service can be used by many customers. SLOs also express a commitment to maintain a particular state of the service in a predefined period of time. For example, (SLO) gold in Table 1 indicates that the SellSolution will start within 12 seconds from the initial request and every transaction will be processed in less than 3 $\mu$s. The customer is limited to perform 1000 transactions. In this service level the application will be available to the user 97% of time and the cost for this type of service is $150.00. The validation time period has to be specified during the negotiation phase, i.e., when the customer and the service provider agree to the specific service terms. We will return to this example in section 6.4.

The flexibility of having a pool of SLOs available will result in the existence of a range of service levels and performance metrics for each resource: for each service there will be multiple SLOs on the basis of which SLAs will be offered.

## 4. Intelligent Agents

A negotiation model is an abstract representation of the structure, activities, processes, information, resources, people, behaviour, goals, rules and the constraints of a computing service environment. From the operational perspective, the negotiation model supplies the information and knowledge necessary to support the SLA creation process. There is a wide variety of information systems that participate in business processes and they are aimed at fulfilling different business requirements. Consequently in business, there are widely varying viewpoints and assumptions regarding what is essentially the same subject. A negotiation framework should have a very carefully "engineered" translation of such different reasoning. To deal with the complex representation issue the system should support the appropriate ontology. The purpose is to provide a shared and common understanding of a domain that can be communicated to people, application systems, and businesses giving some specification of the meaning of semantics of the terminology within the vocabulary [6]. The basic concepts of ontology have also been established in works on intelligent agents and knowledge sharing, such as Knowledge Interchange Format (KIF) and Ontolingua languages [7, 8].

The automation of a negotiation process can advantageously adopt the intelligent agent paradigm. The system can contain one super agent that gets its knowledge from other agents: there can be an agent assigned to each sub-domain, such as a business rules agent, a price agent, an obligations agent, and a resource discovery agent. All of the secondary agents would be reporting to the super agent and only the super agent will engage in the decision making and outer interactions. Figure 1 depicts a Negotiation Model Agent assignment.

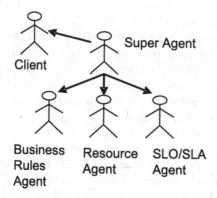

FIGURE 1. Intelligent Agent Assignments

The Negotiation Manager system is based on a multiple agent framework. There should be one agent per every issue that needs an agreement such as resources, price and business policies. Our model is based on a sequential decision making (i.e., as each party presents an offer, a counteroffer or a decision to accept or decline is made in sequence).

## 5. Negotiations

To date, most research in service provision has concentrated on how to manage SLA compliance as well as tracking performance for planning purposes. The existence of a variety of measuring tools allows the service managers to measure and track performance of service levels based on the actual service usage. At the same time the results obtained from such metrics can be used in planning corrective actions.

Automated contract creation enables service providers and their clients to make use of technology to create SLAs within pre-planned and pre-approved parameters. Our goal is to use intelligent agents to provide automation of SLA development and creation, (i.e., the creation of the electronic contracts for computing services), which in addition to giving flexibility to the contracting system will optimize the provider's profits. At the same time it will maximize the customer's satisfaction and the ability to be flexible. We are developing a negotiating tool (SLA Negotiation Manager) described hereafter along with the process of negotiation and creation of a SLA from existing business objectives. The Negotiation Manager is a truth based system and it has a system-wide objective of computing an efficient cost-gain relation. Our goal is to provide an interactive negotiation system that would help a service provider to formulate and evaluate an offer, and then send that offer to the client.

The main module of our system will be dedicated to automate processes on behalf of service provider. The overall negotiation process will be modeled as exchanging proposals and counter-proposals between the provider and the customer. Figure 2 presents a state diagram for a negotiation process.

Each negotiation starts with the customer choosing one service offer from a pool of predefined service packs. Usually such offer depends on service price, delivery, quality etc. The initial offers can be pre-defined and stored in a repository or they can be automatically generated by using existing SLOs and current system's state.

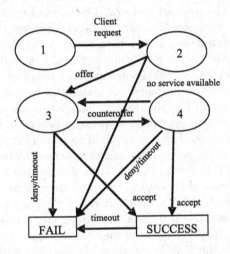

FIGURE 2. Negotiation Process State Diagram

The provider takes all factors into account and calculates the expected pay-off value function associated with possible offers, and selects the offer that maximizes its payoff. When satisfied with an offer, the customer (client) just sends an acceptance message to the provider and a SLA is finalized. In Figure 2, the transition:

$$1 \rightarrow 2 \rightarrow 3 \rightarrow SUCCESS$$

presents such process. If not accepting the first offer, then the client can either abort the negotiations:

$$1 \rightarrow 2 \rightarrow 3 \rightarrow FAIL$$

or can send a counter - proposal:

$$1 \rightarrow 2 \rightarrow 3 \rightarrow \{4 \rightarrow 3\}$$

At this point the service provider evaluates an offer and updates its knowledge about the customer. If the offer is acceptable the Negotiation Manager creates an SLA, otherwise provider sends counter-proposal. Exchange of counter-proposals continues until one of the parties decides to accept an offer or quit. The state SUCCESS or FAIL has to be reached. The essential work in creating SLOs takes place in the business/marketing department. SLOs should aim at achieving the best performance possible, but representing true and real values at all times.

## 6. Implementation

In our system resource specific knowledge inclusion should eliminate many of the inefficiencies in SLA creation. By using templates and SLO libraries SLA Negotiation Manager will ease the contract creation. Our system makes the use of the widely approved contract language Web Service Level Agreement (WSLA). It also provides a user friendly interface for the client to see and choose requested services as well as enabling the exchange of counter-offers. It is anticipated that the contract creation time will be reduced significantly as a result of the usage of templates and pre-approved clauses. By using our system the service provider will be able to ensure consistency and compliance with company's standards. Storing all SLAs in a single repository will provide an additional benefit to the service planning and management tools, so that it is required to search for a contract in only one place. In the SLA creation process, a client is presented with the services that are offered by the provider. Based on the customer's choice the Negotiation Manager aggregates and combines these choices into various SLA parameters, chooses service levels (SLO) for every SLA parameter. Every SLA has to be checked for the resource availability because it defines the agreed level of performance for a particular service. This process is also known as compliance monitoring. It has been our attempt to *teach* the SLA Negotiation Manager the business knowledge, goals, and policies of the party it belongs to. Such knowledge enables the system to choose and combine the set of SLOs that should be specified in the SLA in order to ensure compliance with the business goals.

In [7] it is shown that there are five main components of an enterprise Contract Lifecycle Management strategy:

1. automated contract creation,
2. secure contract negotiation,
3. electronic contract repository,
4. automatic upload of relevant contract data to back-end systems,
5. generation of proactive management reports and alerts to encourage compliance to committed contract terms and conditions.

It is our goal to provide the first four out of the above five directives in the SLA Negotiation Manager. Our system will automate contract creation through a secure negotiation with the customer, then newly created SLA will be stored in a central repository and the back-end system logs will be updated for the usage of resources that are specified in the contract. As for the last component, we leave the generation of relevant reports to the service management tools.

## 6.1. System dependencies

Every SLA consists of at least two signatory parties: the service provider and the customer (client). Both service provider and a client can have multiple SLAs in their internal company's repository. Each SLA can consist of multiple SLOs. There is at least one SLO for each service offered.

As an illustration of these type of situations, hereafter is a typical scenario of a retail store that needs a front end billing transactions handled.

A customer finds a service description and relative URL in the business directory (e.g., UDDI). Then it connects to the company that offers the service. Upon such connection an SLA Negotiation Manager is started. The customer wants to subscribe to a particular service (for example: store customers' billing system). The customer knows that to be successful it needs to have an access to software that can handle 10,000 transactions per day, with an initial transaction response time lower than 5 seconds and the average transaction time not longer than 60 seconds.

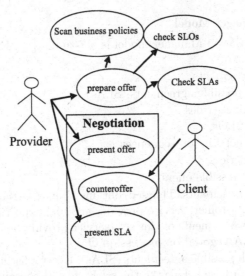

FIGURE 3. Use case diagram for negotiation scenario

The customer is willing to pay $800/month for such service. The SLA Negotiation Manager by examining existing SLOs and existing SLAs checks if such service is available (checking of the existing SLAs is done in order to avoid over-commitment). If the provider's company can provide a service required then a SLA is created accordingly and presented to the customer for an acceptation.

Upon customer's acceptance, the SLA is stored into the repository and the service is made available to the client. It is anticipated that at this point a SLO defining a service of renting a hardware capable of performing 10,000 transactions per day would have to be removed from a resource pool to avoid over-commitment.

This is the best case scenario. Often, the service provider can not commit to the requested service and then the SLA Negotiation Manager would come up with the next best offer. Such decision making might be based on asking customer how much money it is willing to spend or how many transactions its store must absolutely have and based on that and on knowledge of the system the Negotiation Manager can propose a number of options to choose from. The offer can also depend on other parameters as well. Maybe the provider can commit to 10,000 transactions, but the upper limit on the average transaction time will be 90 seconds. One option might be an offer of 8,000 transactions per day with the initial response time lower than 10 seconds and an average transaction time of less than 60 seconds for $650.00/month and/or another offer could be 12,000 transactions per day with the initial response time lower than 5 seconds and the average transaction time of 3 minutes for $1,000.00/month. Ideally the customer chooses one of the offers and a SLA is created. If the customer does not agree to the proposed service then negotiation continues.

## 6.2. Negotiation Manager Model

An Automated Negotiation Manager model is a 7-tuple: { R, K, Z, P, Q, F, M } where:

**R** is a set of participants,
**K** is a set of all possible agreements (SLAs),
**Z** is a set of business rules,
**P** is a set of all SLOs,
**Q** is a set of all negotiation sequences,
**F** is a utility function,
**M** is a set of all possible offers.

1. R is a set of participants. This set contains all parties that can be involved in the contract. The customer, service provider and all supporting parties belong to this set. At least two elements of this set (service provider and customer) must participate in any SLA negotiation process qn Q.

2. K is a set of all possible agreements (SLAs). Every existing SLA agreement that is stored in a data base belongs to the set K. It also contains all the possible agreements that can be created as a result of any successful negotiation process.

3. Z is a set of business rules (also called business knowledge). A business rule that a service cannot cost less than $0.07 per transaction might be an example of $z_i$ Z. Set Z represents corporate preferences and aligns business strategies of a service provider.

4. P is a set of all SLOs. Every SLA contains at least one SLO for the agreed service.

5. Q is a set of all sequences $s$, such that every $s = q1,q2,q3 \ldots qn$ where qi is an action (an offer, a counteroffer, accept or decline). Each $s$ illustrates a negotiation process and every successful negotiation is a finite sequence s. Here, by successful negotiation we mean any negotiation process that resulted in either

accept or decline. Sequence s can also serve as a history log when stored in a repository. The past negotiation procedure can be recreated from such sequence.

6. F is a utility function. This function is customized according to the negotiating party needs and business preferences. For example it might be widely known that the customer offers 10% less for the service than it is really willing to pay. Function f might be used to calculate next offer: f = current offer - 10%.

7. M is a set of all possible offers. Every permutation of elements of P belongs to M. In addition M contains any combination of an offer that has been modified according to one or more business rules from set Z.

There have been many mathematical models developed for negotiations, typically on direct e-commerce negotiations, and often employing game theory algorithms [8, 9]. Although these are not directly applicable to the SLA environment where there are a great deal more factors to consider above the product and price, they are useful for further development of the negotiation system.

A key factor for a Negotiation Manager is the ability to operate in an open environment where the preferences of a client are not known and we can only assume using a common knowledge that client's goal is to get more of a service for less money. This comes from the fact that customer's needs may go beyond specialized capabilities of any single service offerings. Moreover, the participating parties' legacy environments have to be incorporated seamlessly into the system. The Negotiation Manager design will follow the framework of a computational mechanism design which is an aggregation of a game theory, artificial intelligence and algorithmic theory. Mechanism design problem is to implement a system wide solution to a decentralized optimization problem with an intelligent agent representing the service provider and a customer who has private information about its preferences for different outcomes.

### 6.3. Negotiation Mechanism

A negotiation mechanism design is to define the possible strategies and a method used to select an outcome based on client's type and preferences. A negotiation mechanism:

$$M = (\Sigma_1, \ldots, \Sigma_n, g(.))$$

defines a set of strategies $\Sigma_i$ available to the negotiation agent, and an outcome rule:

$g : \Sigma_1 \times \Sigma_2 \times \cdots \times \Sigma_n \to O$, such that $g(\delta)$ is the outcome implemented by mechanism for strategy profile $\delta = (\delta_1, \ldots, \delta_n)$

All of the SLA's components and SLA itself has to be translated into the machine readable format. There are several such specifications resulting from ongoing research at the large software companies such as HP, Sun Microsystems and IBM [10, 11]. For our model we have chosen WSLA expressions. WSLA is based on Extensible Markup Language (XML), and it has the ability to define and describe computing services along with quality of service and service performance parameters. In addition XML is a very flexible text format that was originally

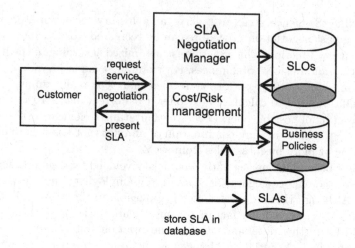

FIGURE 4. Process of creating an SLA

designed to meet the challenges of large-scale electronic publishing, and it can be easily extended to meet one's needs. WSLA is defined as an XML schema therefore the resulting SLOs can be easily translated into system-level configuration and stored in the machine readable format to be used by various system services such as SLA Negotiation Manager. We do not discuss SLOs creation in this paper as this is a research topic of its own, and the scope of this paper does not allow for an elaboration on this process. Here we assume that SLOs are developed by the Business/Marketing department and have already been defined in WSLA.

In our scenario there are two sides of the negotiations. One side, a service provider, has a repository of SLOs that define limits of the resources offered and the cost for each service, and on the other side there is a customer, who also has to define thresholds for acceptable service performance and the price that it is willing to pay.

In our automated SLA Negotiation Manager the system will provide the compliance monitoring according to the customers choices. A base framework for SLA negotiation model is presented in Figure 4.

### 6.4. Service Process Explained

It is very common that the service providers list their service offers in some business directory such as UDDI. A potential customer can find such listing on the web and locate the service. For the clarity of this paper we will continue with our retail store customer who needs hardware and necessary network connections to provide a store front sale billing functionality. Upon the client's choice of a specific vendor (or a specific service) the SLA negotiation manager will be executed. Figure

6 shows a sequence diagram for the SLA creation scenario. Let the application SellSolution serve as an example here.

A financial institution, offers a Web service to private and corporate store owners to perform a number of different types of store transactions (such as bank account transfers, credit card payments, returns, store credit option) and generate the statements needed for tax related and bookkeeping purposes. It is a web service on demand (also called utility service) where the customers can be billed for services used. The computing resource is SellSolution that allows for billing transactions on demand. A potential customer might be a large corporation that has a variety of different types of transactions; a medium size store that uses store credit card charges; or a single private store owner who only wants to use bank account debit charges.

The billing rate might be based on number of transactions, transaction time and/or availability to the customer. In our example the SellSolution has four SLOs specified for different performance levels: platinum, gold, silver and bronze (Shown in Table 1). Every level depends on a number of transactions being performed. The platinum level has an unlimited number of transactions, but instead is bounded by the response time and transaction time.

In our model, every customer no matter how small or how large of an enterprise will be able to take advantage of an automatic SLA creation through our SLA Negotiation Manager. The resulting SLA will be based on the SLOs of the business, and created according to WSLA specifications, which in turn will make them readable for other system utilities such as performance manager or service level manager.

## 7. Conclusion

Even though the software has been around for decades, with passage of time, the complexity of it simply increases. The latest studies show that computing services in combination with software on demand might provide solution for an enterprise level architecture.

Our paper presents a unique approach to the creation of Service Level Agreements. In practice constructing an SLA requires planning and care. While the process can vary among companies, it is often a politically oriented topic. SLAs are known to be used to find blame instead of being a driving force towards a positive change. There is a lot more to SLA Management tools than XML schemas and standards. The combination of information and contract negotiation procedure plays an important role. The system presented in this paper will provide an automated way to create and document SLAs which in turn will increase web service provider's profits, maximize customer satisfaction, and it will open up the way to more flexible service provision.

# References

[1] Christopher Ward, Melissa J. Buco, Rong N. Chang, Laura Z. Luan, Edward So, Chunqiang Tang "Fresco: A Web Services based Framework for Configuring Extensible SLA Management Systems" Proceedings of the IEEE International Conference on Web Services (ICWS'05) 11-15 July 2005 Pages: 237 – 245 vol.1

[2] Buco M.JU., Chang R.N., Luan L.Z., Ward C., Wolf JL., Yu P.S. "Utility computing SLA management based upon business objectives" IBM Systems Journal Vol. 43 No.1 2004 p.159.

[3] Suh, Bob. "Avoiding an Austerity Trap" Outlook Journal, February 2004 http://www.accenture.com/Global/Research_and_Insights/By_Subject/High_Performance_Business/AvoidingtheAusterityTrap.htm

[4] Leopoldi, R. "IT Services Management, A Description of Service Level Agreements", White Paper, RL Consulting, 2002 Retrieved from: http://www.itsm.info/SLA%20description.pdf on June 22, 2005

[5] Sturm, Richard. "Service Level Objectives", Network Word Fusion, 2002 Enterprise Management Associates, Inc. Retrieved from: http://www.slminfo.com/articles/slobjectives.htm on Dec 12, 2005

[6] Gualtieri Andrea, Ruffolo Massimo, "An Ontology-Based Framework for Representing Organizational Knowledge", Proceedings of I-KNOW '05 Graz, Austria, June 29 - July 1, 2005

[7] Weintraub Allan, "Contract Management – A Strategic Asset" CRM Today website, http://www.crm2day.com/highlights/EEplVVVFlpFCMLrUcN.php

[8] Zeng, D., and Sycara, K. "Bayesian Learning in Negotiation" Working Notes of the AAAI 1996 Stanford Spring Symposium Series on Adaptation, Co-evolution and Learning in Multiagent Systems

[9] Oprea M., "An Adaptive Negotiation Model for Agent-Based Electronic Commerce", Studies in Informatics and Control, Vol.11, No 3, September 2002

[10] Dan, A., Ludwig, H., Pacifici, G., "Web Service Differentiation With Service Level Agreements", White Paper, IBM Corporation, March 2003, http://www-106.ibm.com/developerworks/library/ws-slafram/

[11] Sun Microsystems, "Using the Sun ONE Application Server 7 to Enable Collaborative B2B Transactions" Informit Network Website, http://www.informit.com/articles/article.asp?p=100664\&seqNum=2\&rl=1

Halina Kaminski
Department of Computer Science
University of Western Ontario, Canada
e-mail: hkaminsk@csd.uwo.ca

Mark Perry
Department of Computer Science
University of Western Ontario, Canada
e-mail: markp@csd.uwo.ca

Whitestein Series in Software Agent Technologies, 47–64

# A Flexible Approach to Service Management-Related Service Description in SOAs

Christian Schröpfer, Marten Schönherr, Philipp Offermann and Maximilian Ahrens

**Abstract.** In order for service-oriented architectures (SOAs) to deliver their true value for the business, e.g. flexibility and transparency, a holistic service management needs to be set up in the enterprise. To perform all the service management tasks efficiently heavy support by automated processes and tools is necessary. This article describes a service description approach that is based on OWL-S (Web Ontology Language for Services) and focuses on non-functional criteria. It starts with the necessary service management tasks and explains non-functional data elements and statements for its automated support. After covering related work it explains the proposed flexible extension to OWL-S. This extension is twofold. Firstly, simple service lifecycle elements are added using the normal extension mechanism. Secondly for adding QoS (Quality of Service) capabilities, the approach combines this extension mechanism with UML (Unified Modeling Language) Profile for QoS. A prototype delivers the proof-of-concept.

**Keywords.** Service-oriented architecture, semantics, service description, QoS (Quality of Service), service management.

## 1. Introduction

In the last years, a lot of work regarding practical usability of technologies in the SOA (service-oriented architecture) area and especially Web services area has been done. Research work is more and more shifting from the technical areas like reliability and security to the business layer. One of the problems is the operational management – or IT service management – of an actual, implemented service-oriented IT landscape in the enterprise. ITIL (IT Infrastructure Library, see http://www.itil.co.uk/) is a general and widespread IT service management framework. Being a de-facto standard, many other service management frameworks are based on it [1]. Among others, it covers best practices along two areas, *Service*

*Support* and *Service Delivery* including configuration management, incident management, problem management, change management, release management, service level management, capacity management, availability management, IT continuity management, and financial management [1]. Part of the "IT service management" within the SOA is the "service component management" which deals specifically with managing the service components, e.g. Web services, during their lifecycle.

Due to the special characteristics of an SOA, its operational management is different from managing mature architectures. Additional requirements need to be covered. In an SOA, the implemented Web services are most likely much more fine granular than "normal" applications. In one landscape, there exist services that offer similar functionality and have different lifecycle stages. A high number of services need to be managed while a high reuse rate is a primary goal. At the same time in order for SOA to deliver its advantages, changing services and their orchestration should be easily possible. When managed without automated processes, tool support, and centralized repositories, these conditions can lead to confusion and chaos. The contrary of the original goals of SOA, among others more flexibility and more efficient IT, would be the outcome. Hence, an effective and efficient service management framework for SOAs is needed that is supported by automated processes and tools. The following SOA-specific functional blocks should be covered: service definition, service deployment lifecycle, service versioning, service migration, service registries, service message model, service monitoring, service ownership, service testing, and service security [2]. They represent SOA-specific functionality in the broader area of the ITIL processes. Reference [3] highlights the importance of service description and in particular non-functional service description for managing SOAs and mentions in addition service discovery, substitution, and composition. Modeling functional and non-functional information in a machine-readable and semantically enriched way is a basis for a highly automated management of SOAs and in a broader sense of IT service management.

This article looks at a flexible service description approach to non-functional information. In Web services technology, UDDI repositories (Universal Description, Discovery, and Integration) and WSDL (Web Services Description Language) are used for service publication, discovery, and description but do not provide the necessary semantic functionality. Compared to the functional area less work has been done in the area of semantically enriched non-functional service description. Hence, this paper especially deals with the latter part. The approach builds on OWL-S (Web Ontology Language for Services). The two aspects that form the basis in the non-functional area are service lifecycle information and QoS (Quality of Service) guarantees offered by a service. Hence, it is necessary to look at semantic Web service description standards in general as well as description standards in the QoS domain.

The remainder of this paper is organized as follows: In section 2, the requirements for describing services are examined. Section 3 gives an overview over the related work. Section 4 describes the extensions to OWL-S and section 5 the prototype. Section 6 describes the importance of this approach for matching, SLA negotiation, and SLA enforcement.

## 2. Requirements for Service Description

### 2.1. Requirements Overview

In order to support the above mentioned activities, like semi-automatic discovery, service level management, and service migration, several types of information need to be modeled within the service description. The following two sections describe requirements for service description regarding information relevant for service lifecycle management and QoS guarantees. Two aspects have to be considered, the content and the type of statements that can be modeled. The lists contain the most obvious points in both aspects. However, they can not be regarded as complete. The available sources, e.g. [3], [4], [5], and [6], describe very different non-functional characteristics. In order to be future-proof, the approach must allow for extension of both ontological terms and structure of statements used for description. Building on this extensibility, domain specific models can be built that capture most requirements relevant for the domain.

### 2.2. Information Relevant for Service Lifecycle Management

In the area of service lifecycle management, the following most obvious information should be covered as a starting point:

1. Service name
2. Service categories
3. Versioning information
4. Lifecycle status ("Planned", "Design", "Test", "Pilot", "Active – intensive maintenance", "Active – regular maintenance", "Sunsetting candidate", "Sunsetting in progress", "Sunsetted") (based on [2], extended)
5. Service provider information
6. Infrastructure the service runs on: server name, configuration management ID, etc.
7. Link to source code
8. Different responsibilities, roles, persons, e.g. for business aspect or maintenance
9. Link to further business description of the service
10. Pricing information (depending on QoS class)

For lifecycle management, the following obvious statement structures should be covered as a starting point:

1. Parameters with simple values, e.g. versioning information
2. Parameter names with RDF (Resource Description Framework) pointers to terms from predefined ontologies or resources (configuration database IDs for related infrastructure). Technically, this includes 1.

3. Tabular expressions, e.g. listing responsibilities for several areas
4. Free textual statements for a human reader

These statements are not very complex. As shown later, they can be realized relatively simply with OWL-S extensions. Free textual statements are introduced (also for the QoS) because we assume that in the first step it is not reasonable to put semantics behind every statement for automatic processing. Rare statements should be left for a human being to work with.

### 2.3. QoS Guarantees

Table 1 exemplarily describes QoS characteristics to be modeled in the service description.

The following structures of QoS statements should be supported as a basis to facilitate rich QoS specification in service description:

1. *Boolean statements*, e.g. "Component is Basel II certified – yes/no."
2. *Absolute requirements*, e.g. "Reliability should be at least 99.9%."
3. *Composed requirements*, e.g. "On weekdays, between 7am and 8pm, availability should be 99.9%; Otherwise, reliability should be 99%."
4. *Level statements*, e.g. "The QoS requirements as defined in level 'Gold' should be complied with."
5. *Percentile statements*, e.g. "In 95% of the cases, response time should be below 10 ms."
6. *Free textual statements* for a human reader

In addition, it should be possible to specify several sets of QoS guarantees (QoS-level) with added price tags for one Web service that can be referred to during SLA (Service Level Agreement) negotiations.

## 3. Related Work

### 3.1. Standards for Service Description

A number of standards have evolved in the area of semantic service description. A quite mature one by now is OWL-S. OWL-S is an upper ontology language developed by the Semantic Web Services arm of the DAML (Darpa Agent Markup Language) program [7, 8]. Using OWL-S, it is possible to describe Web services, their properties, and capabilities in a semantically enriched form. Given this, we have chosen OWL-S as the basis for our service description approach for two reasons. First of all, it is based on OWL, a well established ontology language. Secondly, there are robust tools available for working with OWL ontologies as well as with OWL-S service descriptions. Both reasons support the intention of this article to show that, based on today's technology, standards, and tools, a reasonable basis for service management can be realized.

Other relevant semantic Web service description standards are WSMO (Web Services Modeling Ontology) and WSDL-S (WSDL with semantic extension).

| QoS area | Explanation/example |
|---|---|
| *General area* | |
| QoS-level | Service level regarding performance and quality ("Gold", "Silver", and "Bronze" are defined in a separate SLA document) |
| Service category | Type of service/service domain (several categories per service possible) |
| Communication | Communication pattern (e.g. real time and batch) |
| *Cost area* | |
| Price | Specification of tariff models, e.g. per period of time, per service call, and volume-fixed |
| *Performance area* | |
| Time | Response time |
| Capacity | Data capacity of a database (normal/max after extension) |
| Accuracy | Accuracy of the result of a calculation |
| Arrival pattern | Jitter; arrival distribution |
| Ratios | Number of service requests per time period (throughput of data sets, calculations per time) – (normal/max after extension) |
| *Quality area* | |
| Functional correctness | Error rate |
| Reliability | Availability, business hours (weekdays/times), incident resolution time |
| End user usability | Rating with respect to ease of use/understanding |
| Security | Security level (high, medium, low – defined in separate document: encryption standard, access rights, and authenticity) |
| *Other boundary conditions* | |
| Organizational | Negative/positive list of partners |
| Cultural | Languages needed for end user communication |
| Normative | Compliance with laws/regulations, certification |

TABLE 1. QoS information

WSMO is a part of the WSMF (Web Services Modeling Framework) [9]. Its distinctiveness lies in its capability to import ontologies specified in other ontology languages, among others OWL, its usage of *mediators* bridging the gap between different Web services, as well as its *goal* concept describing functionality and interfaces from a user perspective.

WSDL-S heavily leverages the existing standard WSDL and is focused on compatibility [10]. It also is very flexible with respect to ontology languages (e.g.

OWL) and mapping languages. However, being so flexible it is also more generic than WSMO and OWL-S.

## 3.2. QoS-Specific Standards – UML Profile for QoS

Specification of QoS characteristics is an important topic in the area of IT systems. The existing standards can be grouped according to their main focus: software design/process description (e.g. UML Profile for QoS and QML – QoS Modeling Language [6]), service/component description (e.g. WS-Policy), and SLA-centric approaches (e.g. WSLA – Web Service Level Agreements [11] [12], WSOL – Web Service Offerings Language [13], SLAng – Service Level Agreement definition language [14], and WS-Agreement [15]). A good overview over most of them can be found in [4].

Several languages have been developed to support SLA negotiation and specification in a service provider/service requestor scenario. The SLA-centric approaches are very much linked to the problem of QoS characteristics specification. The difference to other QoS specification languages is that they are more targeted towards SLA negotiation, specification, and SLA management.

UML Profile for QoS is a comprehensive framework for modeling QoS requirements and offerings in UML models. It extends the reference UML 2.0 meta-model mainly by using stereotypes. The current specification was published by OMG (Object Management Group) in May 2006 [16]. Originally it has been developed for software engineering of object-oriented systems. This article shows that it is also applicable to service description. UML Profile for QoS uses the following approach for QoS description. It describes a QoS model specific to the respective domain separately from the actual elements to be annotated. Then in the actual UML model the elements can be annotated using terms defined in the QoS model.

There are several reasons for choosing UML Profile for QoS for the extension of OWL-S. Firstly, it comes with its own general catalog of QoS characteristics which is not domain- or project-specific. Secondly, it can be well integrated with business process modeling which is part of the Web services matching problem. Thirdly, compared to other specifications, UML Profile for QoS is quite mature and has been accepted by OMG as a standard. Its definition goes back to a thesis by J. Aagedal published in 2001 where a lot of other QoS-related work has been considered [17].

## 3.3. Approaches to Semantic Service Description, Discovery, and Selection

Roy Grønmo and Michael C. Jaeger propose a methodology for Web service composition using QoS optimization [18]. The main focus of their article is on a matchmaking algorithm that uses QoS requirements and offerings for achieving better results. For both, they use UML Profile for QoS. Other than in this article, they use a link from the WSDL operations to a document describing the QoS offerings.

Reference [4] proposes to have functional as well as non-functional specifications in separate repositories. By contrast, we recommend to use a single repository, since we do not see the necessity that a separate organization specifies the

QoS characteristics. In fact, the functional and non-functional properties should be guaranteed together either by the organization itself or a third party. The third party could then be a trusted entity that is responsible for monitoring service levels or even for delivering the service levels itself.

Reference [5] describes a framework and ontology for dynamic Web services selection. It uses an agent-based system to support dynamic service selection and QoS ontologies for describing the non-functional characteristics. Although the approach covers QoS very extensively and comes with a realistic example, it has shortcomings. It uses its own service ontology which makes it proprietary. Also, semantic description of service lifecycle information and functional service description is not explicitly covered by the approach.

WS-QoS is a framework that allows the definition of QoS requirements as well as offerings for Web services and provides an infrastructure for managing those QoS-aware Web services. WS-QoS is based on a WS-QoS XML schema and can be extended. Although it is compatible with UDDI and WSDL by using their extension mechanisms, it is a proprietary approach when it comes to the QoS specification [19].

In [20], Klein and König-Ries present a process and a tool for describing services based on DAML-S. A layered set of ontologies is used and instantiated in a specific service description with the tool. The service description does not specifically deal with service management requirements. In [21], Klein, König-Ries, and Müssig develop an alternative service description language, called DIANE Service Description (DSD) that implements additional requirements that are not covered by OWL-S and WSMO. However, in this article we want to rely on current standards and existing tools as much as possible.

Matching, i.e. service searching, ranking, and selection, is an interesting application of semantically enriched service description. A lot of work is going on in this area. Apart from functional information also the non-functional information is important to be considered as the already mentioned sources [18] and [5] show. However, functional matching is usually the first step to find appropriate services. The recently published OWLS-MX matcher uses a hybrid approach, combining logic-based reasoning and approximate semantic matching, in particular content-based information retrieval techniques for the input and output parameters specified in the service profile of OWL-S [22].

## 4. Extension of OWL-S

The following section describes the proposed extension to OWL-S with respect to service lifecycle management and QoS.

```
<owl:Class rdf:ID="ServiceVersion">
  <rdfs:subClassOf rdf:resource=
   "http://www.daml.org/services/owl-s/1.2/
    Profile.owl#ServiceParameter"/>
</owl:Class>
<owl:Class rdf:ID="ServiceVersionInfo"/>
</owl:Class>
<owl:DatatypeProperty rdf:ID="VersionName">
  <rdfs:domain rdf:resource="#ServiceVersionInfo"/>
  <rdfs:range rdf:resource="http://www.w3.org/
   2001/XMLSchema#string"/>
</owl:DatatypeProperty>
<owl:DatatypeProperty rdf:ID="VersionNumber">
  <rdfs:domain rdf:resource="#ServiceVersionInfo"/>
  <rdfs:range rdf:resource="http://www.w3.org/
   2001/XMLSchema#float"/>
</owl:DatatypeProperty>
```

LISTING 1. Definition of *ServiceVersion* in OWL-S

## 4.1. Extension for Service Lifecycle Management

Extension of OWL-S happens in the *ServiceProfile*, one of the four classes OWL-S uses. It is targeted at describing functional and non-functional aspects for service discovery. For the functional description *Parameter, Input, Output, Condition, Result,* and *Process* are used. The first five refer to the process description in *ServiceModel*. For the non-functional description the following properties/classes are interesting: *serviceClassification, serviceProduct, serviceName, textDescription, ServiceCategory,* and *ServiceParameter*. The first five can be used for the requirements mentioned as they are. The Web service can be classified using *serviceClassification* (mapping to an OWL ontology of services, e.g. NAICS – North American Industrial Classification System), *serviceProduct* (mapping to an OWL ontology of products, e.g. UNSPSC – United Nations Standard Product and Services Classification), as well as *ServiceCategory* (mapping to taxonomies potentially outside of OWL or OWL-S). A semantic name can be given to a service using *serviceName*. Free text descriptions can be represented with *textDescription*.

Especially important for the extension is *ServiceParameter*. With this element the remaining additional service lifecycle characteristics are defined (Table 2). Future extensions also can be realized using *ServiceParameter*.

*ServiceParameter* consists of the *serviceParameterName*, the actual name of the parameter, defined as literal or URI, and *sParameter* a link to the value within an OWL ontology. Listing 1 shows the definition of *ServiceVersion* in OWL-S as an example. *VersionName* and *VersionNumber* are defined as datatype properties (type *xsd:string* and *xsd:float*) of the class *ServiceVersionInfo* (subclass of *owl:Thing*). Listing 2 shows the *ServiceVersion* information in OWL-S in a service description for a logistics Web service *CalculateRoute*. *ServiceVersion_10* and

| Service lifecycle parameter | Explanation | |
|---|---|---|
| **Properties/ subclasses** | **Data type** | **Explanation** |
| *ServiceVersion* | Versioning information | |
| VersionName | String | Version name described as literal |
| VersionNumber | Float | Version number x.x |
| *ServiceLifecycle-Status* | Lifecycle status of the service component | |
| LifecycleStatus (subclass of owl:Thing) | (Enumerated instances) | Enumerated instances: "Planned", "Design", "Test", "Pilot", "Active_intensive_ maintenance", "Active_ regular_maintenance", "Sunsetting_candidate", "Sunsetting_in_progress", "Sunsetted" |
| *ServiceProvider* | Service provider information | |
| ProviderLink | anyURI | Link to external information (name, address, contacts, credentials, etc.) in provider database |
| *Service Infrastructure* | Infrastructure the service runs on | |
| ServerID | anyURI | List of server IDs the service runs on |
| ResourceID | anyURI | List of resource IDs the service uses |
| *SourceCodeLink* | Link to source code in code repository | |
| SourceCode | anyURI | Link to source code |
| *Service Responsibility* | Responsibility for service from business and technical perspective | |
| BizResponsibility | anyURI | Link to organization/person with business responsibility |
| TechResponsibility | anyURI | Link to organization/person with technical responsibility |
| *BusinessDescription* | Information about business background | |
| BizDescription | String | Textual description of business background |
| BizInfLink | anyURI | Link to further information resources |
| *ServicePricing* | Pricing information | |
| PricingModelQ1 | anyURI | Link to pricing model for QoS level 1, e.g. "Gold" |
| ... | ... | ... |
| PricingModelQ5 | anyURI | Link to pricing model for QoS level 5 |

TABLE 2. Defined elements for service lifecycle management

*ServiceVersionInfo_11* are instances that contain the actual version information "Snake" and "5.1".

## 4.2. Extension for QoS with UML Profile for QoS Description

Section 2.3 gives a flavor of what the level of complexity needed is when describing QoS offerings. It shows that a comprehensive and extensible QoS framework that builds on extensive experience needs to be leveraged. UML Profile for QoS is such a

```
<ServiceVersion rdf:ID="ServiceVersion_10">
  <profile:sParameter>
    <ServiceVersionInfo rdf:ID= "ServiceVersionInfo_11">
      <VersionName rdf:datatype=
"http://www.w3.org/2001/XMLSchema#string"
      >Snake</VersionName>
      <VersionNumber rdf:datatype=
       "http://www.w3.org/2001/XMLSchema#float"
      >5.1</VersionNumber>
    </ServiceVersionInfo>
  </profile:sParameter>
  <profile:serviceParameterName rdf:datatype=
   "http://www.w3.org/2001/XMLSchema#string"
   >ServiceVersion</profile:serviceParameterName>
</ServiceVersion>
<profile:Profile rdf:ID= "CalculateRoute_Profile">
  <profile:serviceParameter rdf:resource= "#ServiceVersion_10"/>
[...]
</profile:Profile>
```

LISTING 2. Instance of a service description for *CalculateRoute* with details for *ServiceVersion*

framework that suffices the requirements. Hence we propose to use UML Profile for QoS together with OWL-S to bring QoS functionality to Web services description.

The QoS model does not have to be defined in OWL-S. Its definition remains in UML and can be reused for other services and systems. This is very much in line with the idea of using the same QoS notation on the business process side as well as on the service description side to facilitate service level negotiation. The stereotypes *QoS Characteristic* and *QoS Dimension* are used in the QoS model to specify respectively quantify aspects of QoS. It is possible to use statistical values (maximum value, minimum value, range, mean, variance, standard deviation, percentile, frequency, moment, and distribution) as well as to express preferences about the direction when comparing or optimizing parameters (increasing or decreasing).

For annotating the elements with QoS requirements and offerings UML Profile for QoS uses three types of constraints: *QoS Required, QoS Offered,* and *QoS Contract. QoS Required* and *QoS Offered* describe required and offered limitations of *QoS Dimensions* for annotated elements, either by listing the allowed elements or by stating the limits. *QoS Contract* can be used for agreed limitations. Different QoS levels supported by a system, which can be used in SLAs, can be defined with *QoS Level.*

OCL (Object Constraint Language) expressions are used in the QoS statements. This enables rich expressions as those mentioned in 2.3. The respective *QoS Characteristic* is indicated in the annotation statement via *context.* An example *QoS Offered* statement in OCL is shown below: "From Monday to Friday 8:00am

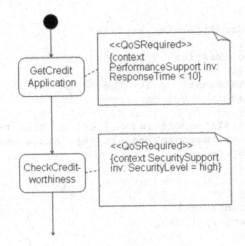

FIGURE 1. Example QoS requirements in a UML Activity diagram

to 8:00pm, the response time can be guaranteed to be below 10 ms."

```
<<QoSOffered>> {context Time_Performance inv:
(Set{'Monday', 'Tuesday', 'Wednesday', 'Thursday', 'Friday'}
->includes(getToday()) and getCurrentTime() > '8:00'
and getCurrentTime() < '20:00') implies responseTime < 10}
```

Introducing such QoS annotations into the OWL-S service descriptions can simply be done by adding *QoSCharacteristics* as a new *ServiceParameter* in *ServiceProfile* and *QoSStatement* as a subclass of *owl:Thing*. *QoSStatement* has the datatype property statement of the type *string*. This field contains the QoS constraints in OCL of the element to be annotated. Figure 1 shows example QoS requirements on the service requestor side in a UML Activity diagram. *responseTime* of *GetCreditService* is required to be lower than 10 ms. Listing 3 shows the corresponding QoS offering in the service description of *GetCreditService* that would be a match during service matching.

## 5. Service Management Prototype

### 5.1. Overview – Architecture and Functionality

The first version of the prototype is a combination of self-developed systems and available open source tools. It is realized as a web application and contains a web browser-driven user interface and two service repositories, one for the standard UDDI publishing and discovery, and one for the semantic search. Two repositories are necessary because the OWL-S-based repository is not UDDI standard compliant, while UDDI as the current standard for service repositories does not offer

```
<profile:Profile
  rdf:ID="GetCreditService_Profile">
  <profile:serviceParameter>
   <QoSCharacteristics rdf:ID="QoSCharacteristics_14">
     <profile:sParameter>
      <QoSStatement rdf:ID= "QoSStatement_15">
        <Statement rdf:datatype="http://
        www.w3.org/2001/XMLSchema#string">
        &lt;&lt;QoSOffered>> {context Time_Performance
        inv: responseTime &lt; 8}</Statement>
      </QoSStatement>
     </profile:sParameter>
     <profile:serviceParameterName rdf:datatype=
     http://www.w3.org/2001/XMLSchema#string>
       QoSCharacteristics</profile:serviceParameterName>
    </QoSCharacteristics>
  </profile:serviceParameter>
  [...]
</profile:Profile>
```

LISTING 3. QoS offering for *GetCreditService* in the service description

semantic support. The UDDI registry can be filled automatically with the information from the OWL-S repository. In order to make that possible, a mapping for many of the repositories' elements has been defined.

Figure 2 gives an overview of the prototype's architecture which is structured in 3 layers. The first layer is the web client and client application. It contains the user interface as a web browser application. Via this web-based front-end the user has access to the functionality described in the next section. User authentication functionality as well as storing the account information in a database is implemented here. The client accesses the UDDI and OWL-S repository on a web application server via SOAP, the standardized XML-based message exchange format for Web services. The UDDI repository is based on jUDDI as persistence layer. The OWL-S repository builds on Jena, a semantic web service framework, for the semantic support. Jena facilitates the usage of internal and external reasoners and access to the database via RDQL (Resource Description Framework Query Language) [23]. The prototype uses it for interfacing with the database where the semantic description is stored and for performing several operations on the ontology database, in this case MySQL. The prototype itself is written in Java. It uses RMI (Remote Method Invocation) for communication between the Java components.

Apart from the self-written parts, the prototype uses the readily available packages Protégé, Protégé-OWL, and OWL-S Editor. Protégé is a free, open source ontology editor from Stanford University [24]. Protégé with Protégé-OWL, a plug-in for defining ontologies in OWL, also from Stanford University (available at [25]),

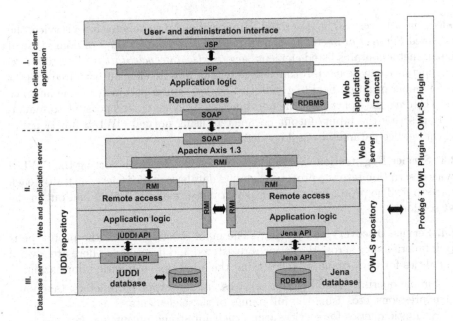

FIGURE 2. Overview of the service management prototype

is used for the taxonomy definition. OWL-S Editor is a Protégé plug-in developed at SRI International (available at [26]). It helps to define services in OWL-S by making available the OWL-S ontology with its predefined elements and a special view on the service, profile, grounding, and process instances.

## 5.2. Functions and Methodology of the Prototype

The first version of the prototype supports the following tasks as a basis for the mentioned service management responsibilities: taxonomy/ontology definition, service description, semantic annotation, service registration, service discovery, service review, and user access control.

### 5.2.1. Taxonomy/Ontology Definition.
The mentioned additions to the OWL-S ontology can be made with the OWL Editor adding new *ServiceParameter* and *owl:Thing* subclasses. Later, service descriptions and ontology extensions can be done using the OWL file. Also, a taxonomy for the service category field and input/output parameters can be developed with Protégé OWL. The generic way of defining/redefining the service taxonomy is an important feature. It is a matter of fact that there is no stable service description in complex environments.

### 5.2.2. Service Description and Semantic Annotation.
Service description and semantic annotations are done with the OWL-S editor by loading the OWL file that contains the ontology extended by the above mentioned elements. It is possible to import existing WSDL descriptions. Once the extended OWL-S ontology is

loaded, the services can be described. For specifying a parameter for a service, the predefined *ServiceParameter* has to be used. There are two ways of doing this. If the parameter contains listed elements, e.g. *ServiceLifecycleStatus*, a link to an existing instance can be used. If the parameter contains an element with free content like a number or a text field (e.g. *ServiceVersion*), a new parameter value instance has to be created. Apart from the non-functional elements, it is possible to semantically describe the input/output parameters using normal OWL-S functionality and the service parameter ontology defined.

**5.2.3. Service Registration.** Service registration is done by importing the OWL-S service description into the prototype and its database. This is necessary after each change to it. The prototype can then perform the search activities laid out in the next section.

**5.2.4. Service Discovery and Review.** The main functionality of the prototype is search functionality across the services registered and described. There are several possibilities for performing searches using the additional semantic information:

1. Simple queries – searching for services, input/output parameters, taxonomy expressions, etc. using the full names of these elements
2. Semantic queries for services using their input and output parameters
3. Semantic queries for services that match other services' input or output parameters
4. Semantic queries for services using taxonomy elements
5. Semantic queries using the other additional parameters such as *ServiceVersion*, *ServiceResponsibility*, and *ServiceLifecycleStatus*
6. Taxonomy tree search – services that belong to one taxonomy can be found by navigating through a simple taxonomy tree (uses Tigra Tree Menu [27]) or a hyperbolic graph (uses HyperGraph [28])

Number 3 refers to a simple matching functionality that can be used for service orchestration and will be extended in the future. To increase the flexibility of the search, it is possible to use the outcome of one search run as the basis for another search.

**5.2.5. User Access Control.** For service management in complex environments it is absolutely necessary to support role-specific views combined with access rights management. The numerous services are the core of an IT system of an enterprise. Therefore they need to be protected against malicious attacks as well as erroneous and uncoordinated activities of careless or unaware users. Hiding unnecessary information improves usability, reduces the number of errors, and is sometimes a must when it comes to confidentiality. The prototype's user authentication module controls the activities of individual users according to the rights associated with their roles. An "Administrator" can add new accounts and associate them to a role. "Users" are only allowed to search and browse through the service repository. "Developers" can in addition perform detailed search operations. The "Architect" is also allowed to register and delete services in the repository.

## 6. Importance for Matching, SLA Negotiation and Enforcement

Currently, the search needs to be done manually. Having visibility about all services implemented and the possibility of managing meta-information of the services centrally and thus in a consistent way is a big advantage and a precondition for the success of an SOA. However, if the IT systems based on the services get bigger and bigger and the number of services is expanding, a process that includes more automated support is necessary. The semantic description of input and output parameters and non-functional characteristics is a prerequisite for that. Only if service requestor and service provider refer to the same ontological concepts, the service matching module can "understand" them. That is why the additional effort of managing the semantic metadata is justified. A common way of performing the matching or SLA negotiation is a two-step approach as proposed by METEOR-S, Grønmo/Jaeger [18], or in "Semantic WS-Agreement Partner Selection" [29]. The first step performs functional matching. We suggest a hybrid semantic matching based on input and output parameters, e.g. by using OWLS-MX. In addition we propose to use the service category. Due to the semantic information not only exact matches of parameters and taxonomies are found but also parameters that stand in a class-sub-class relationship, e.g. car – convertible. The second matching step performs the non-functional matching using particularly the QoS-related information. Constraints about the QoS-characteristics on the service consumer side (*QoS Required*) are compared with the QoS-offerings specified in the service description (*QoS Offered*). The outcome is a ranking of the existing services that perform the desired functionality according to how well they meet the QoS requirements. Once a service is chosen, an SLA, a formal specification of the agreement between service consumer and service requestor (inter- or intra-organizational) can be specified.

It is planned to extend the prototype's service matching functionality and also to introduce an SLA specification, and SLA management module. According to a service request with a set of semantically enriched functional and non-functional information this module will discover existing services in the repository, provide their WSDLs and specify the SLA in a nearly fully automated way. The format for the SLA will be WSLA or WS-Agreement. The machine-readable SLA is a good basis for automated SLA-enforcement and monitoring during run-time. In case of problems, the person responsible can find the respective service in the registry and has access to information, e.g. contact details, infrastructure the service runs on. Matching and SLA specification functionality will ease the life of system developers as well as SLA authors/enforcers. It will also foster reuse, one of the goals of SOAs.

## 7. Conclusion and Outlook

As SOAs will be very complex from an IT service management point of view, in order to deliver their full value automated tool support is necessary. Semantic description of non-functional service characteristics is one important prerequisite for that.

The contribution of the presented work is a practical approach to service description and discovery that is extensible regarding additional future requirements. The article shows that it is possible to build a semantically enriched service repository with OWL-S that supports several tasks that are the basis for higher level service management activities. With the approach, it is possible to describe – along with the functional characteristics – the non-functional characteristics with respect to service management (service lifecycle management and QoS) in a single OWL-S-based repository. The approach is extendable with respect to changes of the used taxonomy as well as the elements used for service description. At the same time it is a compatible upgrade of the existing Web services description standards. Besides the presented approach, the article also gave an overview over relevant standards and related work in the area of non-functional service description.

The prototype will be extended to support better integrated service description functionality. Extensions for automated service discovery, SLA specification, and SLA management are planned.

# References

[1] M. Sallé, *IT service management and IT governance: review, comparative analysis and their impact on utility computing.* 2004. http://www.hpl.hp.com/techreports/2004/HPL-2004-98.pdf

[2] B. Woolf, *Introduction to SOA governance – Governance: The official IBM definition, and why you need it.* IBM, 2006. http://www-128.ibm.com/developerworks/webservices/library/ar-servgov/index.html

[3] J. O'Sullivan, D. Edmond, and A. ter Hofstede, *What's in a service? Towards accurate description of non-functional service properties.* Kluwer Academic Publishers, 2002. http://www.infosys.tuwien.ac.at/Teaching/Courses/IntAppl/Papers/WhatsInAService.pdf

[4] G. Dobson, *Quality of Service in Service-Oriented Architectures.* 2004. http://digs.sourceforge.net/papers/qos.html

[5] E. M. Maximilien and M. P. Singh, *A framework and ontology for dynamic Web services selection.* IEEE Internet Computing 08 (2004), 84–93.

[6] S. Frolund and J. Koistinen, *Quality of Service specification in distributed object systems design.* 1998. https://www.usenix.org/publications/library/proceedings/coots98/full\_papers/frolund/frolund.pdf

[7] DAML, *DAML Services.* 2006. http://www.daml.org/services/owl-s/

[8] D. Martin et al., *OWL-S: Semantic markup for Web services.* Martin, Ed., 2006. http://www.ai.sri.com/daml/services/owl-s/1.2/overview/

[9] *Web Service Modeling Ontology – ESSI WSMO working group.* 2006.

[10] R. Akkiraju et al., *Web service semantics – WSDL-S – W3C member submission 7 November 2005 – Version 1.0.* 2005. http://www.w3.org/Submission/2005/SUBM-WSDL-S-20051107/

[11] *Emerging Technologies Toolkit.* IBM, 2006. http://www.w3.org/Submission/2005/SUBM-WSDL-S-20051107/

[12] H. Ludwig et al., *Web Services Level Agreement (WSLA) Language Specification.*, 2003. http://www.research.ibm.com/wsla/WSLASpecV1-20030128.pdf

[13] V. Tosic, K. Patel, and B. Pagurek, *WSOL – Web Service Offerings Language.* in CAiSE'02 (2002), 57–67.

[14] D. D. Lamanna, J. Skene, and W. Emmerich, *SLAng: A Language for Defining Service Level Agreements.* 2003. http://www.cs.ucl.ac.uk/staff/w.emmerich/publications/FTDCS03/slang.pdf

[15] A. Andrieux et al., *Web Services Agreement Specification (WS-Agreement).* 2005.

[16] OMG, *UML Profile for Modeling Quality of Service and Fault Tolerance Characteristics and Mechanisms – OMG available specification – Version 1.0 – formal/06-05-02.* OMG, 2006. http://www.omg.org/cgi-bin/apps/doc?formal/06-05-02.pdf

[17] J. Ø. Aagedal, *Quality of Service support in development of distributed systems.* Department of Informatics, Faculty of Mathematics and Natural Sciences. Doctor Scientiarium: University of Oslo, 2001.

[18] R. Grønmo and M. C. Jaeger, *Model-driven methodology for building QoS-optimised Web service compositions.* The 5th IFIP International Conference on Distributed Applications and Interoperable Systems (DAIS).

[19] M. Tian, *QoS integration in Web services with the WS-QoS framework.* Department of Mathematics and Computer Science Berlin: Freie Universität Berlin, 2005.

[20] M. Klein and B. König-Ries, *A process and a tool for creating service descriptions based on DAML-S.* 2003. http://hnsp.inf-bb.uni-jena.de/DIANE/docs/TES2003.pdf

[21] M. Klein, B. König-Ries, and M. Müssig, *What is needed for semantic service descriptions – a proposal for suitable language constructs.* International Jounal on Web and Grid Services, 2005.

[22] M. Klusch, B. Fries, and K. Sycara, *Automated Semantic Web Service Discovery with OWLS-MX.* AAMAS 2006, Hakodate, Hokkaido, Japan, 2006.

[23] *Jena – A Semantic Web Framework for Java.* sourceforge.net. http://jena.sourceforge.net/

[24] *Welcome to Protégé.* Stanford Medical Informatics, 2006. http://protege.stanford.edu/

[25] *What is Protégé-OWL?* Stanford Medical Informatics, 2006. http://protege.stanford.edu/overview/protege-owl.html

[26] *The OWL-S Editor.* 2004. http://owlseditor.semwebcentral.org/

[27] SoftComplex, *Tigra Tree Menu.* SoftComplex. http://www.softcomplex.com/products/tigra_tree_menu/

[28] *HyperGraph.* http://hypergraph.sourceforge.net/

[29] N. Oldham et al., *Semantic WS-Agreement Partner Selection.* International World Wide Web Conference Committee (IW3C2), Edinburgh, Scotland, 2006.

Christian Schröpfer
Faculty of Electrical Engineering and Computer Sciences
Technische Universität Berlin
Franklinstr. 28/29
10587 Berlin
Germany
e-mail: `Christian.Schroepfer@sysedv.tu-berlin.de`

Marten Schönherr
Faculty of Electrical Engineering and Computer Sciences
Technische Universität Berlin
Franklinstr. 28/29
10587 Berlin
Germany
e-mail: `MSchoenherr@sysedv.tu-berlin.de`

Philipp Offermann
Faculty of Electrical Engineering and Computer Sciences
Technische Universität Berlin
Franklinstr. 28/29
10587 Berlin
Germany
e-mail: `Philipp.Offermann@sysedv.tu-berlin.de`

Maximilian Ahrens
Deutsche Telekom Laboratories
Ernst-Reuter-Platz 7
10587 Berlin
Germany
e-mail: `Maximilian.Ahrens@telekom.de`

Whitestein Series in Software Agent Technologies, 65–81

# Model Centric Approach of Web Services Composition

Ricardo Quintero, Victoria Torres and Vicente Pelechano

**Abstract.** The development of composite Web Services is being specified in a more declarative way than imperative programming. In this context, conceptual modeling has been the most accepted solution. Conceptual modeling of Web services has been done using behavioral models (like activity diagrams) considering mainly the dynamic view. We believe that, besides the dynamic aspects, the models should capture structural requirements between web service operations. In this way, behavioral models could be complemented with a structural model. In this paper we introduce a Web service composition modeling solution, following the MDA approach, considering both -structural and dynamic properties- enriched with semantic constraints in order to automatically generate composite Web services implemented in BPEL.

**Keywords.** Web Services, Composition, Conceptual Modeling, Web Engineering, MDA.

## 1. Introduction

Current e-business processes have, as an important requirement, the integration (the composition) of diverse application functionalities. The main strategy that has been followed by the industry is the use of Web Services to export the functionality and the use of programming languages to define service composition [11]. Because the majority of them were not designed with this goal in mind, they do not have abstractions for this objective, so usually the composition definitions are cumbersome. In contrast, conceptual modeling offers abstractions and models in order to define this composition at a high level of abstraction [12,13,14]. The main focus of these approaches is on dynamic concerns (as in UML Activity diagrams) forgetting the structural concerns. Although there are some model-driven solutions that generate in a semi-automatic way Web services and WS-BPEL [15], the problem with these modeling approaches is some lack of semantics that makes it difficult to capture the composition requirements in a precise way. This drawback does make it unfeasible to build modeling tools that validate models and generate complete and fully operative implementations. We consider that structural and dynamic models are needed in order to capture these issues, especially static and dynamic binding properties between the Web services that are being composed (the main focus of this work). Moreover it could be used as a way to export the functionality of the application: by means of methodological guidelines it is possible to detect functional groups from the business layer (specified by a structural model) and export them as a set of Web services. These Web services could be consumed by other applications to enable collaboration with other third parties. In this work we introduce, as a main contribution, two models (the Service Model and the Dynamic Model for Service Composition) which allow us specifying the structural and dynamic requirements of Web services compositions by using aggregation/association relationships with a precise semantics, defined in the context of a multidimensional framework [3]. In order to obtain the equivalent software artifacts of these models we follow a Model driven approach where the application of a set of transformation rules generates the corresponding WS-BPEL specification. This solution extends our Web engineering method Object-Oriented Web Solutions (OOWS) [1] in order to capture the collaborative requirements that are necessary to produce (in an automatic way) complete collaborative Web applications. The remainder of the paper is structured as follows: section 2 explains our proposal to conceptual modeling of Services; section 3 shows the introduced models from the point of view of their structural properties; section 4 explains the dynamic properties and the transformation of the models to a specific Web service composition technology (in this case we choose WS-BPEL [4], although it can be another -like BPML [5]); section 5 explains our code generation strategy and finally, section 6 presents conclusions and further work.

## 2. Conceptual Modeling of Services

The Model Driven Architecture (MDA) [2] is a new development strategy in which models are the first order actors within the software development process. MDA has several stages in which specific models are defined: the *platform independent models* (PIM), that describe the system with high-level constructs hiding the necessary technological details of the specific platform; and the *platform specific models* (PSM) which on the contrary, describe the system in terms of a specific technological platform. Besides these models, MDA proposes a strategy that has to be applied in order to transform these models into code. Following the MDA strategy we define two PIM models to capture the requirements of Web services compositions: a *Service Model (hereafter SM)* and a *Dynamic Model for Service Composition (hereafter DMSC)*. As vertical arrows show in Figure 1 each of these models is mapped into a PSM model, the horizontal ones represent the existing relationships between them (both, at PIM and PSM level). The constructs of the PIMs and PSMs (its metamodels) are defined using the Meta-Object Facility (MOF) language.

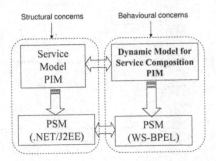

FIGURE 1. MDA strategy to service composition modeling

The SM captures the structural requirements of both, own and external Web services of the application including their ports and operations. This PIM model can be then transformed into several PSMs such as .NET [3] or J2EE [4]. The behavior of the Web services composition is defined by the DMSC. Although traditionally the approach followed has been to compose the new Web services by specifying only the orchestration of the Web service components, we believe that the structural requirements captured in the SM are also needed to have a complete specification in order to enable the automatic code generation.

## 2.1. Service Modeling

The structural requirements of produced and consumed functionality of an application are captured in the SM. Figure 2 shows the SM metamodel foundation. The included metaclasses are the basic constructs needed to model Web services, similar to other works [6,7,8]. The produced functionality is captured in the set of produced Web services from our application (called *Own-services*, see Figure 2). The consumed functionality is captured in the set of consumed Web services of our application (called *External-services*). Each service has one or more access points (Port) where each one has one or more of the following operations: (1) *one-way* (One-way-op), an asynchronous operation invoked by a client without response; (2) *notification* (Notification-op), an asynchronous operation invoked by the service without response; (3) *request-response* (Req-resp-op), a synchronous operation invoked by the client with response from the service and (4) *solicite-response* (Sol-resp-op), a synchronous operation invoked by the service with response from the client. The input and output parameters (Parameter) are one of the two specialized types from the data type (Data-type): simple (Simple-DT) or complex (Complex-DT).

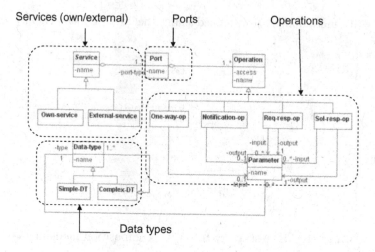

FIGURE 2. The foundation SM metamodel

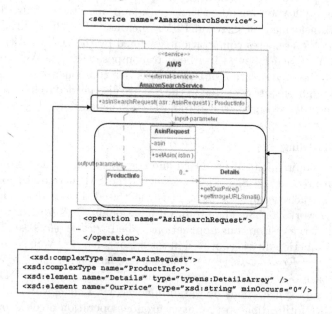

FIGURE 3. SM for Amazon.com (AWS)

Figure 3 shows an instance (an extract) of the SM of Amazon.com (AWS). The operation shown (asinSearchRequest) allows the user to query information about a Product (ProductInfo) from its isbn (AsinRequest). From the point of view of the application, services can be built in one of the following ways: (1) *Own-services*, with two possibilities: (a) those whose operations are views of the pre-existing operations in the logic layer of our application (at conceptual level they may be specified in the structural model) and (b) those whose operations are built from the composition of the operations from other own or external Services; and (2) *External-services* obtained from other applications that publish and produce them.

## 3. Structural Concerns

Services whose operations are built from the composition of own or external services are implemented by orchestrating their operations. This is a way of building *new functionality* (the new own-service) by reusing *functionality* through composition (from the pre-existing own or external services). From this perspective, service composition could be specified by *aggregation relationships of the services components*. Adding this new structural modelling, some tasks will be more easy to do (as we are going to show) than with the traditional dynamic approach, such as the dynamic Web service selection or the automatic and complete code generation contributing to facilitate the maintenance of the composite Service. In order to have a precise definition of the relationships, its semantics needs to be defined. Some works have addressed this problem in the context of object oriented conceptual modeling [9,10]. In this work we follow the multidimensional framework proposed in [3] to characterize aggregation relationships between Web services. The use of this multidimensional framework allows us to capture the structural properties of the composition which are explained in the following subsections.

### 3.1. Service Aggregation

The *structural* properties of the composition are captured in the SM. These properties characterize and define the semantics of the relationships between the Web services being aggregated (its *binding*). In the aggregation relationship, the service defined is called the *composite Service* (an Own-service) and the own or external services that are being aggregated are called the *component Services*.

### 3.2. Properties Specification

The properties are explained with respect to the MOF metamodel in Figure 4.

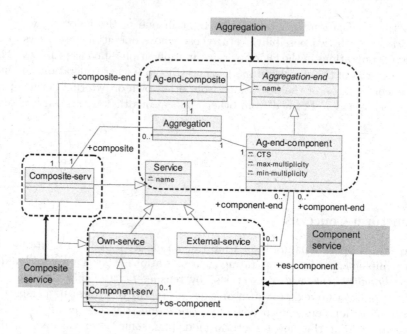

FIGURE 4. Service aggregation MOF metamodel

1. **Temporal Behaviour:**
   **Definition:** specifies if the *composite Service* has (or does not have) permanent *binding* with the *component Service* during its lifetime.
   **Defined over:** aggregation end (*component Service*).
   **Nomenclature:** CTS $_{aggregation-end}$
   **Values:** *Static—Dynamic*
   - *Static*:the *component Service* is bound to the *composite service* during its life.
   - *Dynamic*: the *component Service* is dynamically selected from data values (called *process variables* [11]) obtained during the execution of the composition logic, usually from a UDDI registry.
   **Semantic constraint:** expressed in OCL [9]
   ```
   context Ag-end-component
   inv temporal-value:
   CTS='Static' or CTS='Dynamic'
   ```
2. **Multiplicity:**
   **Definition:** specifies the minimum and maximum number of component services (of the same type) connected with the composite service.
   **Defined over:** aggregation end (*component Service*).
   **Nomenclature:** Min $_{aggregation-end}$, Max $_{aggregation-end}$
   **Values:** nonnegative integers.

**Semantic constraint:** in OCL

```
context Ag-end-component
inv multiplicity-value:
max-multiplicity >=0 and min-multiplicity >=0 and
min-multiplicity <= max-multiplicity
```

### 3.3. Additional Semantic Constraints

One advantage of this multidimensional framework is the additional knowledge implied, which can be used to build better modeling tools with model checking features that assist the modeller in the correct construction of SMs. Some examples of the additional knowledge are as follows (expressed in OCL):

1. Every aggregation includes as a component Service an Own or External service (different from the composite Service):

   ```
   context Ag-end-component
   inv at-least-one-component-service:
   os-component->size()>0 xor es-component-size()> 0
   ```

2. The *Static* value from the *Temporal Behaviour* property implies that the *maximum* and *minimum* values from the multiplicity property are 1 (see Figure 5):

   ```
   context Ag-end-component
   inv static-multiplicity:
   CTS='Static' implies (multiplicity-Max=1 and multiplicity-Min=1)
   ```

3. The *Dynamic* value from the *Temporal Behaviour* property implies that the maximum multiplicity values should be greater than 1. The composite Service could be binding with 2 or more possible component Services, each one dynamically selected, as we are going to show.

   ```
   context Ag-end-component
   inv dynamic-multiplicity:
   CTS='Dynamic' implies multiplicity-Max>1
   ```

### 3.4. Service Aggregation Examples

Figure 5 shows an example of service aggregation to an e-business application that uses the Amazon Web service and B&N Web service. The composite service *Best-StoreService* uses both Web services to get the best store and book price.

The aggregation relationship is defined *Static* because the composite service should have permanent binding with the component services. So they are specified using static *Temporal Behaviour* and multiplicity value equal to 1.

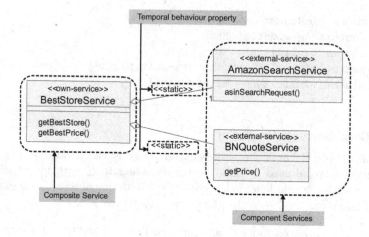

FIGURE 5. SM using static aggregation

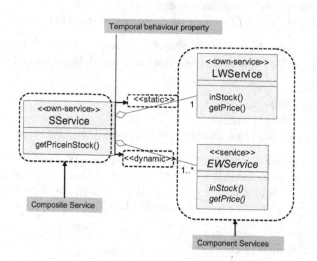

FIGURE 6. SM using static and dynamic aggregation

Figure 6 shows another example. In this case, the composite service (*SSer-vice*) is for a supplier application with the following process: to request the price of a product, the composite service offers the operation (*getPriceInStock*). This operation first checks the stock in the local warehouse using an own service (*LWSer-vice*). If the product is not in stock then it is checked in one of a couple of central warehouses using only one of the services *EWService1* or *EWService2* (specializations of the abstract service *EWService*, see Figure 7). So the binding between the composite service (*SService*) and the own service (*LWService*) is *Static* and to the *EWService* is *Dynamic*. In order to resolve to which concrete *EWService* is going to communicate with the *SService*, a condition is defined in the SM of the dynamic Web service.

Figure 7 shows the SM for the dynamic *EWService*. When a set of Web services (in this case *EWService1* and *EWService2*) are going to be managed dynamically, first they are imported to the SM from a UDDI registry. Then, a facade class (*FEWService*), with an operation `getXService`, is generated into the model in order to delegate it the responsibility of dynamic Web service selection. This operation includes the condition necessary to select the concrete Web service in the dynamic model. This condition can be established in the SM or the DMSC.

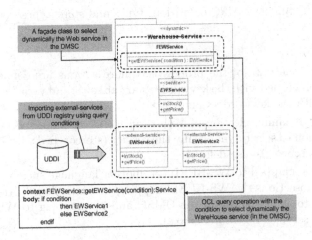

FIGURE 7. Importing Web services to the SM to be used in a dynamic way

In the first case, the condition is based on the different model elements of the application. Because the condition is not defined as part of the DMSC definition, the reuse and flexibility in this model is improved (by example, if a new central Warehouse is added then only a *EWService3* is added to the SM, the DMSC is not changed and the dynamic selection responsibility continues in the SM). In the second case, the modeler defines the condition based on process variables from the DMSC and this condition is passed as parameter to the `getXService` in the SM in order to select the Web service. An example of this mechanism is presented in subsection 4.3.

## 4. Behavioral Concerns

The logic of the composed Web services is captured in the DMSC. This model is defined as an UML activity diagram whose actions define the invocation of some of the component services operations. Each of those operations is defined as one of the types listed in Table 1 which correspond to the possible Web services operation types (see Figure 2).

| Operation Type | Stereotype |
|---|---|
| One-way | <<one-way>> |
| Request-response | <<request-response>> |
| Notify | <<notify>> |
| Solicite-response | <<solicite-response>> |

TABLE 1. DMSC operations types and stereotypes

To manage the data of the process two more actions are defined: variable declaration (stereotyped with the keyword <<variable>>) and variable assignment (stereotyped with the keyword <<assign>>).

In the case of dynamic selection of Web services, we define a special data type *Service*. An action to select dynamically the service (stereotyped with the keyword <<select-service>>) is also defined.

DMSC could be mapped to WS-BPEL (or another language such as BPML). In the following subsections the WS-BPEL mappings are introduced. An example is presented next to show the use of the DMSC and its mapping to WS-BPEL for an e-commerce service (*BestStoreService*).

### 4.1. The BestStoreService Case Study

Once the structural concerns of the *BestStoreService* (see Figure 5) have been defined, the composition logic of each operation needs to be specified by a DMSC. Figure 8 shows the composition logic of the getBestStore operation. Its DMSC is included in an action getBestStore (stereotyped with the keyword <<operation>>). The action has an input-pin, with the input parameter of the operation (isbn), and an output-pin (*BestStore*) with the return value.

The translation of the operation to WS-BPEL needs the structural knowledge captured in the SM (Figure 5) and the composition logic captured in the DMSC (see Figure 8):

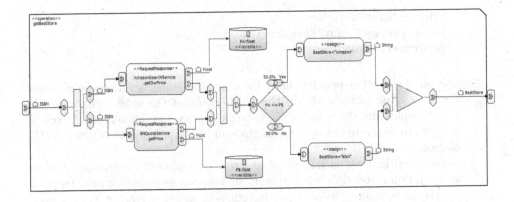

FIGURE 8. DMSC of the getBestStore operation

**Process definition:** corresponding to the main XML element (`<process>`) of the WS-BPEL process. This is obtained from the action name of the operation (getBestStore in Figure 8).

**Partner links identification:** the partner links corresponds to: (1) the client, who invokes the WS-BPEL process and (2) the Web services invoked by the BPEL process. In the first case, the client name of the process is specified with the following syntax: **service-name-clientLT**. The *service-name* is taken from the name of the composite service in the SM. The role corresponds also to the service-name and the *portType* is corresponding from the port name in the SM. Each one of the component services are the Web Services collaborators. Its name has the following syntax: **service-name-clientLT**. For example, from the own-service the following code is generated:

```
<partnerLinkType name="BestStoreService-clientLT">
<role name="BestStoreService">
```

**Operation logic:** is defined in terms of WS-BPEL following this basic template:

```
<process name=..>
<partnerLinks>..</partnerLinks>
<variables>..</variables>
<sequence>..</sequence>
</process>
```

**Client partnerLink definition:** from the client definition as collaborator it is possible to obtain its *partnerLink* in the SM. For example:

```
<partnerLinks>
<partnerLink name="client" partnerLinkType
name="BestStoreService-clientLT"
```

```
myRole="BestStoreService"
partnerRole="'BestStoreServiceClient" />
</partnerLinks>
```

**Definition of the other partnerLinks:** from the component services and its *part-nerLinks* is possible to obtain the *partnerLink* of the other collaborators. For example from the name of the external service `AmazonSearchService` is possible to generate the `<partnerLink>` and the `<partnerLinkType>` XML elements.

**Variable definition:** for each message sent to the collaborators corresponding to an operation invocation it is necessary to define at least one variable (*request* for the invocation) if none value is returned; in other case, it is necessary to define two variables (additionally a *response* for the return value). This can be obtained from the operation definition in the SM and its use in the DMSC.

Declared variables in DMSC actions also can be mapped to variable elements in the process. For example, from the action in the DMSC `PA:Float` is possible to generate the `<variable name="PA" messageType="xsd:float">` XML element.

In operations with response, it is necessary to define two variables: one for the request and one for the response. The SM is used for this mapping.

**Main body process:** which starts with the message reception from the client:

```
<receive partnerLink="client">
operation="getBestStore"
variable="getBestStoreRequest"
createInstance="yes">
```

Each action of the DMSC is mapped to a WS-BPEL activity. For example, a condition action (with a `PA<=PB` boolean condition) in the DMSC comparison is mapping to the following XML element:

```
<switch>
<case condition="getVariableData(PA)<=getVariableData(PB)">
...
</switch>
```

## 4.2. Web Service Dynamic Selection

The dynamic selection of Web services is specified in the DMSC with two special actions: (1) a *variable declaration* action to define a variable of the data type *Service*. This variable will be set using the *select-service* action. And a (2) *select-service* action: in which the `getXService` operation, defined in the facade of the dynamic service in the SM, is invoked in order to select dynamically the Web based on a condition defined by the modeler using an OCL expression.

With respect to the example of dynamic Web service selection of central warehouses from Figure 6, in order to implement the `SService.getPriceinStock` operation and taken into account the SM for the composite Web service (see Figure 7), the actions needed to specify the dynamic selection of web services are: (1) a declaration of a variable of type *Service* (`DService:Service`) (2) a *select-service* action (`DService=FEWService.getEWService(country="Spain")`) and (3) a *request-response* action (`price=Dservice.getPrice()`). In this case the condition has been defined on a DMSC process variable (`country`) which is passed as parameter to the condition in the SM.

## 5. Code Generation

Three steps are included in the code generation strategy to implement our proposal: In the first step we define a set of model to model transformations: from PIM models -SM and DMSC- to PSM models -Java and BPEL-. Both kinds of models are defined using the Eclipse Modeling Framework (EMF) [16] and the transformations are defined using the ATLAS Transformation Language (ATL) [17].

In the second step, another set of model to text transformations are also defined, from PSM models to source code. For each one of the models, a group of templates are defined to enable the complete source code generation (Java and WS-BPEL). We implement this step by using the ERb tool for templates and the Ruby language [18].

In the third step, the Java source code generated from the step 2, is compiled with a common Java compiler (as javac) and is installed in an application server. In the case of WS-BPEL, there is no need to compile; only the code is deployed in a BPEL execution environment. The details about this code generation strategy are given in the following subsections.

### 5.1. Metamodels Definition

The PIM and PSM models are defined using KM3 [19]. Once the metamodels are specified in KM3, then they are transformed to EMF Ecore.

As an example, the following code shows an excerpt of the SM. By using the *transformation* from *KM3 to Ecore* existing in the ATL tool, they are transformed to EMF Ecore.

```
abstract class Service {
attribute name : String;
reference port[1..*]:Port;
}
class EService extends Service { }
class OService extends Service { }
```

```
class Port {
attribute name : String;
}
```

We also define metamodels for the DMSC, PSM-Java (based on platform Axis [20]) and PSM-BPEL. The models are specified in XMI 2.0 format [21].

## 5.2. Model to Model Transformations

The model to model transformations are defined using ATL rules. The Model to Model strategy is shown in Figure 9.

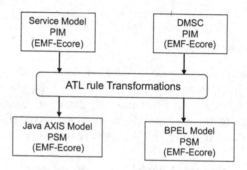

FIGURE 9. Model to model strategy

As an example, the following code is the transformation rule from the SM to PSM-BPEL which implements the transformation defined for the *PartnerLinks identification* step in 4.1 section. This rule matches the Service name in the SM and generates the *Partnerlinks, role* and *PortType* of the PSM-BPEL.

```
rule Service2Partnerlinktype {
from a:Service!Service
to   pl   :PSM_BPEL!Partnerlink(name <- s.name + '_clientLT')
     role :PSM_BPEL!Role(name <- s.name)
     port :PSM_BPEL!PortType(name <- s.name + 'port')
}
```

The input to the rule is a SM and the output is a PSM-BPEL model. From this last model, a model to code transformation algorithm, based on templates, are applied to obtain the final WS-BPEL (or Java) code.

## 5.3. Model to Code Transformations

Figure 10 shows the general Model to Code strategy. From the PSM models a final transformation is needed. For each one of the PSM models a set of templates are designed, depending on the source files needed to the final platforms. So we design templates to the AXIS platform and to the WS-BPEL platform.

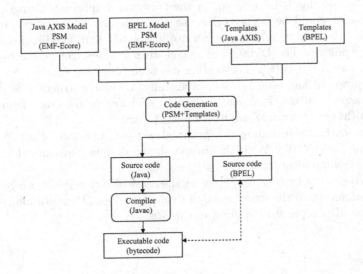

FIGURE 10. From PSM models to target source code

As an example, the following code shows the template (with a format defined by the ERb tool) for the example of the PSM-BPEL in the previous section.

```
<PartnerLinkType name="<%=name_pl%>">
    <role name="<%=name_service%>">
        <portType name="<%=name_port%>">
    </role>
</PartnerLinkType>
```

This template and the XMI model generated in the previous step are inputs to the code generator and the final WS-BPEL is obtained.

In the case of the PSM-Java AXIS Model, the code generator produces Java code that will need a final compilation using the java compiler (javac).

## 6. Conclusions and Further work

In this work we have presented a solution for the conceptual modeling of Web service compositions. The proposed models capture structural (SM) and dynamic

(DMSC) requirements of the composition. As we have shown, the captured aspects in both models are complementary and needed to enable the complete code generation of the composite Web service.

Moreover, with the structural model the modeler gains flexibility and reuse as we have shown in the case of dynamic Web service selection in the DMSC. If a new Web service is introduced, in the traditional approach changes in the dynamic model would be needed. Because our approach follows a polymorphic strategy we only need to add a new Service in the SM and, maybe, a change in the select condition. The DMSC will not change. Finally, from these models a transformation to WS-BPEL specification has been presented too.

This proposal has been proven successfully in the construction of the collaborative aspects of the *Technical University of Valencia General Library* Web application (`http://www.upv.es/bib/index_i.html`).

We are currently including this proposal in the CASE tool of our Web Engineering method OOWS. With this proposal, the designer specifies the *Service view* of the Web application that is being modeled.

As further work we consider exploring the reuse of Web services using specialization relationships in the structural and dynamic models. Presentation concerns should be another topic that we need to explore.

# References

[1] Fons J., Pelechano V., Albert M. And Pastor O. *Development of Web Applications from Web Enhanced Conceptual Schemas.* Proc. of the International Conference on Conceptual Modeling. 22nd Ed. ER'03, pp. 22-45, EEUU, 13-16 october 2003.

[2] OMG. MDA. `http://www.omg.org/mda`

[3] Albert M., Pelechano V., Fons J. Ruiz M. Pastor O. *Implementing UML association, Aggregation and Composition. A particular Interpretation based on a Multidimensional Framework.* CaiSE 2003: 143-148.

[4] Andrews T. Et al. *Business Process Execution Language for Web Services.* Version 1.1. `http://www128.ibm.com/developerworks/library/specification/ws-bpel/`

[5] BPMI. *Business Process Management Language.* `http://www.bpmi.org`

[6] Colombo Massimiliano, Di Nitto Elisabetta, Di Penta Maximiliano, Distante Damiano, Zuccal Maurilio. *Speaking a Common Language: A conceptual Model for Describing Service-Oriented Systems.* ICSOC 2005: 48-60

[7] Gronmo R., Slogan D., Solheim, Oldevik J. *Model-driven Web Services Development.* SINTEF Telecom and Informatics. EEE'04

[8] Bzivin J., Hammoudi S., Lopes D., Jouault F. *Applying MDA Approach for Web Service Platform.* Atlas Group, INRIA and LINA. ESEO. TNI-Valiosys. EDOC 2004.

[9] Warmer J. Kleepe A. *The object constraint language.* Second edition. Addison Wesley. 2003.

[10] Kristensen B. B. Osterbye K. *Roles: Conceptual abstraction theory and practical languages issues. Theory and practice of Object Systems.* 2(3): 143-160, 1996.

[11] Alonso G., Casati F., Kuno H., Machiraju V. *Web Services. Concepts, Architectures and Applications.* Springer 2004.

[12] Object Management Group. *Unified Modeling Language Specification.* http://www.uml.org

[13] Reisig W. And G.R. (editors). *Lectures on Petri Nets I: Basic Models.* Lecture Notes in Computer Science. Springer-Verlag, 1998.

[14] Milner r. Parrow J., Walker D. *A calculus of mobile processes. Information and Computation.* 100(1):1-40, Sept. 1992.

[15] Anzbock R., Dustdar, S. *Semi-automatic generation of Web services and BPEL processes - A Model-driven approach* (Appendix), BPM 2005, 5-7 September, Nancy France. Springer LNCS

[16] Eclipse project. *Eclipse Modeling Framework (EMF).* http://www.eclipse.org/emf

[17] Eclipse project. *ATL Home page.* http://www.eclipse.org/gmt/atl

[18] Herrington Jack. *Code generation in action.* Manning Ed. 2003.

[19] Joualt, F., Bzivin J.: *KM3: a DSL for metamodel specification.* In: Proceedings of 8th IFIP International Conference on Formal Methods for Open Object-Based Distributed Systems, Bologna, Italy (2006).

[20] Apache project. *Web Services - Axis.* http://ws.apache.org/axis

[21] OMG/XMI *XML Model Interchange (XMI) 2.0.* Adopted Specification. Formal/03-05-02, 2003.

Ricardo Quintero
Department of Information Systems and Computation
Technical University of Valencia
Cami de Vera s/n E-46022, Spain
e-mail: iscrquinter@dsic.upv.es

Victoria Torres
Department of Information Systems and Computation
Technical University of Valencia
Cami de Vera s/n E-46022, Spain
e-mail: vtorres@dsic.upv.es

Vicente Pelechano
Department of Information Systems and Computation
Technical University of Valencia
Cami de Vera s/n E-46022, Spain
e-mail: pele@dsic.upv.es

Whitestein Series in Software Agent Technologies, 83–100
© 2007 Birkhäuser Verlag Basel/Switzerland

# Model Driven Design of Web Service Operations using Web Engineering Practices

Marta Ruiz and Vicente Pelechano

**Abstract.** The design of Web Services is nowadays emerging as one of the most important tasks in the development of a Service Oriented Application. Web service designers need some guidelines to achieve a design of quality. In this paper we provide a methodological guide in the context of a Web engineering method called OOWS. Our approach allows identifying the operations of Web services following a model driven approach, taking the OO-Method / OOWS conceptual models as the source. To document our approach, we apply our ideas to a real case study of a Web application to manage University Research Groups.

**Keywords.** Web services design, Service Oriented Architecture, Model Driven, Web engineering, Software Process Engineering.

## 1. Introduction

Web services have emerged as important components of modern Web applications. There are some approaches working on designing services interfaces. Ambler [1] presents several steps for deriving a set of Web services from an object-oriented application, identifying domain packages and the services that each package provides. Papazoglou [8] describes a design methodology for Web services based on business processes. On the other hand, Web engineering methods are extending their proposals to introduce Web services into Web conceptual models. In this context, we can distinguish approaches that introduce some kind of syntactic mechanism to include Web services calls into navigational models like OOHDM [13] and UMLGuide [3]. However, these approaches do not give support to the design and development of Web services. Other methods like OO-H [4] allow Web developers to generate Web services interfaces but they do not give support to their design either. Finally WebML [5] captures Web services invocations by means of visual

This work has been developed with the support of MEC under the project DESTINO TIN2004-03534, cofinanced by FEDER and the PAID-04-06 project by UPV..

representations. They describe the Web interactions using hypertext models but do not follow any strategy or guide to design Web services.

In this work, we present a Web service design guide that extends the OOWS method [10]. OOWS is a Web engineering method that is based on the principles defined by the Model-Driven Development (MDD) [6]. It allows us to automatically obtain fully operative web applications from conceptual models. In order to design the operations of Web services, we consider that the OO-Method [9] / OOWS models are a key point. OO-Method / OOWS models allow us to automatically obtain Web services operations.

The main contributions of this work are:

- Determining which models are useful to obtain Web services operations.
- Proposing a methodological guide to design the operations of Web services.
- Identifying operations that give support to the functional requirements of an application, user identification and management, information retrieval, navigation and presentation. A first approach of this work can be found in [12].
- Providing a Web services design method with tool support to automatically generate the WSDL of the Web services.

The structure of the paper is the following: section 2 introduces a Web service design approach based on the OO-Method / OOWS method. Section 3 presents a methodological guide to obtain well designed Web services in a SOA. In our approach, a set of operations are identified taking the OO-Method / OOWS conceptual models. These operations define the public operations that a Web service can offer to web applications (major web clients). Finally, we present some conclusions and further work in section 4.

## 2. An overview of the Web service design process

In this section, we introduce a Web service design process that takes into account the OO-Method / OOWS models. To present this process we use the notation and terms defined in the Software Process Engineering Metamodel (SPEM) proposed by the OMG [14]. SPEM is a meta-model for defining software engineering process models and their components. First, we present the *Disciplines* that define our process as well as the *Activities*, *WorkProducts* and *ProcessRoles* that are included in each step. Next, we present the *Sequencing of Activities* that defines the design process.

### 2.1. Web Service Design Process

According to SPEM, an Activity is a piece of work performed by one ProcessRole in order to obtain a WorkProduct. A Discipline partitions the Activities within a process according to a common 'theme'.

Our Web service design process is defined from the following disciplines: Requirements Elicitation (see figure 1-A), OO-Method (see figure 1-B) and OOWS (see figure 1-C) conceptual modeling and code generation.

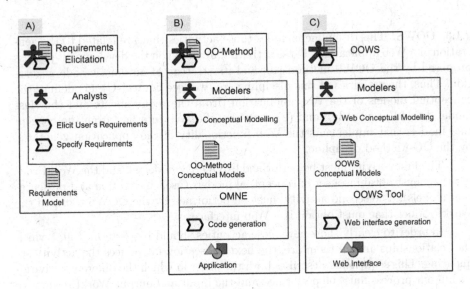

FIGURE 1. Requirements Elicitation, OO-Method and OOWS Disciplines

**2.1.1. Requirements Elicitation.** This discipline includes those activities that are related to the elicitation of the user's requirements. These activities are two (see figure 1-A): (1) elicit the user's requirements and (2) specify requirements. The activities must be performed by Analysts.

The WorkProduct that the analysts must obtain after performing the activities is a requirements model: one task diagram for each kind of user, and a textual and a graphical description for each leaf task. Figure 1-A shows the definition of this discipline by means of the notation proposed in the SPEM.

**2.1.2. The OO-Method.** This discipline includes those activities that are related to the model and generation of applications. These activities are based on the development process of the OO-Method [9] and its strategy of automatic code generation. Nowadays, the OO-Method approach has an industry-oriented implementation called OlivaNova Model Execution (ONME) [7] that has been developed by CARE Technologies S.A.

Thus, the activities of this discipline are two (see figure 1-B): (1) define a conceptual schema to represent the application requirements (from the requirements model defined by analysts); and (2) generate code from the conceptual models that implements an application. The first activity must be performed by OO-Method modelers, and the WorkProduct that must obtain is a set of conceptual models:

class, dynamic (state transition and sequence diagrams) and functional models. The second activity must be performed by ONME and the WorkProduct that must obtain is the final application.

**2.1.3. OOWS.** This discipline includes those activities that are related to the generation of a Web application. These activities are based on the development process proposed by the OOWS method [10] and its strategy of automatic code generation. Thus, the activities of this discipline are two (see figure 1-C): (1) defines the conceptual models of the Web application (from the requirements and the class model defined previously); and (2) generates the Web interface from the conceptual models that implements the Web functionality of the application generated by the OO-Method discipline.

The first activity must be performed by OOWS modelers, and the WorkProduct that must obtain is a set of conceptual models (user, navigation and presentation models). The second activity must be performed by the OOWS tool and the WorkProduct that must obtain is a Web interface.

In order to clearly show how these activities should be performed and which the relationships among them are, the next subsection introduces the activity sequencing. This sequencing describes both the order in which the different activities within our process must be performed and the input and output WorkProducts of each activity.

## 2.2. Sequencing of Activities

Figure 2 shows the activity sequencing of our process (following the activity diagram notation proposed by SPEM). According to this figure, our Web service design process is defined as follows: first, analysts create a requirements model after analyzing the user's needs. Then, on the one hand the OO-Method modelers define the OO-Method conceptual models of the application from the requirements, and the ONME tool automatically generates a software application. On the other hand, OOWS modelers model the Web application and then the OOWS tool generates the Web interface of this application. Finally, the operations of the Web service are designed.

As we can see, there are dependencies between activities: the OO-Method modelers need the requirements models to model the application; the OOWS modelers need the requirements and the OO-Method models to model the Web interface; and the Web service designer needs the requirements models, the class models of the OO-Method discipline, and the user, navigation and presentation models of the OOWS discipline to identify the operations of the Web service to be published.

In the next section, we introduce a guide to support Web service designers in the achievement of their activity.

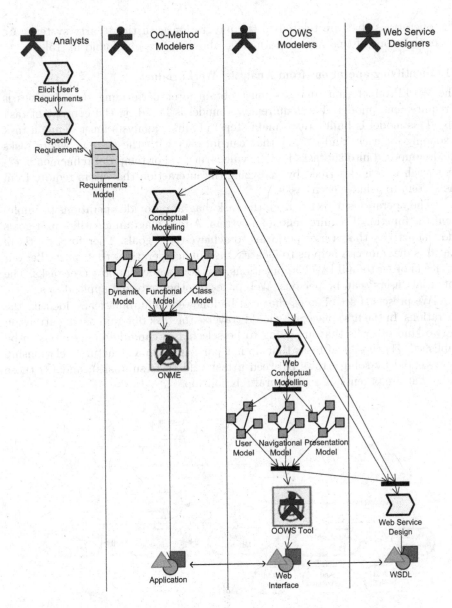

FIGURE 2. Activity sequencing

## 3. The Web service design activity

In this section we present a methodological guide to obtain, in a systematic way, the operations that implement the requirements of a Web application in a SOA.

The operations that are related to the integration with third party systems are out of the scope of this work. Information about this can be found in [15].

### 3.1. Identifying operations from Analysts' WorkProduct

The WorkProduct that analysts must obtain after performing the activities is a requirements model. The requirements model is based on the concept of task [16]. This model is built in two main steps: (1) first, analysts must define a task taxonomy for each kind of user that can interact with the system, where tasks are decomposed into subtasks by following structural or temporal refinements; (2) next, each task is described by analyzing the interaction that users require from the system to achieve each tasks.

The operations detected from the task diagram provide operations to implement the functional requirements of a system. A task diagram identifies user goals and the activity that a user performs to achieve these goals. Therefore, we think that this diagram can help us to identify the public operations that must offer our service in order to build Web applications that completely support user tasks. The potential "users" can be persons, Web pages or other external applications.

We present a set of steps that can be followed to automatically identify the operations. In the first place, we should traverse the task diagram paying attention to two kind of tasks that are going to be selected as candidate operations to be published: (1) those leaf tasks that do not participate in a structural relationship (represented by solid arrows between a task and their subtasks); and (2) those tasks that are parents of a structural relationship.

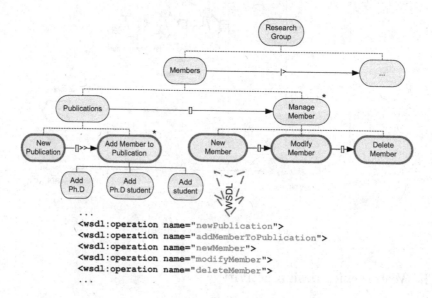

FIGURE 3. Operations detected in the task diagram

In figure 3 we have a partial view of the description of how a researcher can manage a research group. Following the steps previously presented, we define the next operations: newPublication, addMemberToPublication, newMember, modifyMember and deleteMember.

Each task has associated: (1) a *textual description* that defines the goals and the users that can achieve this task; and (2) a *graphical description* by means of activity diagrams.

Operations arguments should be detected from the graphical descriptions associated to tasks. In the graphical description, each node of the activity diagram defines: (1) a system action (stereotyped with <<function>> or <<search>> keyword); or (2) an *interaction point* (IP) (nodes stereotyped with <<input>> or <<output>> keyword). Each IP defines an instant in the achievement of a task where the user interacts with the system. In this context, the system actions performed after a <<output>> IP, allow Web services designers to identify the entity involved in the task. Thus, using this <<output>> IP and the <<input>> IP from the *graphical description* together with the *class diagram* (a WorkProduct of the OO-Method modelers), we can obtain the arguments of each operation. We detect each participant class in an operation by matching the entities that are specified in the node with the class diagram. For each identified class we add its type to the arguments of the operation detected from this branch of the task tree.

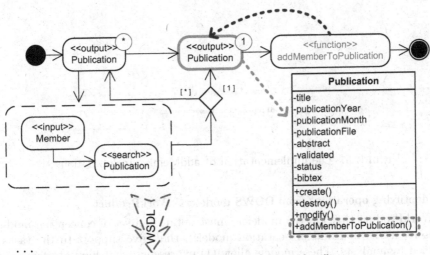

```
...
<wsdl:operation name="addMemberToPublication">
  <wsdl:input message="tns:addMemberToPublicationSoapIn" />
  <wsdl:output message="tns:addMemberToPublicationSoapOut" />
</wsdl:operation>
...
```

FIGURE 4. Arguments of addMemberToPublication

Figure 4 shows the arguments for the operation addMemberToPublication that has been previously defined. This operation is detected from the task *Add Member to Publication*, so the arguments of this operation are taken from the graphical description of this task. This graphical description has the <<output>> IP *Publication* which maps with the Publication class in the class diagram. Matching the *addMemberToPublication* task with the function of the Publication class that is associated, we obtain the arguments for our Web service operation. So we add the argument of Member type to the arguments of the operation addMemberToPublication.

Figure 5 shows the Web page that gives support to the execution of the addMemberToPublication operation.

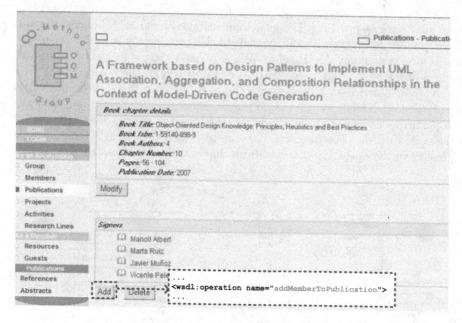

FIGURE 5. The implementation of addMemberToPublication

## 3.2. Identifying operations from OOWS modelers' WorkProduct

The WorkProduct that OOWS modelers must obtain is a set of conceptual models (users, navigation and presentation models), that give support to the tasks identified by analysts. These models allow (1) expressing what kind of users can interact with the system and what system visibility they can have; (2) defining the navigational semantics of the system; and (3) specifying its presentational requirements.

**3.2.1. User Model.** The OOWS user diagram is used to detect kinds of users (roles) and assign to them permissions to interact with the system, providing a role-based access control (RBAC) [2]. The RBAC model gives us a guideline to perform the access control in an application. This model requires a minimum of five elements: users, roles, objects, operations and permissions. This model also provides functions to define the functional specifications.

Afterwards, the operations of this group are detected from both the user diagram and the RBAC model and are classified into three types:

- Those that provide support for the user identification: loginUser, logoutUser, obtainRol, changeRol and remindPassword.
- Those that give support for the generic user administration: newUser, modifyUser, deleteUser.
- Those that give support to the management of user's permissions and roles: newRol, deleteRol, addUserToRol, removeUserToRol, addPermission and removePermission inherited from the RBAC model

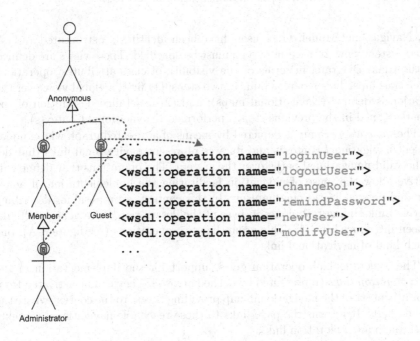

```
<wsdl:operation name="loginUser">
<wsdl:operation name="logoutUser">
<wsdl:operation name="changeRol">
<wsdl:operation name="remindPassword">
<wsdl:operation name="newUser">
<wsdl:operation name="modifyUser">
...
```

FIGURE 6. WSDL based on the User Diagram

It is not necessary to publish all this functionality for every implementation. So the Web service designer must decide which operations should be published. We implement the following six operations in our running example (see figure 6): loginUser, logoutUser, changeRol, remindPassword, newUser and modifyUser.

Figure 7 shows the Web page that gives support to the execution of the loginUser operation.

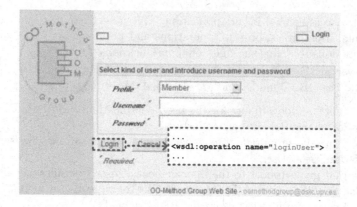

FIGURE 7. The implementation of loginUser

### 3.2.2. Navigational Model.

Once users have been identified, a structured and organized system view for each user type must be specified. These views are defined over the Class Diagram, in terms of the visibility of class attributes, operations and relationships. This model is built in two steps: (1) first, a global view over the navigation is defined (Navigational maps); and (2) a detailed description of the elements defined in the previous step is performed (Navigational Contexts).

The *navigational map* is depicted by means of a directed graph whose nodes represent navigational contexts and its arcs represent navigational links that define the valid navigational paths over the system. The operations that define this primitive allow the reuse of navigation facilitating the implementation of adaptation and personalization mechanisms. In this context, a proposal for describing Adaptive Link-Hiding techniques in base of the description of Navigational Links has been introduced in [11]. This group has two operations (see figure 8-A), one for each kind of navigational link:

1. The explorationLink operation gives support for the implementation of the *exploration links* (represented by dashed arrows). They can be activated from any context of the navigational map providing access to the context where the link ends. It returns the page links to those reachable navigational contexts through an exploration link.

2. The sequenceLink(context) gives support for the implementation of the *sequence links* (represented by solid arrows). They represent a reachability relationship between two contexts. This kind of link can be activated from the context that defines the link source and provide access to the context where the link ends. It returns the set of page links of the navigational contexts accessible by the user from a specific context.

Figure 8-B shows the Web page where the result of the call of the explorationLink operation is shown. This operation returns the page links (contexts) that are reachable from somewhere of the Web application.

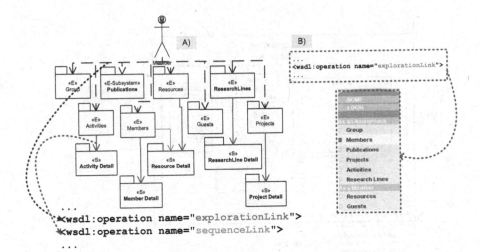

FIGURE 8. Operations detected from the *Client* navigational map
and the implementation of the explorationLink operation

The *navigational context* defines operations to retrieve the information that
must be shown in each navigational context (a web page in the running example).
For each navigational context, we can define (see figure 9):

1. The retrieveViewName ([attributeID]) operation allows us to obtain the information specified in the navigational context views. This operation returns (1)
   a set of instances or (2) a specific instance of the classes defined in the context
   view. We define an operation of this kind for each view defined in a navigational context. Figure 9 shows the operation detected from the navigational
   context *Members*: retrieveMembers.

2. The getIndexedIndexName (attributes) operation gives support for the *index
   mechanisms*. They provide an indexed access to the population of objects.
   This operation returns the list of the resumed information defined in a given
   index allowing the user to choose one item (instance) from the list. It is
   defined for every index in a navigational context. An example of this operation
   is shown in figure 9, where the operation getIndexedMember is identified from
   the index of the context *Members*.

3. The retrievePopulationViewName (attribute*) operation gives support to *population condition* mechanisms. They define an object retrieval condition that
   must be satisfied. This condition can be specified to any navigational class.
   The operation can need one or more attributes, depending on the definition of the population filter. This operation returns a set of instances of the
   class where the population filter is defined that fulfil the condition specified
   by the user. We define an operation of this kind for each view defined in a
   navigational context that has defined a population filter. Figure 9 shows the

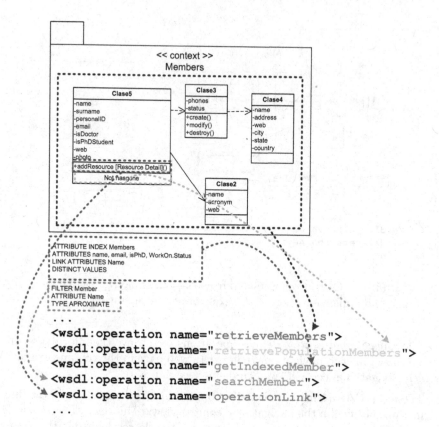

FIGURE 9. Operations detected from the navigational context

operation detected from the navigational context *Members*: retrievePopulationMembers.

4. The searchFilterName (value) operation gives support to *search filters* mechanisms. They allow filtering the space of objects that retrieve the navigational context. This operation returns the set of instances of the manager class (and its complementary classes) that fulfil the search conditions specified by the user. An operation is obtained for each filter of a navigational context. Figure 9 shows the detection of the operation searchMember from the filter defined in the context *Member*.

   Moreover, the navigational map can also provide operations that support part of the implementation of the navigation defined in the navigational model.

5. The operationLink (service) operation gives support to the implementation of the operation links. Operation links represent the target navigational context that the user will reach after an operation execution. This operation

returns the context (Web page) that the user accesses before one specific operation is activated. Figure 9 shows operationLink detected from the operation AddResource defined in the class Product.

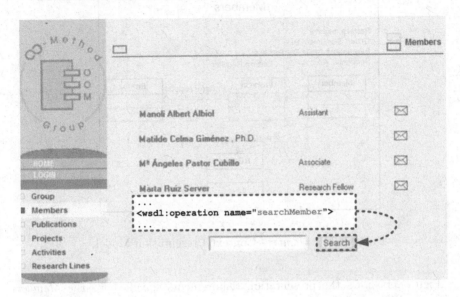

FIGURE 10. The implementation of searchMember

Figure 10 shows a Web page in which the result of the operation searchMember can be seen (defined from the filter of the *Member* Context in figure 9). In this case, the filter condition is that the name of the member has the letter "M". Then, the web page of this figure shows all members related with "M".

**3.2.3. Presentation Model.** Once the navigational model is built, modelers must specify presentational requirements of web applications using a presentation model. It is strongly based on the navigational model and it uses its navigational contexts to define the presentation properties. Presentation requirements are specified by means of patterns that are associated to the primitives of the navigational context. The basic presentation patterns are:

- *Information Paging.* This pattern allows defining information "scrolling". All the instances are "broken" into "logical blocks", so that only one block is visible at a time. Mechanisms to move forward or backward are provided. The required information is: (1) cardinality represents the number of instances that make a block; and (2) access mode (sequential or random).
- *Ordering Criteria.* This pattern defines a class population ordering (ASCendant or DESCen-dant).
- *Information Layout.* OOWS provides 4 basic layout patterns: register, tabular, master-detail and tree.

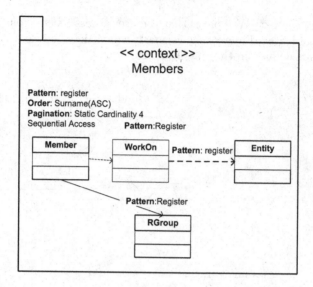

FIGURE 11. *Members* Context Presentation Model

Figure 11 shows the presentation requirements specified for the *Members* Navigational Context. According to these requirements the list of members provided by the context is shown in a register format. This list is grouped in blocks of four members. The surname of each member is used to order them in an increase way.

These presentation patterns, together with the specified navigation features, capture the essential requirements for the construction of web interfaces. Thus, Web service designers can identify two operations from this model:

1. The presentationInfo (operation, operationAttributes, pagination, order, patter) operation, where operation is an operation published by the Web service, operationAttributes is the set of attributes of that operation, and pagination, order and patter are the values for the presentation patterns. This operation returns a piece of Web page with the information retrieved presented with the values defined by the user at the call.

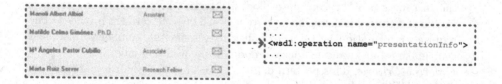

FIGURE 12. The result of presentationInfo(searchMember)

Figure 12 shows the result of the operation searchMember. In this case, the result must be presented as a piece of a Web page where the products are shown in register, in groups of three elements and ordered by ascending price.

2. The operation presentationContext (context) returns a Web page created for the context attribute. This Web page follows the presentation patterns indicated in the presentation model. To create the Web page, this operation uses some the operations presented in this article: retrieveViewName for each view defined in the context and explorationLink and sequenceLink for the link pages. Moreover, if the context has some filter or index, then the Web page will show these operations.

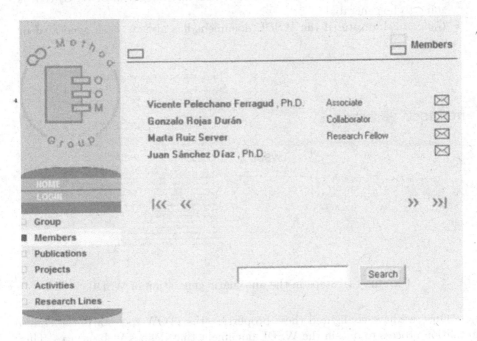

FIGURE 13. presentationContext(Members)

Figure 13 shows the Web page created as a result of the presentationContext(Members) operation. The information retrieved from the *Members* view is shown in register, in groups of four and ordered by surname increasing. In addition, it shows links to those pages reachable since this context.

## 3.3. Tool support

In this section, we present a tool that helps Web service designers in the identification and design of the Web services operations. This tool also allows Web service designers to associate a WSDL specification to a specific application. This tool, which is called ITOW, automatically generates the WSDL specification of the application modeled by the ONME and OOWS CASE tools (see figure 14).

ITOW provides an easy-to-use graphical interface. Before ITOW generates the WSDL specification, it is necessary to configure the following properties:

- *Load Project*: Defines the XML file where the OO-Method and the OOWS models are stored.
- *Save Project*: Defines the target location where the generated WSDL document will be stored.
- *URL*: Defines the namespace of the Web application to be included in the WSDL file.
- *Kind of WSDL*: Specifies the kind of WSDL file (document or RPC) that is going to be generated.
- *Generate*: Indicates if the WSDL document has already been generated or not.

FIGURE 14. Steps in the automatic generation of WSDL

Once we have configured these properties, the ITOW tool starts the transformation process to obtain the WSDL document that defines Web services. This transformation process follows the approach presented in this work.

## 4. Conclusions and Further Work

This article has presented an approach to introduce SOA and the Web services technology as an extension of the OO-Method / OOWS method. We have presented a methodological guide to help Web service designers to obtain the operations that define the Web services from models. This guide can be generalized to other Web Engineering Methods, because the OO-Method / OOWS method shares with them the most common models and primitives taken as source to obtain the Web services.

The ideas presented in this work have been already applied to the development of several applications like the Web site http://oomethod.dsic.upv.es, which supports the management of our research group and in the intranet management system for the General Library of the Technical University of Valencia. Nowadays, we are developing an e-commerce system and a travel agency. These two systems, in addition to provide Web services, integrate functionality of third parties applications.

Several extensions to this work are under development. We are working on integrating this approach on the ONME tool [7]. For this purpose, we are analyzing the models provided by OO-Method / OOWS methods. Our intention is determine how operations presented in this work can be implemented from the functionality generated by the ONME tool. This allows us to provide a Web service with fully operative operations.

We are also working on providing mechanisms that facilitate the integration of Web applications with Third parties systems at the conceptual level [15]. When third parties provide us their functionality as Web services, we proceed to the Web service composition to achieve integration.

We have used the presentation model defined within the OOWS approach to enrich the code generation process providing Web services that include presentational aspects. Our final objective is to generate reusable Web functionality that provides relevant information (content and presentation) to potential consumers [11].

## References

[1] Ambler, S.W., Deriving Web services from UML models, Part 1: Establishing the process. http://www-106.ibm.com/developerworks/webservices/library/ws-uml1/, March 1, (2002).

[2] ANSI. Incits 359. American National Standard for Information technology. Role-Based Access Control, (2004).

[3] Dolog, P., Model-driven navigation design for semantic web applications with the UML-guide. In Maristella Matera and Sara Comai (eds.), Engineering Advanced Web Applications. (2004)

[4] Gómez, J., & Cachero, C. , OO-H Method: extending UML to model web interfaces. In information Modeling For internet Applications. P. van Bommel, Ed. Idea Group Publishing, Hershey, PA, (2003). pp. 144-173.

[5] Manolescu, I., Brambilla, M., Ceri, S., Comai, S., & Fraternali, P., Model-driven design and deployment of service-enabled web applications. ACM Trans. Inter. Tech. 5, 3, (2005) pp. 439-479.

[6] Mellor, S.J., Clark, A.N., Futagami, T.: Model-driven development - Guest editor's introduction. IEEE Software, 20 (5):14- 18, Sept.-Oct. (2003).

[7] OlivaNova Model Execution System. CARE Technologies. Retrieve November 3, (2005), from: http://www.care-t.com.

[8] Papazoglou, M.P. and Yang, J. Design methodology for Web services and business processes. In Proceedings of the 3rd VLDB-TES workshop (Hong Kong, August, 2002). Springer, (2002), 54-64.

[9] Pastor, O., Gomez, J., Insfran, E., & Pelechano, V. : The OO-Method approach for information systems modelling: from Object-Oriented conceptual modeling to automated programming. Information Systems 26, (2001).pp 507–534.

[10] Pastor, O., Fons, J., Pelechano, V., & Abrahão, S. Conceptual modelling of Web applications: the OOWS approach, book chapter in Web Engineering - Theory and Practice of Metrics and Measurement for Web Development, Mendes E. (Eds.), Springer 2005, (2005). pp. 277-302.

[11] Rojas, G., Pelechano, V., & Fons, J.: A Model-Driven Approach to include Adaptive Navigational Techniques in Web Applications. V International Workshop on Web Oriented Software Technologies - IWWOST, Porto, Portugal. (2005).

[12] Ruiz, M., Valderas, P. & Pelechano, V.: "Applying a Web Engineering Method to Design Web Services". 6th International Conference on Service Oriented Computing (ICSOC). Lecture Notes in Computer Science Vol. 3826/2005. (2005).

[13] Schwabe, D., Rossi, G. & Barbosa, D.J.: Systematic hypermedia application design with OOHDM. Proc. ACM Conference on Hypertext. (1996). pp.166.

[14] Software Process Engineering Metamodel, version 1.1. Object Management Group. http://www.omg.org/technology/documents/formal/spem.htm

[15] Torres, V., Pelechano, V., Ruiz, M., & Valderas, P.: A model driven approach for the integration of external functionality in Web applications. The Travel Agency System. Workshop on Model-driven Web Engineering (MDWE). (2005).

[16] Valderas, P., Fons, J., Pelechano, V.: Developing E-Commerce Application from Task-Based Descriptions. 6th International Conference on Electronic Commerce and Web Technologies (EC-WEB). (2005).

Marta Ruiz
Universidad Politécnica de Valencia
Camí de Vera s/n
Valencia-46022
Spain
e-mail: mruiz@dsic.upv.es

Vicente Pelechano
Universidad Politécnica de Valencia
Camí de Vera s/n
Valencia-46022
Spain
e-mail: pele@dsic.upv.es

Whitestein Series in Software Agent Technologies, 101–116

# A Logic-based Approach for Service Discovery with Composition Support

Adina Sîrbu, Ioan Toma, Dumitru Roman

**Abstract.** Web service discovery given a user request becomes a fundamental challenge in a service-oriented world. The overall success of Service Oriented Architectures (SOA) however will very much depend on automatic and accurate solutions for the discovery problem. Furthermore such solutions need to be efficiently integrated with other service related tasks (e.g. service composition). In this paper we propose a logic based approach for service discovery with composition support. First, we provide a formal model for service discovery based on semantic description of services and then we show how such an approach can be integrated with service composition. Furthermore we provide a prototype implementation that validates our theoretical solution.

## 1. Introduction

Service Oriented Architectures are emerging as a new computing paradigm for realizing distributed applications. They promote a service-based view on the world, where providers and clients are exposing and invoking functionalities in a standardized manner. Web services are one possible approach for implementing SOA ideas. They are based on technologies like WSDL [3], SOAP [14] and UDDI [2]. Despite their increasing acceptance in industry, Web services have some important drawbacks which stem mainly from the lack of machine understandable descriptions. More precisely, service related tasks like discovery, negotiation, adaptation, and composition cannot be performed by machines without the explicit intervention of a human programmer. Semantic Web services were proposed as a new paradigm that helps overcome current Web service technology limitations by providing semantically richer service descriptions. This enables machines to reason on these descriptions and to perform service related tasks in a more autonomous and accurate manner.

Service discovery, the task of finding relevant services given a user request, is one task where semantic based approaches can bring more automatization and accuracy. Solutions for discovery were proposed in [1, 9, 11, 12, 13]. However, most of the existing literature in this field refers to detecting matches by comparing the inputs and outputs of requested, respectively provided services. For example, the matching algorithms described in [11] and [9] depend only on the logical relation between the concepts associated with the inputs and outputs. Moreover, many of the proposed solutions are lacking a suitable integration with other service related tasks. Our solution is focused exactly on these two aspects. We provide a formal model for service discovery based on semantic description of services and we show how such an approach can be integrated with service composition. Furthermore we provide a prototype implementation that proves our ideas.

The paper is organized as follows: Section 2 provides the technical solution for our service discovery approach. It first gives some insights on the service model we are using for semantically describing Web services - the Web Service Modeling Ontology (WSMO) and its associated language - the Web service Modeling Language (WSML). The formal model for our discovery approach is described then in the rest of the section. Section 3 presents the prototype we have developed based on the technical solution provided in Section 2. The prototypical solution is described in terms of architecture and behavior. Furthermore a concrete run through a scenario is presented in order to exemplify the work of our prototype. Finally, Section 4 discusses the related work and Section 5 concludes the paper and presents our future work.

## 2. Discovery Approach

The conceptual model and the language we are using for semantically describing Web services is introduced in section 2.1. Based on this model, we present in section 2.2 two alternatives for Web service matchmaking, and for each of them the corresponding algorithm.

### 2.1. Modeling services

The discovery process in general, and service discovery in particular, depends heavily on how the entities that are to be discovered, in our case Web services, are modeled. For our logic based service discovery solution we adopt the Web Service Modeling Ontology (WSMO) [8] as conceptual model for services and its associated Web Service Modeling Language (WSML) [4] as a language for semantically describing Web services. Some of the reasons behind this decision are: (1) WSMO is one of the major initiatives in Semantic Web services area. It provides a semantic-based solution for describing services which is crucial for a logic-based discovery approach such as ours, (2) WSMO provides a clean modeling solution for services, making a clear distinction between the user requests (*goals* in WSMO) and the services descriptions (*Web services* in WSMO), (3) WSML provides different semantic expressivity support for describing services. For our approach we consider one particular variant of the WSML languages family, namely WSML-Flight which offers a reasonable compromise between expressivity and decidability.

In a nutshell, WSMO provides an overall framework for Semantic Web services that aims at supporting automated Web service discovery, selection, composition, mediation, execution, monitoring, etc. It follows the design principles from the Web Service Modeling Framework (WSMF) [5] and provides four top-level notions related to Semantic Web services: (1) *Ontologies* that define a common agreed upon terminology used in the description of all others WSMO elements, (2) *Goals* which are descriptions of the objectives a client may have when consulting a service in terms of functionality, behavior and quality of service, (3) *Web services* are descriptions of services and (4) *Mediators* which address heterogeneity problems that occur between descriptions at different levels: *data, protocol* or *process level.*

For our discovery approach, the first three top-level WSMO elements, namely ontologies, Web services and goals are considered. Although we don't use the mediation support, our solution can be easily extended to integrate mediation aspects. In the following, all Web services, goals and ontologies are specified using WSML. Furthermore, since our approach matches goals and Web services based on the functionality requested, respectively provided, we focus on describing the functional aspects of Web services and goals. Therefore, we leave aside the description of the interfaces, which by definition provide information on how the functionality of a Web service can be achieved. In WSMO, the functional aspects of a Web service or a goal are grouped under an element called *capability*. A *capability* captures in terms of *preconditions* and *assumptions*, on one hand, and *postconditions* and *effects*, on the other hand, a set of conditions that have to hold before and respectively after the execution of the service. More precisely, the pre/postconditions refer to the information space of the Web service, while the assumptions and effects refer to the state of the world.

For exemplification purposes we introduce service and goal descriptions from the real-world use cases developed in the EU project Adaptive Service Grid (ASG)[1].

In this particular use-case, we consider a domain ontology that models a telematics domain. Listing 1 displays a fragment of this ontology, defining the top-level concepts of person, phone number, location, and a relation that holds between an entity and its location. Furthermore, this fragment includes an axiom stating that the location of a phone is also the location of the owner of the phone.

```
ontology _"domainOntology.wsml"
  nonFunctionalProperties
    dc#title hasValue "Telematics domain ontology"
  endNonFunctionalProperties

  concept person
    name ofType _string
    number ofType phoneNumber

  concept phoneNumber

  concept location
```

---

[1]http://asg-platform.org

```
    hasCoordinates ofType coordinates

relation hasLocation/2
   nonFunctionalProperties
     dc#relation hasValue hasLocationDef
   endNonFunctionalProperties

axiom hasLocationDef
   definedBy
     ?person[number hasValue ?phoneNr] memberOf person
     and ?loc memberOf location
     and hasLocation(?phoneNr, ?loc)
        implies hasLocation(?person, ?loc).
```

LISTING 1

Based on this ontology, a telecommunication company offers a phone location service. This service requires as input the number of a mobile phone. This can be seen as a condition over the information space before the execution of the service and therefore is modeled as a *precondition*. The service invoker receives as result the location of the mobile phone. This can be seen as a condition over the information space after the execution of the service and therefore is modeled as a *postcondition*. The complete WSML description of the service is provided in the Listing 2.

```
webService _"MobTelPhoneLocationService"
   nonFunctionalProperties
     dc#title hasValue "MobTel phone location service"
     dc#publisher hasValue "MobTel"
   endNonFunctionalProperties
   importsOntology _"domainOntology.wsml"
   capability phoneLocationServiceCapability
     sharedVariables {?phoneNumber}
     precondition
        definedBy
          ?phoneNumber memberOf dO#phoneNumber.
     postcondition
        definedBy
          dO#hasLocation(?phoneNumber, ?location)
          and ?location memberOf dO#location.
```

LISTING 2

Further on, consider the generic goal of finding the location of a person, knowing the name and the phone number of this person. A goal in WSMO is described in a similar manner to a Web service. Listing 3 represents the formal description of the goal template. A concrete request can then be defined at runtime, by instantiating the goal template with concrete inputs.

```
goal _"findPersonLocation.wsml"
   nonFunctionalProperties
     dc#title hasValue "Find person location goal"
   endNonFunctionalProperties
   importsOntology _"domainOntology.wsml"
   capability findPersonLocationCapability
     sharedVariables {?person}
     precondition
        definedBy
```

```
?person[
    dO#name hasValue ?name,
    dO#number hasValue ?phoneNr
] memberOf dO#person.
postcondition
    definedBy
        dO#hasLocation(?person, ?location)
    and ?location memberOf dO#location.
```

LISTING 3

The user can specify conditions on the information space that hold before the invocation of the matching service, in this case, that the name and phone number of the person are known. These aspects are modeled as *preconditions* in the goal. In the state of the world after the execution of a suitable service, the location of the person is known. Therefore we model this as a *postcondition* of the goal.

The discovery solution we are introducing in this paper will identify, using the background ontology, that the listed Web service represents an exact match for the goal. More details on how services and goals descriptions are used by our solution are provided in Section 3.2.

## 2.2. Matching Web services and requests

We consider two alternatives for Web service matchmaking, each of them applying a different algorithm. They correspond to different phases in the Web service composition process.

The first matchmaking alternative is to locate the Web services that directly match a user request in a given state. If no Web services are discovered, the composer can construct a valid solution that fully satisfies the goal using the second alternative, which identifies all the Web services that are relevant to the request in the given state. More specifically, the service composer can construct a solution by successively discovering the executable services and virtually executing them until the state satisfies the goal. For a description of the service composer used in the context of ASG, we refer the reader to [10].

In section 2.1, we have presented our state-based approach to describing Web services and goals, which allows us to express Web services that can change the state of the world. This approach is characterized by the use of pre-state and post-state constraints for specifying the intended execution of the Web service. In WSMO, the pre-state constraints correspond to postconditions and assumptions, while the post-state constraints correspond to postconditions and effects. In this context, we have not made explicit distinction between effects and postconditions. Together, they represent the outcome of the service execution.

Both matchmaking algorithms take into account the dependence of outputs and effects of the service execution on the concrete input provided by the user. Therefore, they operate at the level of rich semantic description of services, as introduced in [6].

## 2.2.1. Matching based on capabilities.
The first algorithm for service matchmaking identifies the Web services whose capabilities fully match the requester goal.

Of the four possible types of match described in [6], we are taking into consideration only *exact-match* (the Web service description and the goal description coincide) and *plugin-match* (the sets of objects that the Web service claims to deliver is a superset of the set of objects that are relevant to the requestor). The other two cases (*subsumes-match* and *intersection-match*) are not considered valid matches in this context, because the services cannot fully satisfy the goal.

We consider the states of the world to be logical theories. A state of the world comprises the set of registered ontologies and, optionally, an additional set of facts. These facts can be given explicitly by means of an initial state. They can also be the outcome of previous virtual execution of services, because the execution of a service in a given state is considered to change the state of the world, resulting in an update to the logical theory.

In order to determine if the capability of a service satisfies a requester goal one must reason about the resulting updates. Reasoning about updates raises the frame problem. A solution to avoid the frame problem is offered by Transaction Logic, an extension to First-order Logic that allows to specify the dynamics of knowledge bases in a declarative way. The theoretical approach employing Transaction Logic for Web service discovery that has been used as theoretical foundation for the implementation of this matchmaking algorithm can be found in [7].

The algorithm for service matchmaking based on capabilities implemented in our prototype is presented in Listing 4. The ontologies, the Web services and the goal are assumed to be loaded prior to the invocation of the matchmaking process.

```
1   algorithm Matchmaking based on capabilities
2   input: initial state I, goal G
3   output: map of <Web service S, set of <variable binding β>>
4
5   register state I
6   for each registered Web service S
7       if holds pre_S then
8           for each variable binding β
9               if not holds ( eff_S(β) and out_S(β)) then
10                  insert ( eff_S(β) and out_S(β))
11                  if holds ( eff_G and out_G) then
12                      add β to set of <β>
13                  endif
14                  delete ( eff_S(β) and out_S(β))
15              endif
16          endfor
17          if not empty (set of <β>) then
18              add (S, set of <β>) to result map
19          endif
20      endif
```

```
21  endfor
22  unregister state I
23  return result map
```

LISTING 4

We consider a "stateless" functioning of the prototype, meaning that the relevant state information is given as input to each state-dependent operation. The state is loaded and respectively unloaded (Listing 4: lines 5, 22).

The available information sources at this point are:

- the set of ontologies referred to by both goal and Web service descriptions
- the knowledge encoded in the state given as input to the matchmaking process
- the information that may be provided by the goal description itself

We select those registered Web services that are executable. In this context, a Web service $S$ is considered executable if there exist input information in the available information sources such that the preconditions (what must be valid in order for the service to be executed) are fulfilled, while the effects and the postconditions (what the service guarantees after its execution) are not yet fulfilled. The assumptions describe conditions on information that is available only at run-time, and thus are not checked.

Therefore, $S$ is executable if there exists at least one variable binding that satisfies the preconditions $pre_S$, but not the effects $eff_S$ and the postconditions $out_S$ (Listing 4: lines 6-9). Checking that the effects and the postconditions of the Web service are not satisfied for the input that satisfies the preconditions is necessary due to the fact that in this context we wish to allow only a single execution of a Web service for a given input. Note however that a Web service can be executed an arbitrary number of times, with different input information.

A variable binding is a set of $< variable, value >$ pairs capturing the input information for which the service preconditions hold. More precisely, a variable binding is a complete set of bindings

$$< x_1, v_1 >, < x_2, v_2 >, ..., < x_n, v_n >$$

where $x_1, ..., x_n$ are the variables occurring in the precondition, and $v_1, ..., v_n$ is a set of constants. There can be several variable bindings for the same service, and all further tests on the service effects and postconditions will depend on the particular variable binding (Listing 4: line 9).

An executable service is considered a match if, for at least one of the variable bindings, the outcome of the service $S$ satisfies the outcome requested in the goal $G$. We perform this test by assuming the effects and the postconditions of the service for each variable binding and verifying if the effects and the postconditions of the goal hold in the resulting state (Listing 4: lines 10-14).

The set of matching services, and for each service all valid variable bindings, is then returned (Listing 4: line 23).

**2.2.2. Matching for Web service composition.** The second matchmaking algorithm queries for the Web services that are relevant to composition. In this context, we consider a Web service to be relevant if it is executable in the given state.

```
1   algorithm Matchmaking on preconditions
2   input: initial state I
3   output: map of <Web service S, set of <variable binding β>>
4
5   register state I
6   for each registered service S
7       if holds pres then
8           for each variable binding β
9               if not holds ( effs(β) and outs(β)) then
10                  add β to set of <β>
11              endif
12          endfor
13          if not empty (set of <β>) then
14              add (S, set of <β>) to result map
15          endif
16      endif
17  endfor
18  unregister state I
19  return result map
```

LISTING 5

Listing 5 presents the algorithm. Similar to the previous algorithm, the ontologies and the services are assumed to be loaded in the reasoner prior to invocation of the matchmaking process. The state is loaded and respectively unloaded (Listing 5: lines 5, 18).

The available information sources for this second algorithm are:

- the set of the ontologies referred by the Web service descriptions
- the knowledge encoded in the state given as input to the matchmaking process

A Web service is considered a match in the context of this algorithm if it is executable. As already defined, a Web service $S$ is executable if there exists input information such that the preconditions $pre_S$ are fulfilled, while the effects $eff_S$ and the postconditions $out_S$ are not yet fulfilled (Listing 5: lines 6-9).

The set of executable Web services, and for each Web service all corresponding variable bindings, is then returned (Listing 5: line 19).

## 3. A Prototype System for Service Discovery

We have developed a prototype system that implements the matchmaking algorithms presented in Section 2.2. Furthermore we have tested and validated our prototype on a real-world scenario developed in the ASG project, called Attraction Booking Scenario. We now provide a high level overview of our system in terms of its architecture, components and interaction between them. The discovery process is afterwards exemplified with a run-through of the previously mentioned scenario.

### 3.1. System overview

The high level architecture of our prototype system is provided in Figure 1. It consists of a set of loosely-coupled components which includes: a *System Interface*, a *Semantic Matchmaker*, a *Reasoner* and a *Repository*.

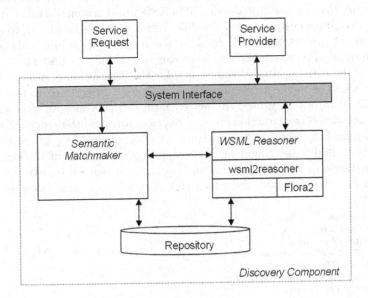

FIGURE 1. Discovery system architecture.

The system itself acts as a component having a defined *System Interface*. This interface offers a programmatic access to the system. Agents that act on behalf of service providers or service requestors can invoke functionalities exposed through this interface. The interface includes methods for managing semantic descriptions (e.g. register, unregister ontologies, services, goals), methods for querying the reasoner and methods for matching goals against registered services.

The *Semantic Matchmaker* is one of the core components of the Discovery System. It implements the matchmaking algorithms described in Section 2.2. It uses the reasoner to determine if the requested capability specified in a goal matches the capabilities of registered services.

The *Reasoner* provides querying and inference support required by the Semantic Matchmaker component. More precisely it supports a set of reasoning tasks like query answering with ontologies. As a backbone reasoner we have used the

$\mathcal{F}lora - 2$ system[2], integrated into the overall discovery system by using a generic framework called *wsml2reasoner*[3]. The framework allows easy integration of different reasoning engines for WSML language.

The *Repository* stores semantic descriptions like ontologies, goals and Web services. It provides methods to register and unregister the semantic descriptions mentioned before. Additionally, sets of facts that represent the states of the world at certain points in time can be registered or unregistered.

## 3.2. Application to use case scenario

The use case presented in the following paragraphs is a simplified fragment from the *Attraction Booking* scenario developed in ASG[4]. In this scenario taken from the telematics domain, a customer uses a mobile device, such as a handheld, to retrieve information on the attractions located in the nearby surroundings. Depending on the information received, the customer can additionally request for attraction details (e.g. the starting time of the event), for the description of a route leading to the attraction or, if the attraction is bookable, for a reservation to the event.

The domain ontology used in this scenario defines concepts, relations and instances associated to attractions (e.g. *attraction, attractionBag, attractionCategory*), locations (e.g. *city, street, coordinates*), mobile devices (e.g. *phoneNumber*). Listing 6 is an additional fragment of the ontology introduced in Listing 1, that refers to attractions. Besides concepts and instances associated to attractions and the search for attractions, we introduce an axiom which specifies that all events are bookable.

```
concept attraction
   name ofType _string
   description ofType _string
   bookingPossible ofType _boolean
   priceRangeA ofType priceRange
   categories ofType (1 *) attractionCategory
   locationA ofType location

concept event subConceptOf attraction

concept attractionBag
   nonFunctionalProperties
      dc#description hasValue "a list of attractions"
   endNonFunctionalProperties
   members ofType (1 *) attraction

concept attractionQuery
   keyword ofType _string
   numberOfResults ofType _integer
   attractionCategories ofType (1 *) attractionCategory

concept attractionCategory

instance categoryCinema memberOf attractionCategory
```

---

[2]http://flora.sourceforge.net
[3]http://dev1.deri.at/wsml2reasoner/
[4]https://asg-platform.org/

```
instance categoryMusic memberOf attractionCategory
instance categoryEatAndDrink memberOf attractionCategory

axiom allEventsAreBookableDef
    definedBy
      ?attraction memberOf Event implies
        ?attraction[bookingPossible hasValue _true].
```

LISTING 6

Further on, we introduce two Web services from the Attraction Booking service space, that provide information about attractions.

**CinemaxXAttractionInformationService.** - modeled after CinemaxX.de, this service retrieves a set of cinema events using as search criteria the location and an attraction query. The service requires that the cinema category is explicitly specified in the attraction query.

```
webService _"CinemaxXAttractionInfoService.wsml"
    nfp
      dc#title hasValue "CinemaxX Attraction Information Service"
      dc#publisher hasValue "CinemaxX.de"
    endnfp
    importsOntology _"domainOntology.wsml"
    capability CinemaxXAttractionInfoCapability
      precondition
        definedBy
          ?location memberOf dO#location
          and ?query[dO#attractionCategories hasValue dO#cinema] memberOf dO#attractionQuery.
      postcondition
        definedBy
          ?bagOfEvents[dO#members hasValue ?event] memberOf dO#attractionBag
          and ?event memberOf dO#event.
```

LISTING 7

**StarbucksAttractionInfoService.** - similar to the CinemaxX Web service, this service retrieves a set of bookable attractions if a location and an attraction query are given. The service requires that the attraction category list present in the query to contain the "eat-and-drink" category.

```
webService _"StarbucksAttractionInfoService.wsml"
    nfp
      dc#title hasValue "Starbucks Attraction Information Service"
      dc#publisher hasValue "Starbucks.com"
    endnfp
    importsOntology _"domainOntology.wsml"
    capability StarbucksAttractionInfoCapability
      precondition
        definedBy
          ?location memberOf dO#location
          and ?query[dO#attractionCategories hasValue dO#eatAndDrink] memberOf dO#attractionQuery.
      postcondition
        definedBy
          ?attrBag[dO#members hasValue ?attraction] memberOf dO#attractionBag
          and ?attraction[dO#bookingPossible hasValue _true] memberOf dO#attraction.
```

LISTING 8

**3.2.1. Matching based on capabilities.** Consider a generic goal of finding attractions that can be booked, located in the nearby surroundings of the user. The user request we wish to model is equivalent to the following natural language specification: "Given a query that specifies the categories of attractions, the problem is solved when the list of bookable attractions is known." The formal specification of the request is given in Listing 9.

```
goal _"findBookableAttractionsGoal.wsml"
  nfp
    dc#title hasValue "Find Bookable Attractions Goal"
  endnfp
  importsOntology _"domainOntology.wsml"
  capability findBookableAttractionsCapability
    precondition
      definedBy
        ?query[dO#attractionCategories hasValue ?category] memberOf dO#attractionQuery.
    postcondition
      definedBy
        ?bookableAttrBag[dO#members hasValue ?bookableAttr] memberOf dO#attractionBag
        and ?bookableAttr[dO#bookingPossible hasValue _true] memberOf dO#attraction.
```
LISTING 9

The user input is captured in the initial state of the problem (Listing 10), which defines a person, a location and an attraction query specifying a list of categories.

```
ontology _"initialState.wsml"
  importsOntology _"domainOntology.wsml"

instance me memberOf dO#person
instance myLocation memberOf dO#location
relationInstance dO#hasLocation(me, myLocation)

instance myQuery memberOf dO#attractionQuery
  dO#attractionCategories hasValue {dO#cinema, dO#music}
```
LISTING 10

The discovery process starts by checking if the goal holds in the initial state. Since the goal postcondition is not satisfied for the initial state, the next phase is service matchmaking based on capabilities, according to the algorithm presented in 2.2.1.

The algorithm analyzes every registered Web service. The preconditions in the CinemaxX Web service are fulfilled, and using the background ontology we determine that the outcome advertised in the Web service satisfies the outcome requested in the goal. The CinemaxX attraction information service is thus considered a match. On the other hand, even though it advertises only attractions that can be booked (and thus meets the goal postcondition), the Starbucks Web service is not a valid match, because its preconditions are not satisfied.

The algorithm returns the identifier of the matching Web service, together with the corresponding variable binding.

```
Service:
        CinemaxXAttractionInfoService.wsml
Service Variables Binding:
        location = initialState#myLocation
        query = initialState#myQuery
```

LISTING 11

**3.2.2. Matching for Web service composition.** Further on, we present a run-through that uses for matchmaking the algorithm defined in 2.2.2.

In order to simulate the Web service composition, we add to the service repository the phone location service introduced in section 2.1.

We consider the same generic goal of finding attractions that can be booked. For this second example, the initial state specifies the user, the phone number and the attraction query. However, in this initial state, no information related to the location of the user is known.

```
ontology _" altInitialState.wsml"
    importsOntology _"domainOntology.wsml"

instance myNumber memberOf dO#phoneNumber
instance me memberOf dO#person
    dO#number hasValue myNumber

instance myQuery memberOf dO#attractionQuery
    dO#attractionCategories hasValue {dO#cinema, dO#music}
```

LISTING 12

The simulation of the service composition process consists of one or more iterations through a series of steps. The steps are executed in the following order:

1. check if the goal holds in the current state. If true exit, else go to 2;
2. query for executable services. If no service is discovered exit, else go to 3;
3. virtually execute one of the discovered services.

**First iteration:** Testing whether the goal is reached in the initial state returns false. We proceed to the next step, finding executable services. The result contains only the phone location service, as it is the only Web service whose preconditions are satisfied (Listing 13).

In case more executable Web services are found, the composition planner can employ a complex approach for selecting the best matching Web service, while also taking into consideration non-functional properties like optimization criteria (e.g. price or speed) and static restrictions (e.g. only services from provider X).

```
Service:
    MobTelPhoneLocationService.wsml
Service Variables Binding:
    phoneNumber = altInitialState#myNumber
```

LISTING 13

We start constructing the first alternative with the virtual execution of the phone location service. By assuming the outcome of this service, a dummy instance of type location is created and related to the phone number. Listing 14 gives the equivalent WSML description of the inserted facts.

```
domainOntology#location1 memberOf domainOntology#location.
domainOntology#hasLocation(altInitialState#myNumber, domainOntology#location1).
```

LISTING 14

**Second iteration:** The test whether we have reached the goal returns false.

The result of querying for the executable services in the current virtual state is the CinemaxX Web service, as it is the only service whose preconditions are satisfied.

```
Service:
        CinemaxXAttractionInfoService.wsml
Service Variables Binding:
        location = domainOntology#location1
        query = initialState#myQuery
```

LISTING 15

The virtual execution of the CinemaxX service adds a new dummy instance of the attraction bag concept, containing one dummy instance of the event concept. Listing 16 displays the WSML description of the added facts.

```
domainOntology#event1 memberOf domainOntology#event.
domainOntology#attractionBag1[
    domainOntology#members hasValue domainOntology#event1
    ] memberOf domainOntology#attractionBag.
```

LISTING 16

**Third iteration:** Testing whether the goal was reached yields true.

```
Goal Variables Binding:
        bookableAttrBag = domainOntology#attractionBag1
        bookableAttr = domainOntology#event1
```

LISTING 17

The output of the presented run-through is a possible service execution plan that can be constructed by a service composition planner. In this execution plan Mobtel phone location service and CinemaxX attraction information service are composed in order to achieve the user goal. Alternative service execution plans can be achieved in case more executable services are discovered at each step.

## 4. Related Work

The automatic discovery of services is nowadays a very popular research topic. Many solutions have been proposed ranging from pure syntactic to highly logic based approaches. However many of them lack a clear discovery model and a formal specification of the discovery process. Furthermore many of them cannot be easily integrated with solutions for other service related tasks.

Approaches like [9, 11], although logic-based, are missing a clear discovery model. These approaches are also too general and is not clear how they can support other service related tasks like service composition.

Same holds for other approaches (e.g. [13, 1])that were mainly provided to work in distributed environments like P2P. Besides the lack of clear discovery model and support for other service related tasks, many of these approaches also lack a formal, concise algorithms for service discovery.

## 5. Conclusions and Future Work

In this paper we presented a logic based approach for service discovery that can be easily used by service composition modules. Two kinds of algorithms for service discovery were presented, one based on capability matching, the other on supporting service composition. Furthermore we have implemented a proof of concept prototype that validates our solution on real use-case scenarios. As future work we plan to compare our solution and implementation against other service discovery solutions. Also, we plan to refine our solution to include the possibility of ranking the matching Web services, the problem of ranking being one of the main challenges in Web service discovery. Performance and scalability tests are also left as future work.

### Acknowledgements

The work is funded by the European Commission under the projects ASG, DIP, enIRaF, InfraWebs, Knowledge Web, Musing, Salero, SEKT, Seemp, Semantic-GOV, Super, SWING and TripCom; by Science Foundation Ireland under the DERI-Lion Grant No.SFI/02/CE1/I13 ; by the FIT-IT (Forschung, Innovation, Technologie - Informationstechnologie) under the projects Grisino, $RW^2$, SemNet-Man, SeNSE and TSC.

## References

[1] Rama Akkiraju, Richard Goodwin, Prashant Doshi, and Sascha Roeder. A method for semantically enhancing the service discovery capabilities of UDDI. In Subbarao Kambhampati and Craig A. Knoblock, editors, *Proceedings of the IJCAI-03 Workshop on Information Integration on the Web (IIWeb-03)*, pages 87–92, 2003.

[2] T. Bellwood, L. Clment, D. Ehnebuske, A. Hately, Maryann Hondo, Y.L. Husband, K. Januszewski, S. Lee, B. McKee, J. Munter, and C. von Riegen. Uddi version 3.0. http://uddi.org/pubs/uddi-v3.00-published-20020719.htm, July 2002.

[3] E. Christensen, F. Curbera, G. Meredith, and S. Weerawarana. Web services description language (wsdl) 1.1. http://www.w3.org/TR/wsdl, March 2001.

[4] Jos de Bruijn, Holger Lausen, Reto Krummenacher, Axel Polleres, Livia Predoiu, Michael Kifer, and Dieter Fensel. The Web Service Modeling Language WSML. Technical report, WSML, 2005. WSML Final Draft D16.1v0.21. http://www.wsmo.org/TR/d16/d16.1/v0.21/.

[5] Dieter Fensel and Christoph Bussler. The Web Service Modeling Framework WSMF. *Electronic Commerce Research and Applications*, 1(2):113–137, 2002.

[6] Uwe Keller, Ruben Lara, Axel Polleres, Ioan Toma, Michael Kiffer, and Dieter Fensel. WSMO discovery. Working Draft D5.1v0.1, WSMO, 2004. http://www.wsmo.org/TR/d5/d5.1/v0.1/.

[7] Michael Kifer, Rubén Lara, Axel Polleres, Chang Zhao, Uwe Keller, Holger Lausen, and Dieter Fensel. A logical framework for web service discovery. In *ISWC 2004 Workshop on Semantic Web Services: Preparing to Meet the World of Business Applications*, volume 119, Hiroshima, Japan, 2004. CEUR Workshop Proceedings.

[8] H. Lausen, A. Polleres, and D. Roman (eds.). Web Service Modeling Ontology (WSMO). W3C Member Submission 3 June 2005, 2005. http://www.w3.org/Submission/WSMO/.

[9] Lei Li and Ian Horrocks. A software framework for matchmaking based on semantic web technology. In *Proceedings of the 12th International Conference on the World Wide Web*, Budapest, Hungary, May 2003.

[10] Harald Meyer and Mathias Weske. Automated service composition using heuristic search. In *Proceedings of the Fourth International Conference on Business Process Management*, volume 4102 of *Lecture Notes in Computer Science*, Vienna, Austria, 2006.

[11] M. Paolucci, T. Kawamura, T. Payne, and K. Sycara. Semantic matching of web services capabilities. In I. Horrocks and J. Handler, editors, *1st Int. Semantic Web Conference (ISWC)*, pages 333–347. Springer Verlag, 2002.

[12] K. Sycara, S. Widoff, M. Klusch, and J. Lu. Larks: Dynamic matchmaking among heterogeneous software agents in cyberspace. *Autonomous Agents and Multi-Agent Systems*, pages 173–203, 2002.

[13] K. Verma, K. Sivashanmugam, A. Sheth, and A. Patil. Meteor-s wsdi: A scalable p2p infrastructure of registries for semantic publication and discovery of web services. *Journal of Information Technology and Management*, 2004.

[14] W3C. SOAP Version 1.2 Part 0: Primer, June 2003.

Adina Sîrbu, Ioan Toma, Dumitru Roman
Digital Enterprise Research Institute
University of Innsbruck
Technikerstrasse 21a
6020 Innsbruck, Austria
e-mail: adina.sirbu@deri.org, ioan.toma@deri.org, dumitru.roman@deri.org

Whitestein Series in Software Agent Technologies, 117–133

# Mobile and Dynamic Web Services

Elena Sánchez-Nielsen, Sandra Martín-Ruiz and Jorge
Rodríguez-Pedrianes

**Abstract.** Making mobile phones capable of consuming Web services over wireless networks is a challenging task because of the different issues to be addressed and the limited resources of mobile devices. In this paper, we focus on the issue of how to perform dynamic discovery and invocation of Web services from mobile phones when a J2ME wireless middleware is used. In order to solve the limitations of the middleware platform when mobile phones act as Web services requestor we propose a Web service based dynamic proxy between service providers and mobile consumers. With this approach, we provide the following features to mobile devices: (1) support of dynamic binding, (2) support of UDDI specification, (3) support of SOAP messages with encoded representation and (4) handling of complex data types. The paper includes the description of the dynamic proxy, implementation and experimental results with the performance of the approach proposed.

**Keywords.** Web services, mobile phones, dynamic discovery, dynamic invocation.

## 1. Introduction

The use of Web services (WSs) in mobile phones allows users to discover and access to digital content and services anywhere and anytime. The access to these resources in a wired-wireless system involves: service provisioning, service discovery and service execution.

The need of service providers to add new capabilities at any time and in turn give mobile consumers a huge choice of available services at runtime requires a dynamic discovery and invocation process. The use of this process brings a number of benefits to mobile users such as to require no prior knowledge of available services nor to require updating clients applications when new services are incorporated at runtime.

Dynamic adaptive middleware for mobile computing has been proposed with the purpose of adapting applications to the current context [18, 19], frameworks for

Web services provisioning in a static environment of fixed and mobile computing have been described in [22] and approaches for provisioning mobile services in critical environments have been outlined in [23]. However, no significant frameworks with experimental results have been carried out to allow access to Web services from mobile phones at runtime without prior knowledge of available services due to the current limitations of extending the Web service technology into the wireless world by the key commercial players.

This paper describes our approach to addressing dynamic discovery and invocation when mobile phones act as WS requestor at runtime, its implementation and performance when J2ME middleware platform [10] is used.

The remainder of this paper is organized as follows. Section 2 introduces the different issues related to invoke Web services from mobile phones and the related work about mobile devices acting as WS requestor. Section 3 describes the current restrictions to design mobile client applications to access to Web services when J2ME development platform is used. Focused on these limitations, we propose to introduce a Web service based dynamic proxy. The use of this component allows service providers to create, update and change services anytime and mobile users to locate new services at runtime without adapting the application of their devices. Section 4 describes our approach and conceptual model to dynamically discover and invoke Web services from mobile phones. Section 5 illustrates the implementation and performance of the approach proposed. Comparisons with common scenarios based on the use of static stubs are performed. Discussion of the advantages and disadvantages of the use of J2ME as wireless middleware is included. Section 6 gives concluding remarks and future work.

## 2. Related Work

This section provides a brief summary of Web services standards related to our work, scenarios of using Web services in mobile phones, and ongoing specifications related to it. Discussion on whether it is appropriate to adopt common scenarios to support services on wired networks in mobile phones is included.

### 2.1. Web Services Standards

The WS paradigm [6] involves three types of participants: WS provider, WS requestor (also referred to as service consumer or client) and WS registry or broker. The infrastructure necessary to implement a WS based approach requires: a way to communicate (SOAP) [7], a way to describe services (WSDL) [8], and a name and directory server to publish and advertise available services (UDDI) [9]. In middleware terms, a service is a procedure, method or object with a published interface by a service provider that can be invoked by service clients. Using SOAP-based interaction, the client makes a procedure call that looks like a local call. As a result, clients can invoke Web services by means of standardized conventions to convert procedure calls into an XML message, to exchange this message through HTTP or other protocols, and to turn the XML message back into an actual service invocation. The structure of a SOAP message is influenced by: two different inter-action styles and encoding rules. Then, four different types of SOAP messages are possible: RPC/encoded, RPC/literal, document/literal and document/encoded.

WSDL is an XML-based interface definition language. This interface is spec-ified in terms of methods supported by the Web service. This interface can be compiled into the appropriate programming language to generate the stubs and intermediate layers that make calls to the Web services transparent. Invoking Web services with clients can be carried out by static stubs, dynamic proxies and dy-namic invocation interface (DII) according to client applications having knowledge of the WSDL URL at development-time or runtime.

- Static stubs: a procedure call of a client application is an invocation of a proxy procedure located in a stub appended to the client at compile time. Then clients invoke methods of a WS directly via the stub.
- Dynamic proxies: the client application calls a remote procedure through a dynamic proxy that is created at runtime. The dynamic proxy needs to be re-instated whenever the service endpoint interfaces are changed.
- Dynamic invocation interface (DII): this approach enables dynamic invoca-tion of Web services without having to know interface details at compile time.

## 2.2. Scenarios of using Web services in mobile phones

The possible scenarios of using Web services in mobile phones are [17]: (i) mobile device acting as WS requestor, (ii) mobile device acting as WS provider and (iii) a mixed combination of the previous approaches. The approach proposed in this paper is related to the first scenario.

In the following sections we describe existing and ongoing work related to the two possible architectural configurations for the first scenario.

**2.2.1. WS-aware mobile device.** In this architectural configuration, the entity that plays the role of the WS requestor is the mobile device itself. This device needs to dispose a WS client application in order to enable the provision of services to mobile users. It interacts with the service provider and the service broker using WS-aware protocols over the wireless network (eg., WLAN, GSM/GPRS).

TinyXML [20] can be used to present data and VoiceXML [21] allows user to listen to data instead of viewing it. Figure 1 illustrates how to access to Web services functionalities from mobile phones using a WS based service oriented architecture with static stubs.

**2.2.2. WS-agnostic mobile device.** This configuration introduces a proxy entity that plays the role of the mobile device representative in the fixed network in-frastructure. This scenario is applicable in the case where the mobile user moves into an unfamiliar environment and obtain services for which it has no previous knowledge. For example, we could consider a mobile user entering an airport and obtaining access to services such as flight information, special offers and promo-tions in the duty free shops, etc. The proxy interacts via WS-aware protocols with

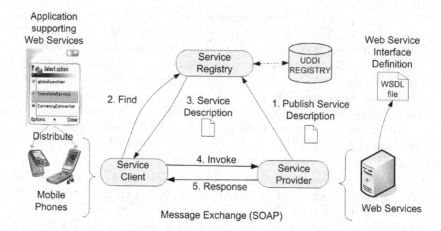

FIGURE 1. Mobile phone as a service requestor. The device hosts WS client code

the service broker and the service provider and returns the results to the mobile device using WS-agnostic protocols such as WAP/WML, i-Mode/cHTML over a wireless network [17]. The proxy may also perform various tasks such as conversion and content adaptation in order to adjust the WS result to different terminal and network environments.

### 2.3. Specifications

Two specifications related to implement services in mobile phones are being developed: (i) OSGi Alliance [2] and Liberty Alliance Project [3]. The OSGi Service Platform defines a standardized, component oriented, computing environment for networked services, where software components can be installed, updated or removed. These components are libraries or applications that can dynamically discover and use other components. The design of this platform is not targeted to Web services solutions. Therefore, there is ongoing work in order to provide the OSGi Service Platform as a platform for Web services such is illustrated by Hall and Cervantes work [4]. On the other hand, the Liberty Alliance Project proposes a federated network with an authentication mechanism that makes use of a Web services framework. However, the usage, advantages and disadvantages of dynamic binding are not mentioned in this specification.

### 2.4. Discussion

In order to provide an admissible solution to dynamic services from mobile devices, the following considerations must be taken into account:

- Standard WS infrastructures to support services on wired networks (e-services) [5] are not appropriate because they are based on the use of static stubs. As a result, the slightest change of Web service definition leads to the stub being useless and a generation of a new stub. Also, each WS to be invoked by a client application requires a stub appended to the client at compile time. Therefore, in order to support a dynamic infrastructure where new services can be provided to mobile clients at runtime requires that the client downloads a new application to its device each time a new service is provided to the marketplace when a static stub based approach is used.

- The main usage mode of UDDI today is focused on design-time discovery and not on dynamic binding [5]. That is, users browse or search the content of a registry for services of interest, read the service descriptions, and subsequently write clients that can interact with the discovered services.
- The WS-aware mobile device based configuration presents several issues which come from the fact that mobile devices are characterized by limited resources such as processing power and memory. Also, CPUs in mobile phones are restricted to handle complex XML parsing and in general to handle the processing need of Web services.
- The WS-agnostic mobile device based configuration is characterized by an increase of the amount of interactions between the mobile device and the network. Also, at the present time commercial middleware based solutions make not possible a DII based approach.
- Also, the specifications supporting these scenarios are still or just emerging.

In this context, we propose a framework based on a dynamic proxy entity. The main contribution of our approach is that we propose the proxy component as a Web service that makes use of dynamic binding and that act as client over the network of services and as server to the mobile devices. With this approach, we compute at runtime WS descriptions from service providers, UDDI registry and invoke services selected by mobile users using WS technology.

## 3. Client Applications with J2ME

The Java Platform, Micro Edition (Java ME) provides an environment for applications running on consumer devices, such as mobile phones. This platform is divided into configurations, profiles and optional packages. Configurations are specifications that detail a virtual machine and a set of class libraries which provide the necessary APIs that can be used with a certain class of device. A profile is a set of higher-level APIs that further define the application life-cycle model, the user interface, persistent storage and access to device-specific properties. Optional packages extend the Java ME platform by adding functionality to Web services.

MIDP profile with CLDC configuration, KVM virtual machine and JSR-172 specification is required as development environment to design mobile client applications to access to Web services using Java ME. JSR-172 specification provides the necessary APIs to access from J2ME applications to remote SOAP/XML services and parsing XML data. This specification provides two optional packages based on XML: Java API for XML Processing (JAXP) and Java API for XML-based

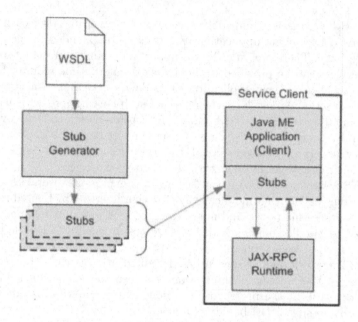

FIGURE 2. Generating the JAX-RPC Stub

RPC (JAX-RPC). JAXP provides the XML parsing functionality to process XML data received in a mobile phone. JAX-RPC is an implementation of RPC technology (Remote Procedure Call), where the client makes a procedure call that looks like a local call. This call is an invocation of a proxy procedure located in a stub appended to the client at compile time. Currently, designing client applications using JSR-172 specification presents the following restrictions:

- There is no support for dynamic proxies or dynamic invocation interface. That is, the Java ME subset supports only static stubs. The developer is responsible of generating the stubs using a WSDL-to-Java mapping tool. Figure 2 illustrates the process. The Sun Java Wireless Toolkit includes a stub generator. In this context, as many stubs are generated and appended to the client application as different services are provided to the service client.
- There is only support to the document style of operation with literal use.
- Neither capabilities for standard service registration and discovery nor support to UDDI 2.0 specification are provided.
- There is no support to the use of a mobile phone as server of Web services. That is, the JAXP-RPC for Java ME subset does not support the service endpoint model, only the client service consumer model is supported.

JAX-RPC for Java ME does not support all of the JAX-RPC 1.1 basic types. For example, there is only partial support for complex value types, and mapping of floating-point types depends on the Java ME configuration you use.

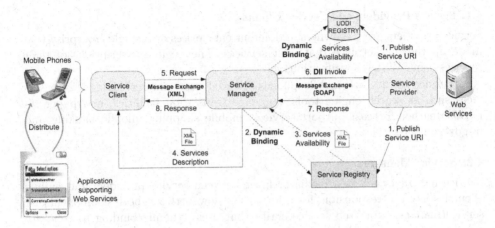

FIGURE 3. Mobile Web services framework

## 4. Mobile Web Services Framework

Commercial middleware such as J2ME and basic infrastructures to support WSs are addressed by employing a static stub approach that guarantees the execution of WSs in a static environment. However, this middleware platform does not take into account basic features that characterize today's mobile phones environments. In this context, we aim to modify traditional WS SOA based approach to enable dynamic discovery and invocation for mobile phones. To be precise, we propose:

- To introduce an intermediate entity between service providers and service clients. This entity consists of a service manager that operates as a dynamic discovery and invocation (DDI) client of the distributed network of Web services offered by the different providers and as server to the mobile phones. With this approach, we delegate the business logic to service managers, solving the problems faced by direct access from mobile devices to Web services and at the same time reducing the number of interactions between mobile phones and the network.
- An XML based infrastructure as format data exchange with two purposes: (i) to define a service registry structure to locate services that allows service providers to create, update and change services at any time and (ii) to establish the communication between the service manager and mobile phones. This infrastructure is described in [1].

Figure 3 illustrates the framework proposed. In the following sections, we describe the components of our approach illustrated in Figure 3, the interactions among the different components and the UML class diagram for the conceptual model of the service manager.

## 4.1. Service Providers and Service Clients

Service providers are the owners of different enterprises or a single enterprise who made up the marketplace that offer services. They define descriptions of their services using WSDL specifications [8].

Service clients are mobile phones-oriented users interested in diverse services such as search engine tools, language translation facilities, newspaper reports, weather forecast, airport services, mobile shopping, mobile banking and m-government services.

## 4.2. Service Managers

Service managers act as a mediator layer between service providers and mobile clients. They are responsible for information flow between both components. A service manager is a Web service entity that uses dynamic binding to compute service descriptions and dynamic invocation interface (DII) to query for services to service providers.

With the use of DII, we allow service managers to invoke WS without knowing their communication interface at compile time. As a result, we obtain several advantages: (i) invocations of Web services not known prior can be computed by the service manager (ii) service providers can create, update and change their services at runtime, (iii) no static stub generated manually for the service manager at compile time is required and (iv) a single stub appended to the Java ME client application is required. This appended stub corresponds to the service manager.

According to the structure of marketplace, one or multiple service managers can be supported. The use of a single service manager involves a centralized marketplace. If multiple service managers are used, different operators or third parties can be incorporated at anytime, where each one can support different service providers. The integration of service managers into a service oriented architecture leads to mobile client applications to only interact with these components and not with the different service providers. This way, a single stub corresponding to the service manager is needed to be appended to the client application and no several stubs corresponding to the different services available on the marketplace. At the same time, the interactions between mobile phones and the network are considerably reduced. The conceptual model of a service manager is described in section 4.5.

## 4.3. UDDI Registry

UDDI service directory can be used by mobile users to locate new services. Discovery is computed at runtime by the service manager, once the user has sent their request of new services at UDDI registry.

## 4.4. Interactions

Interactions between service providers and mobile clients using a service manager consist of the following processes:

- **Start up:** When the service manager starts up, it processes a service registry. This registry is a structure that enables service providers to store their list of URL addresses (URI) of accessible services made available. New URI can be incorporated anytime. The service manager maintains an XML based structure as registry. Dynamic binding is used by the service manager in order to obtain the service descriptions at runtime.
- **Service delivery descriptions:** the description (operations provided, parameter...) of available Web services set is sent from service manager to mobile client according to an XML format.
- **Request Service:** once mobile clients have received the description of available services, they send requests for services of their interest.
- **Service invocation:** service manager receives a request encoded as an XML message with the necessary information (Web service name, selected operation, parameter values introduced...) from a mobile device when a user is interested in some service. Dynamic invocation is used by service manager in order to invoke Web services functionalities to service providers.
- **Results transmission:** the service manager sends the information encoded as an XML message to the mobile user, when it receives the response of the corresponding service provider. This information is shown on the screen display of the mobile device.
- **UDDI services:** mobile clients can also demand services supported by UDDI registry. In this context, a client makes a request to the service manager using keyword in order to discover a particular service at UDDI registry. Then, the service manager uses dynamic binding to discover services at UDDI registry that match with the user search criterion. The description of these services is sent from the service manager to the mobile application. The user selects the service of its interest and finally the service manager processes this request at the same way as the request and invocation of services previously described.

## 4.5. Conceptual Model of Service Manager

Figure 4 depicts the UML class diagram for the conceptual model of the service manager. The different classes and relationships are illustrated. Following, the different classes are described.

The *WebService class* corresponds to the service manager that processes the requests of mobile clients. In order to avoid a new creation of instance every time the user performs an invocation of some operation of this class and reduce computational costs, two different classes were developed (*StandardServices* and *UDDIServices*). These classes were implemented using a singleton pattern. As a result, a single instance is present every time. The client application invokes the corresponding operation according to the selection achieved by the mobile user:

- **updateStandardServices:** this operation allows mobile users to check the current version of downloaded services. If the version of the mobile application does not correspond to the service manager version, a new version with the new services incorporated at runtime is sent to the mobile client in an XML format.

- **invokeStandardService:** this operation allows mobile users to invoke any WS registered at the service registry of the service manager. Input parameters are: URL address of WSDL file, QName of portType, operation name to invoke and parameter values of the operation. Once the results of the invocation of the Web service have been processed by the service manager, this one transforms these results to an appropriate XML format, which is sent to the mobile application.

- **processUDDISearch:** this operation allows mobile users to request a search at UDDI registry. Once the search is computed by the service manager using dynamic binding, the results of available services are encoded as an XML message to the client application.

- **computeUDDISearch:** once client application receives services located at UDDI registry as a result of the **processUDDISearch** operation, the user selects the appropriate Web service for its interest. The input parameter of this operation is the service selected. An XML document is generated with the service description which is sent to the client application.

- **invokeUDDIService:** with this operation, services searched at UDDI registry are invoked using dynamic invocation.

The *StandardServices* class is responsible of the management of all the operations related to the processing of Web services, such as: computation of the Web services to offer to mobile clients, making of the XML document to be sent to the mobile application with the new services incorporated at runtime and invocation of the operation of a specific WS selected by a mobile user.

The *UDDIServices* class corresponds to the operations related to Web services searched at UDDI registry: Web services list that matches with the search criterion of the user and invocation of the corresponding operation. The search of Web services at UDDI registry is computed by *locateUDDI* method. This method makes use of the *locateUDDIService* class that computes the search at UDDI registry according to the search criterion detailed by the mobile user. After the search has been performed, services found at UDDI registry are checked in order to detect inconsistencies.

The *ManagerOperations* class manages the operations related to Web services such as operations of incorporation, searching and invocation. The attributes of this class are the *operations* set and the *dynamicInvoker* object. Attribute *operations* contains the description of operation of Web services: URL address of WSDL document, parameters required and description of the operation. The *dynamicInvoker* object is an instance of the class *DynamicInvoker*.

The *DynamicInvoker* class is designed with the purpose of achieving the description of Web services from WSDL files and invocating them at runtime. Apache Axis [11] is used to implement this class. In order to make dynamic invocation, we use the *call* interface provided by Axis. Invocation of an operation implies to generate an instance of this class. With the purpose of reducing computational costs and avoiding the generation of a new instance with every invocation, we use a structure with a *call* instance for every operation created. This way, a single instance is generated for every operation, using this instance every time that it is necessary to invoke the same operation.

Following, the parameters of the operation selected must be checked. The parameters to be processed can basically be simple or complex. However, the *call* interface does not provide support to handling complex data type. That is, if the *call* object receives as input parameter a complex type, this object has not the sufficient information to the serialization and deserialization process of this parameter.

At the present, Axis interface provide the *invoke* method to compute the invocation of the service. Once the operation and service to be computed has been indicated, the method *invoke* can basically be used by two different ways:

- *invoke (Object[] arg0)*: service invocation is computed by means of the use of arg0, which represents a set of parameters of the operation to be computed. Every element of this array is an instance of a Java class that represents every parameter of the operation.
- *invoke (Message arg0)*: service invocation is computed by a message, which represents a SOAP message, that is, an XML format with the operation to be invoked and their parameters.

To handling the complex data types, we use the first option of the *invoke* method. However, there is not a representation for a complex data type in a structure that can be used by the invoke method. Therefore, in this situation, the service cannot be invoked. To solve this problem, we generate at runtime a *JavaBeans* software component that represents each one of the different complex types that appears on the WSDL files analyzed. As a result, the bean associated to each complex parameter type allows that the *call* instance will be able to catch and modify the fields of the parameter at the invocation time by means of the instance of Axis *BeanSerializerFactory* and *BeanDeserializerFactory* classes.

The *BeanJavassistUtils* class produces at runtime the beans necessary to make invocations of operations that contain parameters with complex data types. In order to produce a class at runtime, we use the class library *Javassist* (*Java Programming Assistant*) [16]. It enables Java programs to generate a new bytecode at runtime. *Makebean* method of *BeanJavassistUtils* class (Figure 4) is responsible of generating the corresponding beans. It is implemented in a similar way as the beans are generated by the mapping tools of stubs of Axis.

## 5. Development and Results

The framework described in section 4, allows mobile users to access to Web services published at World Wide Web by means of requesting a service manager entity. No update of client application is required when new services are provided at runtime.

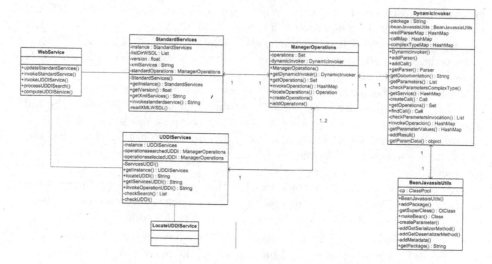

FIGURE 4. Class diagram of service manager

The framework has been implemented using the following open source software: Apache Tomcat 5.0.28 for application server [15], J2ME Wireless Toolkit (WTK) [13] for developing wireless applications and designed to run on cell phones, and Eclipse 3.1 development platform with WTP (Web Tools Platform) plug-in [14] for building software and developing Web applications. Axis [11] and UDDI4J [12] Java libraries have been used as SOAP motor and Java implementation of UDDI protocol. Javassist (Java Programming Assistant) [16] has been used as a class library for editing bytecodes in Java. It enables to define a new class at runtime and to modify a class file when the JVM loads it. The client application has been implemented as a MIDlet using J2ME Wireless Toolkit. That is, a Java application developed with MIDP profile and CLDC configuration.

In order to test the Web services framework for mobile devices, we have implemented on mobile phones different scenarios services using a service manager entity. The following services have been implemented and tested: (1) searching with Google engine, (2) text translation from one language to another, (3) newspaper reports from different sources, (4) temperature converser, (5) weather forecast, (6) calculator operations and (7) dynamic binding with UDDI registry.

We have developed the Java client application and tested it on the Sun emulator. Also, with the purpose of testing correct performance, we have tested the client application with mobile emulators of commercial trademarks.

### 5.1. Performance

The core of our framework is the Web service based proxy (service manager). An important part of this component is the ability of processing requests from mobile phones. In order to measure and compare the running of our proxy, we compute the performance of the service manager invoking services over the wired network under two approaches: (i) static stub and (ii) DII.

Different qualities or properties defined by Quality of service (QoS) [24] are used in order to evaluate the performance of the Web service based proxy from the perspective of the users of services (in this case, the users with mobile phones).

WSTest [25], a benchmark developed at Sun Microsystems is employed with the purpose of computing two aspects of QoS. WSTest benchmark simulates a multi-thread server program that makes multiple Web services calls in parallel. WSTest reports the *Throughput* (average number of Web service operations per second) and the *Response Time* (average time taken to process a request).

**5.1.1. Test Description.** With the purpose of computing the performance of the service manager, we consider the invocation of three operations of a Web service with the following types of parameters:

- **echoVoid:** sends and receives an empty message.
- **echoStruct:** sends and receives an array of size 20, where each element is a structure composed of one element each of an integer and string data type.
- **echoSynthetic:** sends and receives a string and a complex parameter (struct).

For the results reported, WSTest was run with the following parameters set, specified in an initialization file:

- **Agents:** this is the number of client threads and is set to maximize CPU utilization and system throughput. The number of concurrent threads is set to 8.
- **Execution time:** 300 seconds.
- **The same number of calls** for each of the 3 types of operations tested.

WSTest was run on the following system configuration:

- **Service manager and Web service invoked:** Intel Pentium 2GHz. 1GB DDR2, 1 processor.
- **Client of service manager:** Intel Pentium 2GHz. 512MB DDR2, 1 processor.

**5.1.2. Results.** The measured throughput and response times were computed for four different scenarios:

- **Static stub:** invocation of the Web service from the service manager using a static stub approach.
- **DII1:** invocation of the Web service with a standard DDI service manager.
- **DII2:** invocation of the Web service with a DDI service manager. The first time the service manager employs standard DII. In the successive times the service manager computes and caches the *call* class. This consideration will allow the invocation for each of the different operations that support the service. As a result, it will be not necessary to generate the *call* objects every time a client of the service manager processes a request of the same Web service.

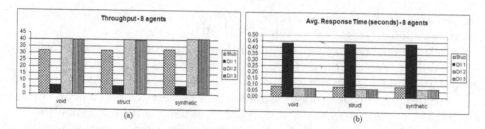

FIGURE 5. Throughput and average response time for service manager using three different parameter types (echo, struct and synthetic) and four different approaches: (1) static stub, (2) standard DII (DII1), (3) standard DII for the first time and a memory cache for the successive times (DII2) and (4) DII with a cache memory (DII3)

- **DII3:** it is assumed that the service manager has a cache memory with the *call* objects.

The graph in Figure 5 shows the performance for each of the four scenarios. The x-axis indicates the types of parameters such as void, struct and synthetic. The y-axis in Figure 5.a indicates the throughput, the number of Web service operations executed per second (higher is better) and the y-axis in Figure 5.b indicates the response times measured in seconds (lower is better).

In order to compare the results between a static stub approach and a DII improved approach with cache memory, Figure 6 shows the results performed with both approaches.

Although a better performance could be supposed with a static stub approach, a DII approach with cache memory offers better results. Initially, the DDI service manager client needs an additional cost for discovering the service to be invoked, for processing the WSDL document, for obtaining the description of the service and for the generation of the necessary structures for the invocation. This is illustrated in Figure 5 with the DII1 scenario. However, this computational cost is only assumed the first time by the service manager for every service invoked. All the knowledge acquired by means of the use of a cache memory of *call* objects is used in successive invocations. With this approach, we compute a better performance in contrast to a static stub approach (Figure 6).

### 5.2. Discussion

At present, we found that open source development tools for building, deploying and testing production quality work well together. Using a dynamic binding based approach and MIDlets as client applications allows users to download a single time the application directly to their device over-the-air or via their PC. As a result, no update of the client application is required when new services are provided.

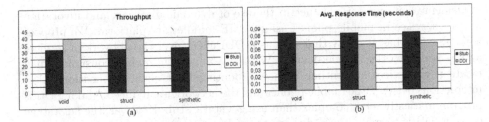

FIGURE 6. Throughput and average response time for service manager using three different parameter types (echo, struct and synthetic) and two approaches: (1) static stub, and (2) DII with a cache memory (DII)

In order to develop client applications using J2ME middleware platform, we have found the following drawbacks:

1. The Java Specification Request 172 (JSR-172) required for invocating Web services from a mobile J2ME application does not support UDDI specification and SOAP encoded messages.
2. There is only support to static stubs. Therefore, new stubs must be manually generated when new services are incorporated at runtime and clients need to download a new application in order to incorporate the new services.
3. Specific implementations must be developed in order to handling complex data types when dynamic invocation interface is used.

Also, we have found that the use of UDDI registry provides high rate of time responses and many of the services published at UDDI registry are not correctly published. Thus, all the services located through UDDI registry must be verified by the service manager, before the results are sent to the mobile user. However, these checking operations increase the response time to mobile users.

In order to provide flexibility in an environment with high rate of change we design a dynamic discovery and invocation (DDI) service manager. We have found that the use of DII is more complex for the software developer because a more complex interface is required in relation to the use of static stubs or dynamic proxies. We have compared the performance of the service manager under a static stub and a DII approach. The results show that DII approach offers better performance than static stub approach when a cache memory is used.

## 6. Conclusions and Future Work

Standard Web services infrastructures are focused on static stub based invocation of Web services. However, this scenario is not appropriate for mobile environments, where services and clients have a high rate of change. In order for Web services to expand across the mobile phones, users need to be able to efficiently discover and access to Web services at runtime. In this paper, we address the issues, challenges, implementation and performance in the use of dynamic discovery and invocation of Web services in mobile phones using J2ME middleware platform. We propose a Web service based proxy that acts as a DDI client over the network of services and as server to the mobile devices. With this approach, mobile consumers may locate new services at runtime without updating their client application. Also, interactions between the mobile phones and the network are reduced. Making DII is programmatically more complex than using a static stub. However, the advantage of using DII is to make the code easy to modify if the Web service details change and/or new services are offered. We have measured the performance using Sun benchmark with the purpose of comparing Web service proxy performance under a static stub and a DII approach. The results show that DII approach offers better throughput and average response time than the static stub approach when a cache memory is used.

Once we have tested the viability of dynamic mobile services, our future work will be focused on extending our approach in order to explore other approaches to handling complex data types based on XML messages when dynamic invocation is used, to perform more complex services and incorporate semantics, context-awareness and security aspects.

# References

[1] Elena Sánchez-Nielsen, Sandra Martín-Ruiz, Jorge Rodríguez-Pedrianes. *An open and dynamical service oriented architecture for supporting mobile services.* Proceedings of ACM ICWE 2006, pp. 121-128, Palo Alto, California, July 2006.

[2] OSGi Alliance. http://www.osgi.org/

[3] Liberty Alliance Project. https://www.projectliberty.org/

[4] R.S. Hall and H. Cervantes. *Challenges in Building Service-Oriented Applications for OSGi.* IEEE Communications, Volume 42, Number 5, May 2004.

[5] Gustavo A.., Casati, F., Kuno H., Machiraju, V. *Web Services: concepts, architectures and applications.* Springer-Verlag Publications, Berlin 2004.

[6] Vinoski, S,. *Web Services Interactions Models, Part 1: Current Practice.* IEEE Internet Computing, 6(3), 2002.

[7] W3C: World Wide Web Consortium. Simple Object Access Protocol (SOAP). http://www.w3.org/TR/soap/

[8] W3C: World Wide Web Consortium. Web Services Description Language (WSDL). http://www.w3.org/TR/wsdl

[9] UDDI. Universal Description, Discovery and Integration. http://www.uddi.org/

[10] Java Platform, Micro Edition (Java ME). http://java.sun.com/javame/index.jsp

[11] Apache Axis. http://ws.apache.org/axis

[12] UDDI4j. http://uddi4j.sourceforge.net

[13] Sun Java Wireless Toolkit. http://java.sun.com/products/sjwtoolkit

[14] Eclipse. http://www.eclipse.org

[15] Apache tomcat. http://tomcat.apache.org/index.html

[16] Javassist - Java Programming Assistant. http://www.jboss.org/products/javassist

[17] T. Pilioura, A. Tsalgatidou, S. Hadjiefthymiades. *Scenarios of using Web Services in M-Commerce*. ACM SIGecom Exchanges, Vol. 3, Number 4, January 2003, pp. 28-36.

[18] V. Sacramento, M. Endler, H. K. Rubinsztejn, L.S. Lima, K. Gonalves, and F.N. do Nascimento. *MoCA: A Middleware for Developing Collaborative Applications for Mobile Users*. IEEE Distributed System Online, 2004.

[19] J. keeney, V. Cahill. *Chisel: A Policy-Driven, Context-Aware, Dynamic Adaption Framework*. IEEE 4th International Workshop on Policies for Distributed Systems and Networks, June 2003.

[20] TinyXML. http://www.grinninglizard.com/tinyxml/

[21] VoiceXML. http://www.w3.org/TR/voicexml20/

[22] Z. Maamar, Q.Z. Sheng and B. Benatallah. *On composite Web Services Provisioning in an Environment of Fixed and Mobile Computing Resources*. Information Technology and Management 5, 251-279, 2004. Kluwer Academic Publishers.

[23] F. Papadopoulos, A. Zarras, E. Pitoura, P. Vassiliadis. *Timely Provisioning of Mobile Services in Critical Pervasive Environments*. Lectren Notes in Computer Sciences LNCS 3760, pp. 864-881, 2005.

[24] Daniel A. Menascé. *QoS Issues in Web Services*. IEEE Internet Computing, pp. 72-75, December 2002.

[25] WSTest. Sun Microsystems. https://wstest.dev.java.net/

Elena Sánchez-Nielsen
Dpto. E.I.O. y Computación – Escuela Técnica Superior de Ingeniería
Informática, Universidad de La Laguna
38271 La Laguna
Spain
e-mail: enielsen@ull.es

Sandra Martín-Ruiz
Dpto. E.I.O. y Computación – Escuela Técnica Superior de Ingeniería
Informática, Universidad de La Laguna
38271 La Laguna
Spain

Jorge Rodríguez-Pedrianes
Dpto. E.I.O. y Computación – Escuela Técnica Superior de Ingeniería
Informática, Universidad de La Laguna
38271 La Laguna
Spain

Whitestein Series in Software Agent Technologies, 135–152
© 2007 Birkhäuser Verlag Basel/Switzerland

# Software Metrics for the Efficient Execution of Mobile Services

Pablo Rossi and Zahir Tari

**Abstract.** This paper presents a suite of software code metrics, developed specifically for service-oriented systems with a well-defined methodology, which can be used as indicators of runtime efficiency. Existing literature on software metrics is mainly focused on centralized systems, while work in the area of distributed systems, particularly in service-oriented systems, is scarce. Firstly, a critical analysis of the problem domain identifies a number of software attributes which are likely to have an impact on efficiency. Secondly, concrete metrics are defined and evaluated (theoretically and empirically) for all identified attributes, with results showing that these software metrics are strongly correlated to typical efficiency metrics. Finally, a simple algorithm, which facilitates the runtime adaptation of service-oriented systems via service redeployment, illustrates a practical application of the metrics.

## 1. Introduction

Existing literature on software metrics is mainly focused on centralized systems (e.g. [1]), while work in the area of distributed systems, particularly in service-oriented systems, is scarce. Systems with distributed components differ from traditional non-distributed systems along a number of dimensions including communication type, referencing/parameter-passing strategies, partial versus total failure, latency and concurrency [2]. Distributed systems with service-oriented components are even more complex, since efficiency and other quality attributes must be achieved in a typically more heterogeneous networking and execution environments. Given these differences, this paper argues that it is necessary to extend established software measurement and related techniques before applying them to the emerging domain of service-oriented systems (SOS). Note that it has been argued before, in the domain of web systems, that traditional techniques and metrics should be re-assessed before being applied to a new domain [3].

This work is part of a project whose aim is to design an efficient middleware infrastructure to support highly adaptable mobile services. This infrastructure will provide robust and efficient management of business processes across different enterprises. In this context, adaptation refers to the ability of the software, or the underlying middleware, to modify its behaviour in response to changes in the environment. In this project, adaptation can be achieved, among others, via service mobility, where individual services can migrate through the system nodes. The decision of when and how service migration should be performed is dependent on factors such as available resources and the nature of the interaction between services. As such, this provides a practical application for the metrics proposed in this paper.

This paper presents a suite of software code metrics that can be used as indicators of runtime efficiency of service-oriented systems. These metrics were developed taking into account the particular characteristics of service-oriented systems (SOS) and following a well-defined methodology. The availability of well-defined metrics is crucial for middleware infrastructures to make dynamic decisions at run-time that are objective and robust.

The rest of this paper is organized as follows: Section 2 begins with a review of related work, with an emphasis on prior studies involving the specification of metrics for distributed systems. Section 3, through a critical analysis of the problem domain which provides face validity [4], identifies a number of specific software attributes that are likely to have an impact on efficiency, with a concrete metric defined for each. Since theoretical validation of software measures provides supporting evidence as to whether a measure really captures the internal attributes they purport to measure, metrics are theoretically validated in section 4. Section 5 evaluates empirically the relationships between software and efficiency metrics in the context of SOS. To illustrate the potential practical applications of the metrics, a simple strategy is presented in section 6, with the intention of facilitating runtime decisions concerning the adaptation of SOS via service mobility. Finally, section 7 closes with a summary, conclusions and discussion of future work.

## 2. Related Work

Although many software metrics have been defined for traditional systems [5], a much smaller number relates to distributed systems in general, and few, if any, consider the unique characteristics of SOS as is the subject of this paper. This section provides a review of related work in terms of the measurement of software attributes of distributed systems.

Shatz [6] proposed a metric for measuring communication complexity in distributed Ada programs, describing total complexity as the weighted sum of two components. Firstly, local complexity, which reflects the complexity of the individual tasks (disregarding their interactions with other tasks), was measured using traditional metrics such as lines of code or cyclomatic complexity. Secondly, communication complexity, which reflects the complexity of interactions among tasks, was derived by representing the programs as Petri nets and measuring the number of rendezvous which can be executed concurrently at a given point in time. Neither theoretical/empirical evaluation nor discussion about the practical utility was presented.

Cheng [7] also proposed a set of complexity metrics for distributed programs. Like Shatz [6], the metrics were defined based on graph representations for 1) multiple control flows (non-deterministic parallel control-flow net), 2) multiple data flows (non-deterministic parallel definition-use net) and 3) various program dependencies (process dependency net). As above, no empirical support was provided, nor was a discussion of how the metrics could be used within the software engineering process.

Based on the smallest event communication group (SECG) concept, Tsuar and Horng [8] suggested a metric to quantify the complexity of distributed programs, which was defined in terms of the number of events of a SECG. Although, the metric was experimentally evaluated with a moderately complex example, they were not evaluated theoretically, and it was not made clear how it could be used by practitioners.

Morasca [9] put forward a set of measures for capturing a number of internal attributes (namely size, length, complexity, and coupling) of software specifications written with Petri nets for concurrent systems. These measures were theoretically evaluated, but empirical evaluation was not provided.

A measurement suite to quantify design attributes of distributed systems was presented by Rossi and Fernandez [10]. The proposed measures were obtained from formal models derived from an analysis of the problem domain. Although these measures were theoretically evaluated, only a small subset was subject to empirical evaluation [11].

Arguably the closest study to our work are the metrics proposed by Ryan and Rossi [12], since they were defined and empirically evaluated for distributed systems with mobile components. However, this work focuses on the specific characteristics of software objects and, as such, may not be directly applicable to services.

In summary, existing studies suffer at least one of the following shortcomings: 1) metrics are not theoretically or empirically evaluated, 2) metrics have no clear practical applicability, or 3) metrics do not capture the particular nature of SOS. Therefore, given these shortcomings, it seems appropriate to develop and evaluate a new suite of software metrics to support the unique aspects of SOS.

## 3. Analysis of the Problem Domain

Here we are concerned with the impact of software attributes on the efficient execution of services in a mobile computing context. For the purpose of this paper, in line with ISO 9126-1 [13], efficiency is considered to be a high-level quality attribute comprising the attributes performance (or time behaviour) and resource utilization. Software is considered to be more efficient as performance increases and resource utilisation decreases. These attributes are quite broad and, as such, were decomposed into particular sub-attributes of interest:

P1. *Service Migration Cost:* the cost of moving a service between hosts.

P2. *Operation Execution Cost:* the processing cost of an operation, ignoring any overhead associated with its call.

P3. *Operation Call Cost:* the cost of calling a service operation, independent of its actual execution.

R1. *Memory Utilisation:* the current memory usage on a host.

R2. *Network Utilisation:* the current unavailable network bandwidth of a host.

R3. *Processor Utilisation:* the current processing load of a host

It should be noted that other resources such as mass-storage capacity and power consumption are also considered important but due to space constraints will be studied in future work.

From a critical analysis of the problem domain a number of software attributes were identified that were likely to have an impact on the efficiency of SOS in a mobile environment. In this context, the size and coupling of a service were identified as the key software attributes that represent most of the impact on efficiency. As size and coupling are also generic attributes, they were refined to capture more precisely the specific characteristics of services as software components:

S1. *Service Implementation Dimension:* the size of the service executable code; the larger the Service Implementation Dimension, the longer the Service Migration Time and the higher the Network Utilisation.

S2. *Service State Dimension:* the size of a service execution state; the larger the Service State Dimension, the higher the Memory Utilisation.

S3. *Operation Interface Dimension:* the aggregated size of the parameters of a service operation interface; the larger the Operation Interface Dimension, the higher the Operation Call Cost and the higher the Network Utilisation.

S4. *Operation Execution Length:* the length of a service operation implementation; the larger the Operation Execution Length, the higher the Operation Execution Cost and the higher the Processor Utilisation.

C1. *Service Collaboration Coupling:* a service degree of connection to other services; the higher the Service Collaboration Coupling, the higher the Operation Execution Cost, and the higher the Network Utilisation.

C2. *Operation Call Occurrence:* the call frequency of a service operation; the higher the Operation Call Occurrence, the higher the Network Utilisation and Processor Utilisation.

The model depicted in Figure 1 summarizes the studied relationships between software and efficiency attributes — additional attributes such as probability of service execution were identified but considered beyond the scope of this paper.

Furthermore, the authors identified other potential relationships that are not expressed explicitly. For example as memory utilisation increases, paging could affect performance; as processor utilisation increases there will inevitably be an effect on attributes such as Operation Call Cost. However since these factors were not expected to have a primary effect, and in the interests of studying a manageable set of metrics in this paper, the analysis of such attributes and relationships is left to future work.

The final stage of the analysis process was to derive concrete metrics for each of the attributes in a form that could be measured at runtime within a middleware infrastructure. The complete set of metrics and their units of measurement are listed in Table 1. A formal definition of the metrics is presented in the next section, while details of how each metrics can be measured in practice can be found in the appendix.

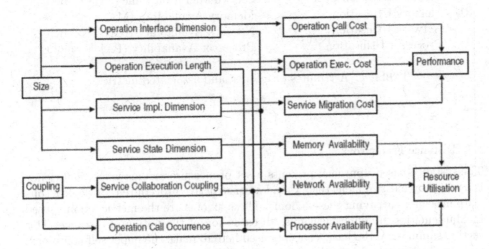

FIGURE 1. Summary of the relationships between software and efficiency attributes for SOS

## 4. Theoretical Evaluation

Since theoretical validation of software measures provides supporting evidence as to whether a measure really captures the internal attributes they purport to measure, we consider this validation as a necessary step before empirical validation takes place. The distance framework [14] is briefly introduced in sub-section 4.1 and it is then used to define the proposed metrics formally in the following subsections. This framework has been employed to theoretically validate software measures previously (e.g. [15, 16]).

| | Attribute | Metric | Unit |
|---|---|---|---|
| S | Operation Interface Dimension | Operation Interface Size (OIS) | byte |
| | Service Implementation Dimension | Service Code Size (SCS) | byte |
| | Service State Dimension | Service State Size (SSS) | byte |
| | Operation Execution Length | Operation Number of Statements (ONS) | int |
| C | Operation Call Occurrence | Operation Call Number (OCN) | int |
| | Service Collaboration Coupling | Collaborator Service Number (CSN) | int |
| P | Operation Execution Cost | Operation Execution Time (OET) | ms |
| | Operation Call Cost | Operation Call Time (OCT) | ms |
| | Service Migration Cost | Service Migration Time (SMT) | ms |
| RU | Memory Utilisation | Memory Availability (MA) | byte |
| | Network Utilisation | Network Availability (NA) | byte/s |
| | Processor Utilisation | Processor Availability (PA) | int/s |

TABLE 1. Attributes of interest and associated metrics

## 4.1. Distance Framework

The distance-based approach presents a set of measure axioms whose sufficiency is assured by measurement theory, and a constructive procedure that defines software measures satisfying these axioms. These axioms are the metric axioms, used in Mathematics to define measures, an extension of the notion of distance. This section summarizes the basic concepts used here to make the paper self-contained. (For more details refer to the original work [14]). The distance-based measure construction process consists of five steps:

1. For the set of software entities $E$ and for the internal attribute $a$, select a set of software entities $M$ that can be used as measurement abstractions to emphasise $a$, and define a function $\alpha : E \to M$.
2. Define a set $T$ of elementary transformation types on $M$ that is constructively and inverse constructively complete to model the conceptual distances between measurement abstractions.
3. Quantify distances between measurement abstractions defining a metric $\delta : M \times M \to R$ such that $(M, \delta)$ is a metric space.
4. Select a reference model $r \in M$ that is the software entity abstraction for which it holds that for all $e \in E$ with $\alpha(e) = r$, $e$ has the lowest value of $a$.
5. Define a function $\mu : E \to R$ such that for all $e \in E$, $\mu(e) = \delta(\alpha(e), r)$ which is a measure of distance from $\alpha(e)$ to $r$.

## 4.2. Coupling Metrics

Here we provide the formal definition of CSN that demonstrates its theoretical validity. OCN was formally defined and validated following an analogous process

**Step 1.** The set of software entities $E$ is the universe of services $(US)$ that is relevant for some system domain and $S$ is a service (viz. $S \in US$). The attribute of interest $a$ is the number of services that collaborate with $S$ via operation calls. The set of services that collaborate with service $S$ is then a subset of $US$. All the sets of services with collaboration coupling within $US$ are elements of the power set of $US$, denoted by $P(US)$. Consequently we can associate the set of measurement abstractions $M$ to $P(US)$ and define the abstraction function $\alpha_{CSN} : US \rightarrow P(US)$ as:

$$\forall S \in US : \alpha_{CSN}(S) = \{R \in US | R \text{ collaborates with } S \text{ via an operation call}\}$$

This function maps a service $S$ onto the set of collaborator services that are called by $S$.

**Step 2.** The next step is to model the distance between elements of $M$. It is necessary to find a set of elementary transformation types for $P(US)$ such that any set of services can be transformed into any other set of services by way of a finite sequence of transformations. Since the elements of $P(US)$ are sets of components, $T$ must only contain two types of elementary transformation. $T = \{\theta_{CSN1}, \theta_{CSN2}\}$ where

$$\forall s \in P(US) : \theta_{CSN1}(s) = s \cup \{m\} \text{ and } \theta_{CSN2}(s) = s - \{m\}, \text{ with } m \in US$$

Given two sets $s$ and $s'$ of $P(US)$, $s$ can always be transformed into $s'$ by first removing all services from $s$ that are not in $s'$ (through $\theta_{CSN2}$) and then adding all services to $s$ that are in $s - s'$ (through $\theta_{CSN1}$).

**Step 3.** The distance between two sets of services $s$ and $s'$ can be measured by the length of the shortest sequence of elementary transformations taking $s$ to $s'$. As exactly one elementary transformation will be needed for each service of $US$ that is contained in either $s$ or $s'$, but not in both sets, the distance value is equal to the cardinality of the symmetric difference between $s$ and $s'$:

$$\forall s, s' \in P(US) : \delta_{CSN}(s, s') = |s - s'| + |s' - s|$$

**Step 4.** The reference abstraction is the empty set of services. It is desirable that a service $S$ without service collaborations will have the lowest possible value for the $CSN$ measurement. Hence we define the following function: $r_{CSN} : US \rightarrow P(US) : S \rightarrow \emptyset$.

**Step 5.** The number of services called by service $S \in US$, can be formally defined as the distance between its set of collaborator services and the empty set. Therefore, formally CSN can be defined as $\mu_{CSN} : P(US) \to R$:

$$\forall S \in US : \mu_{CSN}(S) = \delta_{CSN}(\alpha_{CSN}(S), r_{CSN}) = |\alpha_{CSN}(S)\Delta\emptyset| = |\alpha_{CSN}(S)|$$

### 4.3. Size Metrics

Here we theoretically validate ONS by presenting its formal definition. SCS, SSS and OIS were formally defined and validated following an analogous process.

**Step 1.** The set of software entities $E$ is the universe of Operations ($UO$) that is relevant for some Service domain and $O$ is an Operation (viz. $O \in UO$). Let $UES$ be the Universe of Executable Statements relevant to $O$. The attribute of interest $a$ is the number of Executable Statements that are part of Operation $O$. The set of Executable Statements $ES$ that are part of Operation $O$ is then a subset of $UES$. All the sets of Executable Statements that are part of Operations within $UO$ are elements of the power set of $UES$, denoted by $P(UES)$. Consequently we can associate the set of measurement abstractions $M$ to $P(UES)$ and define the abstraction function $\alpha_{ONS} : UO \to P(UES)$ as:

$$\forall O \in UO : \alpha_{ONS}(O) = \{ES \in UES | ES \text{ is part of } O\}$$

This function maps an operation $O$ onto its set of Executable Statements.

**Step 2.** The next step is to model the distance between elements of $M$. It is necessary to find a set of elementary transformation types for $P(UES)$ such that any set of Executable Statements can be transformed into any other set of Executable Statements by way of a finite sequence of transformations. Since the elements of $P(UES)$ are sets of Executable Statements, $T$ must only contain two types of elementary transformation. $T = \{\theta_{ONS1}, \theta_{ONS2}\}$ where:

$$\forall es \in P(EUS) : \theta_{ONS1}(es) = es \cup \{m\} \text{ and } \theta_{ONS2}(es) = es - \{m\},$$
$$\text{with } m \in UES$$

Given two sets $es$ and $es'$ of $P(UES)$, $es$ can always be transformed into $es'$ by first removing all Executable Statements from $es$ that are not in $es'$ (through $\theta_{ONS2}$) and then adding all Executable Statements to $es$ that are in $es' - es$ (through $\theta_{ONS1}$).

**Step 3.** The distance between two sets of Executable Statements $es$ and $es'$ can be measured by the length of the shortest sequence of elementary transformations taking $es$ to $es'$. As exactly one elementary transformation will be needed for each statement of $UES$ that is contained in either $es$ or $es'$, but not in both sets, the distance value is equal to the cardinality of the symmetric difference between $es$ and $es'$:

$$\forall es, es' \in P(UES) : \delta_{ONS}(es, es) = |es \Delta es'|$$

**Step 4.** The empty set of statements is the reference abstraction $r$. It is desirable that an Operation $O$ without Executables Statements will have the lowest possible value for the $ONS$ measurement. Hence we define the following function: $r_{ONS} :$ $UO \rightarrow P(UES) : O \rightarrow \emptyset$.

**Step 5.** The number of Executable Statements that are part of Operation $O \in UO$, can be formally defined as the distance between its set of Executable Statements and the empty set. Therefore, formally $ONS$ can be defined as $\mu_{ONS} : P(UO) \rightarrow$ $R$:

$$\forall O \in UO : \mu_{ONS}(O) = \delta_{ONS}(\alpha_{ONS}(O), r_{ONS}) =$$
$$|\alpha_{ONS}(O) - \emptyset| + |\emptyset - \alpha_{ONS}(O)| = |\alpha_{ONS}(O)|$$

## 5. Empirical Evaluation

This section provides experimental results to support the relationships between software and efficiency metrics described in section 3. We have followed some of the guidelines provided in the literature [17] on how to perform and report controlled experiments. (Please note that not all available information has been included in this paper due to space constraints.)

### 5.1. Definition

Following the GQM template [18], our experiment goal can be summarised as follows:

  *analyse* SOS software measures,
  *for the purpose of* evaluating,
  *with respect to* their capability of being used as indicators of efficiency,
  *from the point of view of* SOS engineers,
  *in the context of* wireless and mobile environments.

### 5.2. Planning

In order to evaluate software measurement hypotheses empirically, it is possible to adopt two main strategies [19]: (a) small-scale controlled experiments, and/or (b) real-scale industrial case studies. In this case we chose the first alternative, since it is more suitable to study the phenomena of interest in isolation, without having to deal with other sources of variation, such as co-existing systems, security mechanisms, etc. However, we envisage that after several experiments the suite of measures will be shown to be robust, and we intend to test the measures following the second strategy.

    The hypotheses to be tested were derived from the attribute relationships discussed in section 3 as part of the analysis of the problem domain. The dependent (efficiency) and independent (software) variables are quantified by the metrics shown in Table 1. Details of how each measure was quantified can be found in the Appendix.

For each hypothesis, experimental data was collected using a synthetic Java system, with the measurement of metrics obtained either through internal instrumentation of the code, or from the operating system via a native interface. All tests were executed in an isolated network using two identical laptops in a client server configuration via a wireless link.

## 5.3. Operation

Before the actual experiment, several pilot experiments were run to make sure that there were no apparent anomalies, and the system behaved in the same way as before the measurement code was introduced.

The experiment was conducted in the Distributed Computing Research Laboratory of our University. The system was executed on an isolated (54 Mbps) wireless network of laptops (Pentium M, 1.6 GHz, 512MB RAM) and running under a Windows operating system. All computers had the same hardware and software, and were configured in the same way. Every service was run on a separate laptop as the only user process, all other processes running were a few system processes started by default. The execution of the system was initiated and terminated by the experiment team, which also controlled that in the meantime nobody else had access to the facilities.

Despite the data being collected reliably and objectively by electronic means, it was thoroughly inspected to assert that it was consistent. For this purpose we run the experiment three different times and compared the three data sets obtained. However, it should be noted that only the first data set was subject to analysis. Finally, there was no need to discard any data, hence all data collected was used.

## 5.4. Analysis and Interpretation of the Results

After the execution of the experiment, all the measures were computed electronically from the recorded data. The empirical data was analysed with the assistance of the statistical software package SPSS [20], and the obtained results are presented in the remainder of this section.

**5.4.1. Correlation Analysis.** Table 2 presents the Pearson correlation coefficients (significant at the 0.01 level) between the software measures and efficiency measures.

|     | OET   | OCT   | SMT   | MA    | PA    | NA    |
|-----|-------|-------|-------|-------|-------|-------|
| SCS |       |       | 0.927 |       |       | 0.928 |
| SSS |       |       |       | 0.959 |       |       |
| CSN | 0.932 |       |       |       |       | 0.938 |
| OIS |       | 0.955 |       |       |       | 0.965 |
| ONS | 0.990 |       |       |       | 0.967 |       |
| OCN |       |       |       |       | 0.931 | 0.984 |

TABLE 2. Pearson correlation coefficients (N = 100)

**Discussion.** The results show that all the associations are statistically significant. The correlation coefficients are significant, indicating a nontrivial association of the software measures with the efficiency measures. This suggests that these variables are candidates for a base regression model to estimate efficiency. Examination of the coefficients indicates that all software measures are positively correlated to the efficiency measures — it should be noted that a higher value of OET, OCT or SMT indicates worse performance.

**5.4.2. Univariate Regression Analysis.** Here we present the results obtained when analysing the individual impact of the software measures on efficiency using Ordinary Least Squares (OLS) Regression [21]. In general, a multivariate linear regression equation has the following form:

$$Y = B_0 + B_1 X_1 + ... + B_n X_n \tag{5.1}$$

where $Y$ is the response variable, and $X_i$ are the explanatory variables. A univariate regression model is a special case of this, where only one explanatory variable appears. Table 3 presents the unstandardised regression coefficients $(B_i)$, the statistical significance of $B_i$ $(p_i)$, and the goodness-of-fit $(R^2)$ of models. Each row contains the statistics of a different univariate regression model.

**Discussion.** The results obtained are remarkably consistent. They indicate that all software measures that we considered in this paper indeed strongly correlate with efficiency. In the best case, in our context, ONS accounted for 98 percent of the variation in performance (measured by OET) — each increase of one unit of ONS increased OET by 16.88 units. In addition, by analysing the trends indicated by the coefficients, we see that the hypotheses underlying the measures are empirically supported.

It should be noted the fact that $p_0 > 0.01$ for some models only means that we cannot really conclude that $B_0 \neq 0$, but this does not affect the fact that we can realistically conclude that it is very unlikely that $B_1 \neq 0$, i.e., it is very likely that the software attribute is correlated to the efficiency attribute.

**5.4.3. Validity.** Four different threats to the validity of the study were addressed [17]:

- *Conclusion validity.* An issue that could affect the statistical validity of this study is the size of the sample data, which may not be large enough for a conclusive statistical analysis. We are aware of this, so we do not consider these results to be final.
- *Construct validity.* The study was carefully designed, and the design was piloted several times before actually being run. The efficiency metrics are obtained from the OS, thus it is assumed they are reliable. The software metrics used in this study were shown to adequately quantify the attribute they purport to measure in section 4.

| $X$ | $Y$ | $B_0$ | $B_1$ | $p_0$ | $p_1$ | $R^2$ | $N$ |
|-----|-----|-------|-------|-------|-------|-------|-----|
| SCS | SMT | 22983 | 3.701 | 0.000 | 0.000 | 0.859 | 100 |
| SCS | NA | 74065 | 2.809 | 0.000 | 0.000 | 0.860 | 100 |
| SSS | MA | 0.000 | 1.044 | 0.000 | 0.000 | 0.920 | 100 |
| CSN | OET | 7.214 | 2.345 | 0.206 | 0.000 | 0.868 | 100 |
| CSN | NA | 32516 | 5311.7 | 0.159 | 0.000 | 0.879 | 100 |
| OIS | OCT | 5059 | 0.436 | 0.000 | 0.000 | 0.912 | 100 |
| OIS | NA | -2463.3 | 2.839 | 0.764 | 0.000 | 0.931 | 100 |
| ONS | OET | -44002 | 16.884 | 0.081 | 0.000 | 0.981 | 100 |
| ONS | PA | 10920 | 65.249 | 0.530 | 0.000 | 0.936 | 100 |
| OCN | NA | -288.2 | 168.239 | 0.462 | 0.000 | 0.968 | 100 |
| OCN | PA | 342.1 | 16.042 | 0.000 | 0.000 | 0.867 | 100 |

TABLE 3. Univariate Regression Models

- *Internal validity.* The study was highly controlled and monitored, so it is very unlikely that undetected influences have occurred without our knowledge. The instrumentation was trustworthy since the data was collected, and the measures computed, electronically.
- *External validity.* Although the study is based on a representative case, more studies are needed using real systems. We are also aware that more experiments with different platforms (e.g. computer and network hardware, operating systems, etc.) and infrastructure (e.g. middleware type, programming language) must also be carried out to further generalize these results.

## 6. Practical Applicability

Software measurement is not merely about defining new metrics, but about building new theories that can help solve practical problems [22]. As stated previously, one of the main goals of this research is to provide middleware support enabling SOS to maintain specified levels of quality, particularly efficiency, in mobile environments.

Consequently, this section defines, and provides initial testing for, an adaptation approach based on the metrics introduced in section 3. In general, the practical application of these metrics is within a middleware infrastructure, which will collect software metrics describing the services that constitute the system, as well as information about the hosts in which the services are running, and will make decisions in terms of service (re) location.

The approach to adaptation developed is decentralized and reactive, involving an individual node making a decision to move one or more services to another host when either a performance or resource utilisation threshold is met. Other approaches to adaptation are possible but are outside the scope of this paper

— for example an alternative approach to adaptation could be centralised and proactive involving the solution of an optimization model.

A reactive/adaptive decision is typically triggered by the utilisation of a resource that at some point in time exceeds a predetermined threshold. The objective of this adaptation approach is to distribute the utilisation of resources whilst maintaining (or improving) performance. However, performance and resource utilisation are attributes that generally conflict with each other and since compromises may have to be reached; this decision is not trivial even for the simplest scenario of two services and two machines. A more typical case may involve numerous services and many nodes, and thus achieving an effective decision requires an appropriate process.

Therefore, in order to test the ability of the metrics to support such decision making, whilst yielding a tangible benefit in terms of efficiency, a preliminary empirical study was conducted by implementing a prototype SOS which consists of five main services executing over Sun System Application Server Platform Edition 9. For the experiment, software and performance metrics were collected directly via instrumentation in the system code and resource utilisation metrics from the Windows Performance Monitor via the Java Native Interface (JNI). The experiment was conducted under the same laboratory conditions, using three nodes of the same specification as described in the previous section.

The adaptation decisions (which determine if and when a given service should migrate to another host) were calculated and executed offline. Therefore, the intention of this experiment is not to evaluate the efficiency of the metric collection and adaptation process itself, although this is the subject of ongoing work. Rather, this experiment aims to demonstrate that the metrics presented herein can support the effective placement of services to hosts in a SOS, in order to improve efficiency compared with the baseline case of no adaptation.

At the abstract level, the adaptation approach operates according to algorithm depicted in Listing 4 in which individual nodes move services to other hosts when some criteria related to efficiency (performance versus resource utilisation) are met. The algorithm evaluates, based on the metric values, possible migration options based on the available local mobile services and remote nodes. The algorithm stops when all possible migrations have been evaluated. An explanation of how the function 'evaluate' produces its indicators is given in Definition 1.

In the initial state all services (i.e. $S_1$, $S_2$, $S_3$, $S_4$ and $S_5$) were residing on node 1 ($N_1$), where the processor was heavily loaded (**PA** around 10%), while $N_2$ and $N_3$ were not loaded at all (**PA** around 99%). Applying the adaptation algorithm to SOS resulted in four cases of service migration: $S_2$, $S_3$, $S_4$ and $S_5$ from $N_1$ to $N_2$. The standard deviation of the processor loads was calculated before and after adaptation. Additionally, response time data was collected for all business processes with each executed and measured 100 times.

The standard deviation of the processor loads before adaptation was around 57% whereas the standard deviation after adaptation was around 48%. Moreover, the average process response time after adaptation was 297 ms versus 321 ms

```
maxIndicator = 0, maxService = null, maxNode = null
for each service s in local node do
   for each remote node n do
      i = evaluate(s, n)
      if (i > maxIndicator) then
         maxIndicator = i
         maxService = s
         maxNode = n
      end if
   end for
end for
if (maxIndicator > 0.5)
   move maxService to maxNode
end if
```

LISTING 1. High-level Adaptation Algorithm

before adaptation. Therefore not only did the adaptation algorithm provide better processor load balance, which was the principal aim of this experiment, but it also provided superior performance and thus greater efficiency as well. The adaptation algorithm was initialised with the following parameters: $W_P = 0$, $W_{RU} = 1$, $k_{RU} = 1$, $max_{RU} = 100$.

Although the presented adaptation algorithm is relatively simple, it illustrates the benefits of applying the metrics proposed in this paper to a practical application. This provides a basis for further large scale studies and the development of advanced adaptation approaches. For example, a more sophisticated approach to adaptation based on these metrics, and a comprehensive evaluation, can be found in a separate study [23].

## 7. Concluding Remarks

Having recognized that distributed systems differ from their traditional centralised counterparts, and that SOS are even more complex, this paper has introduced a suite of metrics for such systems. These metrics aim at estimating the impact of software attributes upon efficiency, in terms of performance and resource utilisation, for SOS operating in mobile environments.

Having defined such metrics from a critical analysis of the problem domain, a series of hypotheses relating the metrics were proposed, and the metrics were evaluated theoretically and empirically. With the results demonstrating the strong correlation between software attributes and efficiency of SOS, an adaptation strategy was developed, in order to illustrate one of the practical applications of the metrics in the context of middleware infrastructures for SOS.

There are a number of possible general approaches to decision making based on multiple attributes, which differ in terms of how they specify criteria for the decision making process. Since this is a proof-of-concept implementation of adaptation, we have selected a simple linear additive approach according to the following equation:

$$I_E = (W_{RU} I_{RU} + W_P I_P) \qquad (6.1)$$

In order to evaluate such function, and thus produce an overall decision making indicator of efficiency ($I_E$) that can be used to rank and runtime actions, the level of satisfaction of the individual indicators ($I_i$) must be calculated — this is done by normalising the values to the unitary interval ($0 \leq I_i \leq 1$). Furthermore, the aggregate decision making function include weights ($W_i$), to represent the relative importance of the individual indicators when calculating the decision making indicator $I_E$. A further requirement of the function is that $(W_1 + W_2 + ... + W_m) = 1$, where $W_i \geq 0$ for $i = 1...m$.

Finally, the resource utilisation ($I_{RU}$) and performance ($I_P$) indicators were calculated as follows:

$$I_P = 0.5 + \frac{0.5 \times (dif_P - k_P)}{2 \times max_P} \qquad (6.2)$$

$$I_{RU} = 0.5 + \frac{0.5 \times (dif_{RU} - k_{RU})}{2 \times max_{RU}} \qquad (6.3)$$

$$dif_P = \left[ \sum_{i=O_S} \left( OCN_i \times (ort_i^C - ort_i^D) \right) \right] - SMT \qquad (6.4)$$

$$dif_{RU} = \left| \frac{ra^C}{rc^C} - \frac{ra^D}{rc^D} \right| - \left| \left( \frac{ra^C + ru_S}{rc^C} \right) - \left( \frac{ra^D - ru_S}{rc^D} \right) \right| \qquad (6.5)$$

where:
- $max_P$ and $m_{RU}$ are maximum values of performance and resource utilisation.
- $k_P$ and $k_{RU}$ are threshold parameters which specify the minimum acceptable value of performance and resource utilisation.
- $O_S$ = number of operations of service $S$.
- $ort_i = \mathbf{OET} + \mathbf{OCT}$ (operation response time)
- $ru_S$ = the resource usage of service $S$: $nu_S = \mathbf{SCS}$, $mu_S = \mathbf{SSS}$, or $pu_S = avg(\mathbf{ONS})$
- $ra_C$ and $ra_D$ = resource (i.e. network, memory or processor) availability of the current and destination nodes of the service; $ra = \mathbf{NA}$, $\mathbf{MA}$ or $\mathbf{PA}$.
- $rc_C$ and $rc_D$ = resource (i.e. network, memory or processor) capacity of the current and destination nodes of the service.

DEFINITION 1. Function Evaluate Description

Although this paper has made a significant incursion into an area that is not yet well understood, there are a number of limitations and opportunities that remain to be explored in the future which include, but are not limited to:

- Evaluation of the software attributes and their associated metrics against other quality attributes such as reliability.
- Analysis of additional resources such as mass-storage and power.
- Evaluation of the overhead of the metric collection and the adaptation strategy.

In closing, the present authors believe this paper to be one of the few reported studies of metrics for distributed software, and the first involving the specific case of SOS. The results encourage further large-scale studies and which will suggest modifications to the metrics suite as additional understanding is achieved.

## Appendix

The contents of this appendix can be obtained from the authors on request or can be found online at http://goanna.cs.rmit.edu.au/~pablo/wewst06/appendix.pdf.

## References

[1] Purao, S. and V. Vaishnavi, Product metrics for object-oriented system. ACM Computing Surveys, 2003, 35(2): p. 191-221.

[2] Emmerich, W., Engineering Distributed Objects, 2000: Wiley.

[3] Ruhe, M., R. Jeffery, and I. Wieczorek. Using Web objects for estimating software development effort for Web applications. Proceedings: Ninth International Software Metrics Symposium. 2003.

[4] Henderson-Sellers, B., Object-Oriented Metrics: Measures of Complexity. 1996, Upper Sadle River, USA: Prentice Hall.

[5] Fenton, N. and S. Pfleeger, Software Metrics: A Rigorous and Practical Approach. Second ed. 1996, London: International Thompson Computer Press.

[6] Shatz, S., Towards Complexity Metrics for Ada Tasking. IEEE Transactions Software Engineering, 1988. 14(8): p. 1122-1127.

[7] Cheng, J. Complexity metrics for distributed programs. Proceedings: International Symposium on Software Reliability Engineering. 1993: IEEE.

[8] Tsuar, W. and S. Horng, A New Generalised Software Complexity Metric for Distributed Programs. Information and Software Technology, 1998. 40(5-6): p. 259-269.

[9] Morasca, S. Measuring attributes of concurrent software specifications in Petri nets. Proceedings: Sixth International Software Metrics Symposium. 1999.

[10] Rossi, P. and G. Fernandez. Definition and validation of design metrics for distributed applications. Proceedings: Ninth International Software Metrics Symposium. 2003. Sydney: IEEE.

[11] Rossi, P. and G. Fernandez. Design Measures for Distributed Information Systems: an Empirical Evaluation. Proceedings: International Workshop on Software Audit and Metrics (In conjunction with ICEIS). 2004. Porto.

[12] Ryan, C. and P. Rossi. Software, Performance and Resource Utilisation Metrics for Context Aware Mobile Applications. Proceedings: Proceedings of International Software Metrics Symposium IEEE Metrics 2005. 2005. Como, Italy.

[13] ISO/IEC, Information Technology - Software Product Quality - Part 1: Quality Model. 2003, International Standards Organisation: Geneva.

[14] Poels, G. and G. Dedene, Distance-based software measurement: necessary and sufficient properties for software measures. Information and Software Technology, 2000. 42(1).

[15] S. Abrahao, et al. Defining and Validating Metrics for Navigational Models. Proceedings: Ninth International Software Metrics Symposium. 2003: IEEE.

[16] Marcela, G., M. David, and P. Mario, Defining Metrics for UML Statechart Diagrams in a Methodological Way, Proceedings: Conceptual Modeling for Novel Application Domains (LNCS 2814). 2003, Springer. p. 118-128.

[17] Wohlin, C., et al., Experimentation in Software Engineering. 2000: Kluwer.

[18] Basili, V. and D. Rombach, The TAME Project: towards improvement-oriented software environments. IEEE Transactions Software Engineering, 1988. 16(6).

[19] Briand, L., S. Morasca, and K. El Emam, Theoretical and Empirical Validation of Software Product Measures. 1995, International Software Engineering Research Network.

[20] SPSS, I., SPSS 8.0: User Guide. 1998, Chicago: SPSS Inc.

[21] Freund, R. and W. Wilson, Regression Analysis: Statistical Modeling of a Response Variable. 1998: Academic Press.

[22] Briand, L.C., S. Morasca, and V.R. Basili, An operational process for goal-driven definition of measures. Software Engineering, IEEE Transactions on, 2002. 28(12): p. 1106-1125.

[23] Rossi, P. and Z. Tari. Software Adaptation for Service-Oriented Systems. Proceedings: Middleware for Service Oriented Computing (MW4SOC'06). 2006. Melbourne, Australia: ACM Press.

**Acknowledgment**

We would like to thank the Australian Research Council (ARC) for supporting this project. This work is funded under ARC Linkage Project scheme no. LP0455234.

Pablo Rossi
School of Computer Science and IT, RMIT University
GPO Box 2476V
Melbourne, Victoria, 3001
Australia
e-mail: pablo@cs.rmit.edu.au

Zahir Tari
School of Computer Science and IT, RMIT University
GPO Box 2476V
Melbourne, Victoria, 3001
Australia
e-mail: zahirt@cs.rmit.edu.au

Whitestein Series in Software Agent Technologies, 153–165

# Dynamically Adapting Clients to Web Services Changing

Mehdi Ben Hmida, Céline Boutrous Saab, Serge Haddad, Valérie Monfort and Ricardo Tomaz Ferraz

**Abstract.** Web Services are the fitted technical solution which provides the required loose coupling to achieve Service Oriented Architecture (SOA). However, there is still much to be done in order to increase flexibility and adaptability to SOA-based applications. In previous researches, we proposed approaches based on Aspect Oriented Programming (AOP) and Process Algebra (PA) to address flexibility and client generation issues in the Web Service context. In this paper, we extend these works in order to automatically create extended BPEL processes and generate clients which dynamically adapt themselves to the service changing.

**Keywords.** Service Oriented Architecture (SOA), Web Services (WS), BPEL, Aspect Oriented Programming (AOP), Process Algebra (PA).

## 1. Introduction

Web Services (WS) are "self contained, self-describing modular applications that are published, located, and invoked across the Web" [1]. They are based on a set of XML [2] standards to make them more portable than previous middleware technologies [3]. WSs need to be composed to fulfill business requirements. The *Business Process Execution Language for Web Services* (*BPEL4WS* or *BPEL*) has been proposed for this purpose and becomes a standard [4]. BPEL supports two types of business processes:

1. *Executable processes* specify the exact details of business processes and are executed by a BPEL engine.
2. *Abstract business processes* specify the public message exchange between the client and the service (the interaction protocol).

Web Service technology has to handle the same features as middlewares such as DCOM [5], J2EE [6] or CORBA [7] already handle. The features, such as security, reliability, or transactional mechanisms, can be considered as non-functional aspects. Obviously, these aspects are crucial for business purposes and we cannot build any genuine IS without consideration for them.

However, managing these aspects is likely to involve a great loss in interoperability and flexibility. This effect has already been experienced with the above middleware technologies. Mostly, middleware delegates these tasks to the underlying platform, hiding these advanced mechanisms from the developer, and then establishing a solid bond between the application and the platform. Moreover, WS providers are faced to some important difficulties to change their services behaviours because WSs are shared by many clients and a minor change leads to client execution problems.

In our previous works, we addressed service adaptability and client interaction issues. We proposed an Aspect Oriented Programming (AOP) [8] approach which aims to change elementary WSs at runtime [10, 9]. We also proposed a Process Algebra (PA) approach which solves the interaction problem between BPEL processes and their clients. In this paper, we extend these works in order to reach the objectives previously discussed.

This paper is organized as follows: section 2 presents the Aspect Oriented Programming (AOP) paradigm. Section 3 briefly presents our previous AOP approach for elementary WSs, then shows its extension to support BPEL processes. We also present the architecture of our *extended BPEL generator* tool which integrates these concepts. Section 4 presents the process algebra formalism which supports change-prone BPEL processes. This formalism leads us to generate clients that adapt themselves to the service changes. Section 5 discusses related work. We conclude and present future works in section 6.

## 2. Aspect Oriented Programming (AOP)

Many researches [12, 13, 14] consider Aspect Oriented Programming AOP as an answer to improve WS flexibility. AOP is a paradigm that enables the modularization of crosscutting concerns into single units called aspects, which are modular units of crosscutting implementation. AOP concepts were formulated by Chris Maeda and Gregor Kiczales [8].

Crosscutting concerns are requirements that cannot be localized to an individual software component and that impact many components. In aspect-speak, these requirements cut across several components. Aspect-oriented languages such as AspectJ [15], JBoss AOP [16], AspectWerkz [17], Spring AOP [18], etc. are implemented over a set of definitions:

1. *Joinpoints*: They denote the locations in the program that are affected by a particular crosscutting concern.
2. *Pointcuts*: They specify a collection of conditional joinpoints.

3. *Advices*: They are codes that are executed *before, after* or *around* a joinpoint.

To better clarify, consider the classical example to implement a logging functionality. Logging code is often scattered horizontally across object hierarchies and has nothing to do with the core functions of the objects it is scattered across. The same is true for other types of code, such as security, exception handling, and transparent persistency. This scattered and unrelated code is known as crosscutting code and is the reason for AOP's existence.

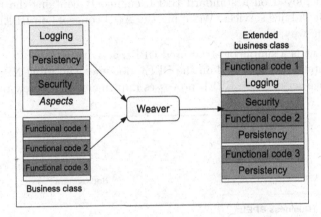

FIGURE 1. The weaving process

Using Object-Oriented Programming, every time we need to introduce the logging functionality in an application, the programmer must add the logging code into the appropriate objects. Using AOP, we can insert the logging code into the classes that need it with a tool called a *weaver*. This way, objects can focus on their core responsibilities. The figure 1 shows the weaving process.

The weaver is in charge for taking the code specified in a traditional (base) programming language, and the additional code specified in an aspect language, and merging the two together. The weaver has the task to process aspects and component code in order to generate the specified behaviour. The weaver inserts the aspects in the specified joinpoint transversally. The weaving can occur at compile time (modifying the compiler), load time (modifying the class loader) or runtime (modifying the interpreter).

## 3. Adapting BPEL processes

**Our previous approach.** We developed an AOP-based tool named *Aspect Service Weaver (ASW)* [10, 9]. The ASW intercepts the SOAP (Web Service communication protocol) messages between a client and an elementary WS, then verifies during the interaction if there is a new behaviour introduced (*advice service*). We use the AOP weaving time to add the new behaviour (*before, around* or *after* an activity execution). The advice services are elementary WSs whose references are registered in a file called "*aspect services file descriptor*". The pointcut language is based on XPath [24]. XPath queries are applied on the service description (WSDL) to select the set of methods on which the advice services are inserted.

**Principles of our current approach.** We extend this approach to BPEL processes. We apply the AOP concepts to BPEL processes in order to automatically generate extended BPEL processes without touching the base implementation. The new document is deployed on a standard BPEL engine. It contains the base BPEL process and the advice services. We apply the AOP concepts on BPEL processes in the following way:

1. A joinpoint is a simple or structured BPEL activity.
2. The pointcuts are specified on the BPEL document by using XPath.
3. The advice services are BPEL processes implementing the new behaviour.

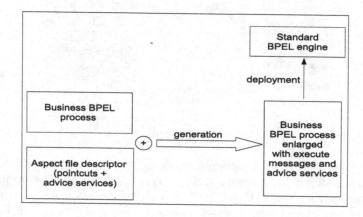

FIGURE 2. The extended executable BPEL process.

We also add to the generated process, an advertising activity before each inserted advice service (figure 2). This activity sends to the client a message called *execute*. This message advertises the client about the execution of a new behaviour. It encapsulates two kinds of information: the identifier of the advice service and its corresponding interaction protocol. This message is necessary since the new behaviour can require new information exchange involving messages unexpected by the client and leading to execution failures. At the client implementation, the developer has to handle this type of message: he has to extract the interaction protocol of the *advice service* and integrate it in its behaviour. This part is detailed in the next section.

## 3.1. Extended BPEL generator

These previous concepts are concretized through the architecture of our tool named *extended BPEL generator*. The tool contains the following components (figure 3):

1. The *BPEL weaver*
2. The *aspect services file descriptor*
3. The *advice service repository* (or the *pattern repository*) which contains the services advices present in the system
4. The *deployment module* which deploys the extended BPEL process executed by a standard BPEL engine.

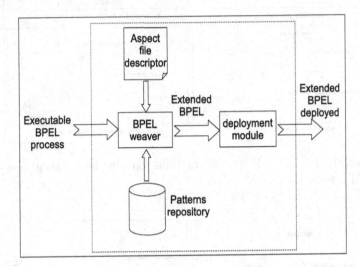

FIGURE 3. The extended BPEL generator.

The BPEL weaver takes as input the base BPEL process and the *aspect services file descriptor*. Then, it performs transformations on the base BPEL process syntactic tree. It inserts the actions of sending *execute* messages and the advices services at the selected joinpoints depending on the kind of the *advice service*. The figure 4 shows the transformations made on the base process $sequence(receive(ResReq), switch(reply(ResResp), reply(error))$ which receives a *ResReq* message then replies by a *ResResp* or *error* message depending on a condition (the switch process). In the case of an around *advice service* (figure 4.d), the specified *joinpoint* is replaced by the advice service and the *execute* message replying activity, because we consider that the *advice service* can encapsulate the joinpoint. In the figure, a triangle represents an advice service and $Q$ its corresponding interaction protocol.

## 3.2. The extended interaction protocol

The extended executable BPEL process interaction protocol is described by an extended abstract BPEL process which integrates the sending of *execute* messages. The extended interaction protocol is generated from the base BPEL process and the *aspect service file descriptor* based on the defined pointcuts and the type of advices (before, after or around).

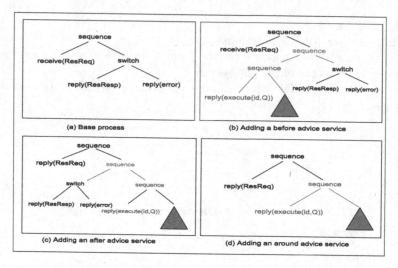

FIGURE 4. Syntactic transformations on the base executable BPEL process.

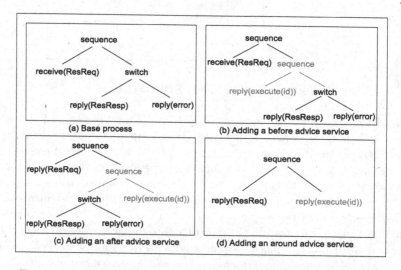

FIGURE 5. Transformations on the syntactic tree of the abstract BPEL process.

The generation process performs transformations on the base abstract BPEL process syntactic tree. It inserts the action of sending *execute* messages in the selected joinpoints depending on the kind of the *advice service* (figure 5). The *execute* messages contain only the identifier of the *advice service id*. The interaction protocol corresponding to that *id* is sent to the client at runtime.

## 4. Generating dynamic clients

BPEL provides a set of operators describing in a modular way the observable behaviour of an abstract process. As shown in [20], this kind of process description is close to the process algebra paradigm illustrated for instance by CCS [21].

However, time is explicitly present in some of the BPEL constructors and thus the standard process algebra semantics are inappropriate for the description of such processes. Thus, we defined a new process algebra semantics that associates a timed automaton (TA) [19] with an abstract process [11]. The theoretical developments follow these steps: associating operational rules with each abstract BPEL construct, defining an interaction relation which formalizes the concept of a correct interaction between two communicating systems (the client and the WS), and designing an algorithm that generates a client automaton which is in an interaction relation with the WS.

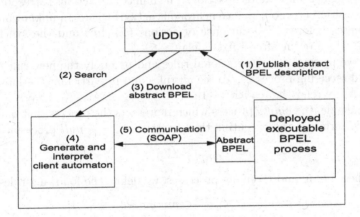

FIGURE 6. Generic client interpreter.

The client automaton is interpreted by our generic client interpreter (figure 6). Our client downloads the abstract BPEL process from an UDDI registry (step 3) and generates its corresponding TA. Then, based on the TA of the service and the interaction relation, it generates the client TA if the service is not ambiguous (step 4). Finally, it executes the client TA (step 5) and displays graphical interfaces allowing to the human user to enter the message parameters.

### 4.1. The dynamic client interpreter

In order to communicate with change-prone BPEL processes, we extend the previous client interpreter. The new client has to achieve the following tasks:

1. When the client receives an $execute(id, Q)$ message, it has to extract the *advice service* interaction protocol $Q$ (identified by $id$) and generates its client TA.

2. It simultaneously executes the client TAs of the main process and its *advice clients* TA.

3. It makes synchronisation between the main client TA and the advice clients TA on the termination of advices service execution.

Furthermore, the generation module of the dynamic client interpreter also integrates new operational rules for the sending and receiving processes in order to handle the *execute(id)* messages.

## 4.2. Formalisation steps

In order to formalize BPEL as timed process algebra, we have to define the actions (alphabet) of the process algebra. The possible actions are message receiving ($?m$) and sending ($!m$), internal actions ($\tau$) (not observable from the client side), raise of exceptions ($e \in E$), expiration of timeout ($to$) and the termination of the process ($\surd$). We distinguish three kinds of actions: the immediate actions corresponding to a logical transition ($\tau, e, \surd$), the asynchronous actions where an unknown amount of time elapses before the occurrence of actions ($?m, !m$) and the synchronous actions ($to$) which occur after a fixed delay.

Now, we present some operational rules and precisely the new rules for the sending and receiving processes. To see all rules and in particular the handling of clocks in TA, we refer the reader to[11].

For example, the *empty* process which represents the process that does nothing can only terminate by executing the $\surd$ action (0 is the *null* process).

$$empty \xrightarrow{\surd} 0 \tag{4.1}$$

For the sending and receiving processes, we define the following rules.

$$\forall m \neq execute, \; *o[m] \xrightarrow{*m} empty \; avec \; * \in \{?, !\} \tag{4.2}$$

$$!o[execute(id)] \xrightarrow{!execute(id)} WaitAdvice(id) \tag{4.3}$$

$$WaitAdvice(id) \xrightarrow{id.\surd} empty \tag{4.4}$$

Rule 4.2 states that the process $?o[m]$ (resp. $!o[m]$) which corresponds to the reception of a message of type $m$ (resp. sending of message of type $m$) executes the action $?m$ (resp. the action $!m$) which corresponds to the message reception action (resp. the message sending action) and becomes the *empty* process. In the case of sending an *execute* message, the automaton evolves to an intermediary state named $WaitAdvice(id)$ (rule 4.3). $WaitAdvice(id)$ waits for the termination of the *advice service* identified by $id$. When *advice service id* terminates, $WaitAdvice(id)$ state executes $id.\surd$ and becomes *empty* process (rule 4.4).

The sequential process $P; Q$ ($P$ and $Q$ are BPEL processes) corresponds to the execution of the process $P$ followed by the execution of the process $Q$. It becomes the process $P'; Q$ if the process $P$ executes an action $a$ different from termination action and becomes $P'$. If $P$ terminates and Q can execute an action

$a$ and becomes $Q'$, the process $P; Q$ executes the action $a$ then becomes the process $Q'$.

$$\forall a \neq \sqrt{} \quad \frac{P \xrightarrow{a} P'}{P; Q \xrightarrow{a} P'; Q} \tag{4.5}$$

$$\frac{P \xrightarrow{\sqrt{}} \text{ and } Q \xrightarrow{a} Q'}{P; Q \xrightarrow{a} Q'} \tag{4.6}$$

Finally, the $switch\{P_i\}_{i \in I}$ process evaluates an internal condition represented by $\tau$ then becomes the process $P_i$.

$$\forall\, i \,\in\, I, \; switch\{P_i\}_{i \in I} \xrightarrow{\tau} P_i \tag{4.7}$$

### 4.3. Execution Scenario

Considering the abstract BPEL process defined in section 2. If we want to add dynamically an authentication process before the *switch* process, the extended abstract BPEL process has to integrate a sending *execute(id)* message process before the *switch* process.

$$?o[ResReq]; !execute(id); switch(!o[ResResp], !o[error])$$

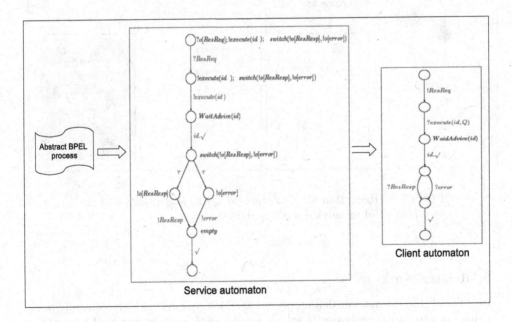

FIGURE 7. Adaptable service and client automata

At the execution, our dynamic client interpreter downloads the extended abstract BPEL specification. Then, it generates the corresponding service TA based on the operational rules previously defined. Then, based on the service TA and the interaction relation, our client generates the client TA and begins its interpretation. Figure 7 shows the generation process.

When our client receives an *execute(id)* message, it extracts the abstract BPEL *advice service* process from the message. In our example, the *advice service* is an authentication process of which the abstract BPEL specification is *!o[authDataRequ est]* ; *?o[authDataResp]* ; *P1*. This process sends an authentication data request to the client asking for authentication data, receives these data then performs some actions to authenticate the user. Our client generates the corresponding advice client automaton, associates with the received *id* and begins its execution (Figure 8.(left), states in grey represent the current execution step).

When the *advice client id* terminates, our client makes synchronisation with the main client automaton. It deletes the *advice client*, performs the *id.√* action and continues the execution of the main client automaton (figure 8.(right)).

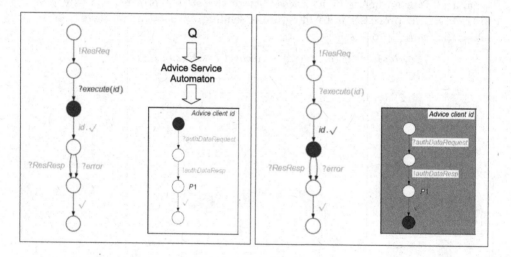

FIGURE 8. Reception of an *execute(id, Q)* message (left) and the termination of an advice service (right)

## 5. Related work

In [12] and [13], the authors define specific AOP languages to add dynamically new behaviours to BPEL processes. However, neither of these approaches addresses the client interaction issue. The client has no mean to handle the interactions that can be added or modified during the process execution.

The Web Service Management Layer (WSML) [14] is an AOP-based platform for WSs that allows a more loosely coupling between the client and the server sides. WSML handles the dynamic integration of new WSs in client applications to solve client execution problems. WSML dynamically discovers WSs based on matching criteria such as: method signature, interaction protocol or quality of service (QOS) matching. In a complementary way, our work proposes to adapt a client to a modified WS.

Some proposals have emerged recently to abstractly describe WSs, most of them are grounded on transition system models (Labelled Transition Systems, Petri nets, etc.) [26, 27, 28]. These works propose to formally specify composite WSs and handle the verification and the automatic composition issues. Still, none of these works propose to formalize the dynamics of SOA architectures and to handle runtime interaction changes.

## 6. Conclusion

In this paper, we proposed a solution based on AOP and PA to handle dynamic changes in the WS context. We extended our previous AOP approach to support BPEL processes and to handle interaction issues. We also use process algebra formalism to specify change-prone BPEL processes and generate dynamic clients.

As future works, we want to extend the work to take into account the client execution context. We also want to formally handle the aspect interactions issue (aspects applied at the same joinpoint). Finally, we plane to improve the current ASW prototype as proof-of-concepts.

## References

[1] Tidwell, D., Web services - the web's next revolution. IBM developerWorks (2000).

[2] Extensible Markup Language(XML) 1.0, W3C Recommendation, February (2004). http://www.w3.org/XML/

[3] Web Services Architecture, W3C Working Draft 14 November 2002. http://www.w3.org/TR/ws-arch/

[4] Andrews, T. et al., Business process execution language for web services (2003). http://www-128.ibm.com/developerworks/library/specification/ws-bpel/

[5] DCOM Architecture, Microsoft Corporation, 1998. http://msdn2.microsoft.com/en-us/library/ms809311.aspx

[6] Java Platform Enterprise Edition(J2EE), http://java.sun.com/javaee/index.jsp

[7] Object Management Group (OMG), Common Object Request Broker Architecture (CORBA/IIOP), revision 3.0.3, 2004. http://www.omg.org/technology/documents/corba_spec_catalog.htm

[8] G. Kiczales et al. , Aspect-Oriented Programming, in proc. of ECOOP'97. LNCS 1241, Springer-Verlag, (1997).

[9] R. Tomaz Ferraz, M. Ben Hmida and V. Monfort. Concrete solutions for web services adaptability using policies and aspects. The International Journal of Cooperative Information Systems (IJCIS), 15(3), pp. 415-438, 2006.

[10] M. Ben Hmida, R. Tomaz Ferraz and V. Monfort. Applying AOP concepts to increase Web Service flexibility. Journal of Digital Information Management (JDIM) 4(1), pp. 37-44, 2006.

[11] S. Haddad, P. Moreaux and S. Rampacek. Client Synthesis for Web Services by way of a Timed Semantics. ICEIS 2006 8th International Conference on Enterprise Information Systems, IEEE Computer Society, pp. 19-26, 23-27 Mai 2006, Paphos - Chypre.

[12] Anis Charfi and Mira Mezini. Aspect-oriented web service composition with ao4bpel. In ECOWS, volume 3250 of LNCS, pages 168-182, Springer, (2004).

[13] Carine Courbis and Anthony Finkelstein. Weaving aspects into web service orchestrations. In ICWS, pages 219-226, (2005).

[14] B. Verheecke, M.A. Cibran and V. Jonckers, AOP for Dynamic Configuration and Management of Web Services, ICWS-Europe, LNCS 2853, pages 137-151, (2003).

[15] R. Laddad, ASPECTJ in Action: Practical Aspect-Oriented Programming, Portland: Book News, Inc, 2004.

[16] JBoss AOP, http://www.jboss.org

[17] AspectWerkz, http://Aspectwerkz.codehaus.org

[18] Spring AOP platform, http://www.springframework.org/docs/reference/aop.html

[19] R. ALur and D.L. Dill, "A theory of Timed Automata", Theorotical Computer Science, 126, pp. 193-235, 1994.

[20] Staab, S., van der Aalst, W., Benjamins, V., Sheth, A., Miller, J., Bussler, C., Maedche, A., Fensel, D., and Gannon, D. (2003). Web services: Been there, done that? IEEE Intelligent Systems, 18:72-85.

[21] Milner, R. (1989). Communication and Concurrency. Prentice-Hall, Englewood Cliffs, NJ, USA.

[22] Hoare, C. (1985). Communicating Sequential Processes. Prentice Hall, Englewood Cliffs, NJ, USA.

[23] Bergstra, J. and Klop, J. (1984). Process algebra for synchronous communication. Information and Control, 60(1- 3):109-137.

[24] XML Path Language (XPath) Ver. 1.0, W3C Recommendation 16 November (1999). http://www.w3.org/TR/xpath

[25] X. Nicollin and J. Sifakis. The algebra of timed process, ATP: Theory and. application. Information and Computation, 114(1):131178, 1994.

[26] R. Hamadi and B. Benatallah, A Petri Net-based Model for Web Service Composition, Proceedings of Australasian Database Conference, pp. 191-200, Australia (2003).

[27] X. Fu, T. Bultan, and J. Su., Analysis of Interacting BPEL Web Services, In Proc. of WWW'04, pp. 621-630, ACM Press, USA (2004).

[28] A. Ferrara, Web Services: A Process Algebra Approach, Proceedings of the 2nd International Conference on Service Oriented Computing, ACM Press, pp. 242-251 USA (2004).

Mehdi Ben Hmida
LAMSADE-CNRS, Université Paris-Dauphine,
Place du Maréchal de Lattre de Tassigny,
Paris 75775 Cedex 16, France
e-mail: mehdi.benhmida@lamsade.dauphine.fr

Céline Boutrous Saab
LAMSADE-CNRS, Université Paris-Dauphine,
Place du Maréchal de Lattre de Tassigny,
Paris 75775 Cedex 16, France
e-mail: celine.boutrous-saab@lamsade.dauphine.fr

Serge Haddad
LAMSADE-CNRS, Université Paris-Dauphine,
Place du Maréchal de Lattre de Tassigny,
Paris 75775 Cedex 16, France
e-mail: haddad@lamsade.dauphine.fr

Valérie Monfort
LAMSADE-CNRS, Université Paris-Dauphine,
Place du Maréchal de Lattre de Tassigny,
Paris 75775 Cedex 16, France
e-mail: valerie.monfort@univ-paris1.fr

Ricardo Tomaz Ferraz
CRI, Université Paris 1 Sorbonne,
90 rue de Tolbiac,
75013 Paris, France
e-mail: ricardo.ferraz-tomaz@univ-paris1.fr

Whitestein Series in Software Agent Technologies, 167–182

# Web Service Standards: Do we need them?

Tosca Lahiri and Mark Woodman

**Abstract.** There is a three-fold argument that there are too many overlapping Web service standards, they are not constraining enough and they exhibit too much proprietary interest. These criticisms suggest a dilemma of whether Web service standards are worth investing time in – which raises the question of whether we should use standards or not. This dichotomy raises issues critical to both software engineering and business. Deciding which standards to adhere to is difficult from the viewpoints of the software developer and the perspective of the business arm. We discuss standards' benefits and downfalls, looking at the implications for stakeholders. For successful uptake standards need precision and flexibility in solutions to common development challenges. Whether there are enough rigorous standards, or whether there are not sufficient robust standards is at the heart of the matter. We will expose different facets of an argument pointing to a standards marshalling framework for easier adherence.

**Keywords.** Web Services. Standards.

## 1. Introduction

Web services are a maturing design option offering substantial benefits to software designers and commercial enterprise process designers alike. Standards for Web services are developing in such a way that they will form part of the "next-generation" web [1].

However, in a recent publication Microsoft presented the results of a survey of senior IT managers in which it emerged that the level of trust in standards was at the root of any slowness to use Web services [2]. If the use of software-to-software Web services across business boundaries is to become commonplace then the standards that govern the transport, storing and handling of data will need strengthening. We will examine some of the reasons why standards are weak in later sections.

## 1.1. Web Service Definition

It is clear from the relevant literature that the definition of a Web service is still developing. In our previous work [3] we identified three "schemes" to describe how Web services are used. In *Scheme I* the developer of systems that consume Web services identifies the exact service they want to use before they have designed their system. Then the developer produces the system to fit the published Web service. In *Scheme II* system developers identify sets of Web services that their system may consume and then develop their software to fit the set of published Web services. *Scheme III* is the Web service ideal in which the developer does not select a Web service for use prior to development and they develop their Web service consuming system for dynamic discovery.

There is disagreement as to whether Web services are revolutionary or evolutionary; whether Web services are a form of distributed computing or not; whether Web services are state-less or state-full. Furthermore, there is the question of whether Web services are just a new means of delivering content or whether their use will actually change the business processes before, after and during content delivery.

So, what is a Web service? At the simplest level it is a software facility, delivered over the Internet, that meets a commercial need.

Web services are used to create systems from independently created and controlled parts that can interoperate according to a variety of standards. The services adhere to a loosely coupled interoperability model, which means that different system parts, whether they are internal business objects or external business entities, have the flexibility to interact with each other programmatically. The ideal model is what we termed *Scheme III*: interoperability at three levels – at a platform level, an operating system level and the programming language level.

## 1.2. Standards Definition

In this sub-section we try to capture what people mean when they talk or write about "standards". The term is now much more loosely used and encompasses a multitude of ideas and practices.

There are at least five categories of the notion of a standard: specifications (which we conflate with *de jure* standards), *de facto* standards, proprietary standards, recommendations, and best practices. A specification is a set of detailed instructions for a specific activity. SOAP is a specification that details how messages are transported across applications. De facto standards are not prescribed but are so commonplace that in reality they are standards. An example of a de facto standard is Microsoft Word for word processing. Proprietary standards are vendor-specific conditions for use. Recommendations may be followed if your situation warrants it. Best practices are guidelines that again may just as well be ignored as followed.

The UK's standards body, the British Standards Institution (BSI [4]), defines a standard as a published document that:

> ... contains a technical specification or other precise criteria designed to be used consistently as a rule, guideline, or definition.

Other similar bodies state something about the process of making a standard, e.g., on the need for consensus, the use of science, and the benefit to the community. For the purposes of this discussion we propose the following definition:

> *A standard is an established or widely recognized specification or statement of practice from an organization whose authority and experience is recognised by the community using the standard.*

## 2. Too Many Overlapping Standards

When a software developer goes to create a system that consumes Web services, such as that described in our *Scheme III*, they are faced with a plethora of standards to choose from. After they have defined the functional requirements, the first choice to make concerns which standards body they would go to. This choice may be based on previous experience. The second choice is about the impact caused on the application architecture. In this section we will discuss some of their overlapping standards from the standards organizations, with some comments about their apparent agenda. We will then discuss the affect on the software architecture from the viewpoint of the software developer and the business manager. Finally, we will identify areas that have overlapping standards.

### 2.1. Standards Organizations

Gordon Bell, states in [5], that "we have far too many standards organizations, each with its own set of internal conflicts and an often inconsistent set of goals." This statement from Bell is worthy of further investigation. How many standard organizations are there? And what are their motivations? There are the W3C, OASIS, The Liberty Alliance and the WS-I to name just a few – and to temporarily ignore long-standing, independent, often government-approved bodies such as ISO, ANSI, CENELEC, ITU, IEEE.

In its own words, "WS-I is an open industry organization chartered to promote Web services interoperability across platforms, operating systems, and programming languages" [6]. WS-I promotes interoperability by devising profiles which are collections of standards and specifications.

W3C "develops interoperable technologies (specifications, guidelines, software, and tools) to lead the Web to its full potential" [7]. OASIS "is a not-for-profit, global consortium that drives the development, convergence and adoption of e-business standards" [8]. The Liberty Alliance Project is a coalition of more than 150 companies, non-profit and government organizations from around the globe. The consortium is committed to developing an open standard for federated network identity that supports all current and emerging network devices [9].

In short, given how many organizations are making standards in these areas, if we were to list all the standards organization and their *raison d'être* we would have a wide spectrum of beliefs and motivations. This may be the root cause of why there are too many and overlapping standards.

A survey of Web services standards offered by these four organizations alone highlights the proliferation of standards. As we discuss later it is difficult sometimes to see where one standard ends and another begins. Examples of overlapping standards that we will look at in this section are as follows:

- For Orchestration: WS-Choreography and BPEL
- For Business Transactions: WS-Transaction and RosettaNet
- For Reliable messaging: WS-ReliableMessaging and WS-Reliability
- For Registries: ebXML and UDDI

## 2.2. Repercussions of Overlapping Standards

It has been suggested [10] that there are too many standards in the field of web services. A situation where we have too many standards has several repercussions for the software developer and the business manager. If there are two standards for one issue in Web services the developer has to decide which standard to follow. It could be that the developer decides not to follow a standard as the existence of two or more standards for the same issue mean that there is in effect no "standard". For business managers, the same dilemma means spending time, and therefore resources, in the decision making process, because they will have to assess each standard and decide which one to adhere to, if any.

With the proliferation of Web service standards we have also seen proposed standards that do not mature into full standard mode. For example, WSCI 1.0 (The Web Service Choreography Interface) is a Note on the W3C web site (dated 2002) but appears to have been superseded by other standards such as the Web Services Choreography Description Language. The repercussions of this pattern of development makes developing software more challenging as the developer finds it hard to decide which standard, or proposed standard, to follow. There is the instinct to use the newest standard as soon as it has been developed and published. This need is fraught with dangers to the development life cycle as immature standards have not had time to cover developmental challenges. The decision point of when to adhere to a standard or not could either bring financial loss or financial growth.

This surfeit of Web service standards naturally raises inconsistencies [11], inconsistencies that can be costly. For example, deciding to use WSCI 1.0 in 2002 would very shortly, when it has been superseded, increase design time, increase the financial risk and decrease interoperability. Design time is increased because code would need to be refactored. The financial risk is increased because as an IT manager you would have to re-allocate resources from one task to the refactoring task required. Interoperability is decreased because a standard has been removed from the design. If the standard has not been replaced, or the replacement is significantly different from the original standard, the same level of interoperability can not be guaranteed.

## 2.3. Examples of Overlapping Standards

Here we sketch the four areas where there are clearly overlapping standards.

**2.3.1. Orchestration.** In the area of Web service orchestration there are at least two standards that assist in the process of coordinating an exchange of information. The first of these is WS-Choreography. It:

> provide[s] an information model that describes the data and the relationships between them that is needed to define a choreography that describes the sequence and conditions in which the data is exchanged between two or more participants in order to meet some useful purpose [12].

WS-Choreography is a W3C initiative. At the time of writing, the working group for this standard is dominated by people from the Oracle Corporation. Does the presence of Oracle on the Working Group influence the pathway to standardization? This would depend on whether Oracle had any plans for products in this area. The influence could be a positive one as well as a negative one.

BPEL (Business Process Execution Language) is a XML-based language designed to enable task sharing for a distributed computing environment, across multiple business boundaries using combinations of Web services. BPEL is an OASIS initiative and has the support of a wide spectrum of corporations as well other interested parties like IONA.

WS-Choreography and BPEL both deal with orchestrating data across business boundaries. They go about the tasks in different ways yet they share a common objective – that of enabling data exchange across business boundaries.

As either a software developer or IT manager the choice of which standard to use for orchestration would mean dissecting WS-Choreography and BPEL in turn to find the similarities and differences. A rationale would then be developed to assist with the decision of which standard is most suitable. "Suitability" would have several criteria by which the underlying principals are formed. These criteria would fall into two groupings; either technical criteria or commercial criteria. It would be common practice that both groupings would be considered when trying to decide which standard to adhere to.

**2.3.2. Business Transactions.** For business process/transactions there are two overlapping standards: WS-Transaction and RosettaNet. WS-Transaction is a collaborative piece of work involving IBM, BEA Systems, Microsoft, Arjuna, Hitachi, and IONA. Three other sub-standards make up WS-Transaction. They are WS-Coordination, WS-AtomicTransaction and WS-BusinessActivity. WS-Coordination creates a context in which software activities take place. It also coordinates the actions of distributed applications. WS-AtomicTransaction defines the atomic transaction coordination type used with the WS-Coordination framework. The WS-BusinessActivity defines the business activity coordination type used by the parent standard [13].

RosettaNet provides standards that work on the global supply chain, addressing the challenges of global networks. RosettaNet provides a language for doing e-commerce in technology-based industries, or those companies that use technology for business processes. RosettaNet provides automated trading partner exchanges which results in considerable financial savings for the partners. The automation requires that applications have a shared understanding of the business process involved. RosettaNet provides this understanding via a set of processes that underlies partner to partner communications [14].

WS-Transaction and RosettaNet both deal with business processes or transactions. Although WS-Transaction may be more generic than RosettaNet both standards focus on B2B (mainly) business transactions and how and where these transactions happen.

**2.3.3. Reliable Messaging.** In the reliability of sending and receiving messages field we have the WS-ReliableMessaging and WS-Reliability standards. WS-ReliableMessaging was co-authored by BEA, IBM, Microsoft and TIBCO before being submitted to OASIS for fine tuning and a stamp of approval. This standard allows messages to be delivered irrespective of any system failures. WS-Reliability has been ratified as a standard by OASIS after being devised initially by Fujitsu, Hitachi, Oracle, NEC, Sonic Software, and Sun Microsystems in March 2003. It too guarantees message integrity.

It seems at odds that there should be two "standards" for essentially the same purpose. However, we can see from the list of authors that each standard comes with its own perspective. These two standards are competing for dominance.

**2.3.4. Registries.** In the area of Web service registries we have two standards: ebXML and UDDI. The UDDI is an attempt to create a platform-independent framework for discovering businesses and the services that they offer. The definition from Microsoft Corp. states that the "UDDI (Universal Description Discovery and Integration) is a public registry, offered at no cost, where one can publish and inquire about Web Services" [15]. UDDI.ORG, the industry repository for UDDI information claims that UDDI has the support of "all major platform and software providers, as well as marketplace operators and e-business leaders". This is a major step towards interoperability for businesses worldwide as they attempt to reach the nirvana of boundary-less business.

The definition given by Sun provides a further insight into the benefits of fully implementing UDDI:

The UDDI specifications define a way to publish and discover information about Web services. UDDI aims to automate the process of publishing your preferred way of doing business, finding trading partners and have them find you, and interoperate with these trading partners over the Internet [16].

Sun sees implementation of UDDI as enabling integration between trading partners. For example, if company A wants to buy product B from company C, without automated interoperability, company A must blindly proceed through company C purchasing procedures. With UDDI implementation, company C would publish these stages for company A to integrate with.

The UDDI specification takes advantage of other standards, such as those from the W3C and the IETF (Internet Engineering Taskforce), in its own development. The standards, such as XML, Hypertext Transfer Protocol (HTTP) and Domain Name System (DNS), provide well-grounded foundations for the UDDI itself.

Since UDDI would allow businesses a much deeper level of integration, B2B e-commerce is sure to benefit when UDDI is fully implemented by all online businesses. This is perhaps a step too far for some of the ultra competitive software industry.

The OASIS ebXML (Electronic Business XML) Registry sets out to realize interoperable registries and repositories, with an interface that allows submission, query and retrieval on the contents of the registry. ebXML is a set of services that supports business integration via the sharing of information. Partners find each other's services with the use of Collaboration Protocol Profile (CPP). The CPP tells the partners how to connect with the service; it describes the services on offer and includes a description of the partner offering the services [17].

The decision of which registry standard to use requires analysis of the benefits each offers. Both ebXML and UDDI offer registries of business services and explain how business transactions can take place. ebXML is more directly focused on e-commerce, which may sway the decision.

There are many other areas that we could have discussed beyond the above four, such as security. Discussing these four, however, already highlights the basic premise that having too many standards for the same issue causes technical and commercial confusion.

## 3. Standards are not Constraining Enough

We now look at the repercussions of standards that do not constrain sufficiently. We shall then look at four examples of such standards.

Ambiguity in standards has consequences for the architecture of software in that interoperability is reduced. Interoperability is based on well-crafted standards. Standards that allow the software developer leeway to make discretionary decisions will mean that the software developed does not interoperate well with other systems. This indistinctness loosens the hold that a standard has on the software developed in that the standard does not proscribe a particular course of action. Whether it is reasonable for standards to be prescriptive is another question that remains unanswered here. What is sure is that standards that allow discretionary decision points are not constraining the software developer. This is of importance when considering the degree of interoperability in a system.

Specifications built on another specification like SOAP for example are in effect a divergence from the original document [18]. It is another way of saying that the standard has deficiencies and this is how a particular task should be achieved. An example of an extension is the SOAP *Security Extensions: Digital Signatures* proposal that describes how to digitally sign SOAP messages [19]. Extensions that address new issues that have arisen since the standard was decreed are acceptable. Standards that have glaring holes that give rise to an extension, are not constraining the software developer. Security is an issue that SOAP, for example, hardly addresses. Security of SOAP messages was an issue while the SOAP specification was designed, yet those on the W3C Working Group, side-stepped the issue. The SOAP specification allows for several different security extensions, e.g., [20]. Having several extensions for the same issue is no constraint.

The interoperability of a piece of software can be reduced if there is more than one standard which the software could employ. For example, either the software designer tries to make the software conform to both standards, or, more likely, the software does not conform to any standard. Trying to make a piece of software conform to two standards will inevitably result in situations where for a particular issue one standard as opposed to the other had to be followed. If for the next issue that comes along you adhere to the other standard then you cannot claim that your piece of software is compliant with standard $X$, because in at least one place it is compliant with standard $Y$. If because of the presence of two standards for the same issue the designer decides that they cannot adhere to any standard, then interoperability is reduced given that interoperability is driven by conformance to standards. In this scenario the number of standards available explains why standards are not constraining enough.

The language of the SOAP specification is riddled with discretionary phrases. Table 1 highlights this.

| CommandWord | Occurrences |
|-------------|-------------|
| recommended | 8 |
| may | 85 |
| optional | 9 |
| should | 23 |

TABLE 1. Discretionary words in SOAP

Eric Newcomer supports this analysis [21]:

> One problem with the SOAP specification is that it contains lots
> of rules that may or may not be enforced. Thus it is very likely
> that two conforming SOAP implementations will not implement
> the same collection of optional features and thus be incompatible.

The rest of this section will briefly look at a few examples of non-constraining standards.

In Section 7 of the SOAP Specification, *Security Considerations*, it says that "SOAP implementors need to anticipate rogue SOAP applications sending intentionally malicious data to a SOAP node It is strongly recommended that a SOAP node receiving a SOAP message is capable of evaluating to what level it can trust the sender of that SOAP message and its contents" [20]. The critical word here is "recommend". A recommendation is not the same as saying that you "must" do something. In this case, the SOAP specification is passing responsibility for assessing and measuring levels of trust to the individual developers. So, SOAP does not prevent users from ignoring levels of trust when they use the SOAP specification.

In Section 1.3 of the SOAP specification, *Relation to Other Specifications*, it says that "a SOAP message is specified as an XML Information Set [XML InfoSet]. While all SOAP message examples in this document are shown using XML 1.0 [XML 1.0] syntax, other representations MAY [*sic*] be used to transmit SOAP messages between nodes " [20]. The keyword here is, of course, "MAY". Thanks to this discretionary word the SOAP specification allows for an infinite number of representation systems.

SOAP does not prescribe that an XML Information Set must be used:

> SOAP Version 1.2 can be used as the basis for other technologies
> that provide richer or more specialized services. To claim confor-
> mance with the SOAP Version 1.2 specification, the specifications
> and implementations of such technologies must be consistent with
> the pertinent mandatory requirements expressed in Part 1 of the
> SOAP Version 1.2 specification (this document). Rules for confor-
> mance with such new specifications are beyond the scope of the
> SOAP Version 1.2 specification; it is recommended that specifica-
> tions for such technologies provide the appropriate conformance
> rules [20].

The keyword in this instance is "recommend". What this extract is saying is that the SOAP specification can be used as the basis for other new sub-specifications. However, this extract is only saying that the new specification *should* have its own conformance rules as opposed to must have its own conformance rules.

Section 4.3.3 of the XML Specification, *Character Encoding in Entities*, says:

> It is recommended that character encodings registered (as charsets)
> with the Internet Assigned Numbers Authority [IANA-CHARSETS],
> other than those just listed, be referred to using their registered
> names; other encodings SHOULD use names starting with an

"x-" prefix. XML processors SHOULD match character encoding names in a case-insensitive way and SHOULD either interpret an IANA-registered name as the encoding registered at IANA for that name or treat it as unknown (processors are, of course, not required to support all IANA-registered encodings) [22].

There are three keywords or phrases in this quotation: *recommended*, *should* (used twice) and *not required*. In this extract the specification gives guidelines for the use of character encodings. It suggests that you refer to character encodings with their registered name. If an encoding does not have a registered name you ought to use names starting with an "x". What happens if you do not use the registered name, or use a name beginning with a letter other than "x"?

In this section we have outlined why we think that Web service standards are not constraining enough. We have then given four examples where the standards allow for various interpretations. In the next section we shall look at why we think that standards are too proprietary and what the ramifications of this are.

## 4. Standards Are Too Proprietary

The proprietary interest seen in standards is a complex issue, but is one that needs to be addressed. Due to space limitations, in this section we will restrict ourselves to an overview of the primary concerns.

When reviewing a standard it is important to consider the list of committee members to see if there is any unwarranted bias in the resulting standard. Obviously a person will always bring their interests to the negotiating table. There are the benefits and disadvantages to having vendors on the committees devising standards.

By the time work on a standard begins there has normally already been people developing software in the area. Committee members bring with them industry experience of the relevant domain – experience that highlights what has happened while they, or their colleagues, have developed software using technology sets before they have been verified by a standard organization. This means that, in effect, for a given area, solutions that have been developed and tested by a few are treated as well-honed design patterns which feed into the "new" specification.

A different way of characterising the impact of limited industry experience is to say that the knowledge pool for a standard is shallow. The knowledge of the new technology is limited within all companies by practical restraints like having to use only particular toolsets. Another restriction in companies will be the money that they have to invest in developing new standards for the benefit of others.

We also have to consider the benefits of significant commercial interest from the industry: a company may support the development of a particular standard because they have products in a particular field that they want to promote. An example of this is Microsoft updating its SOAP toolkit to natively support the SOAP specification. Looking at the SOAP specification one can see that Microsoft make up 40% of the editorial team. This is of benefit to Microsoft in that they have helped devise the SOAP standard.

Another benefit to having proprietary interest in a standard is that the company brings the advantage of strategic thinking to the table. Development of strategy in a particular field is important because it brings a systematic plan of action to achieve particular goals. However, when a particular strategy threatens to overwhelm the standardization process you can see evidence of proprietary interest.

It is also possible that the existence of several company strategies will stall the standardization process. There have been disputes about IPR, patents, licenses and royalties at W3C and OASIS committees for instance. Looking at the IPR statements for BPEL at OASIS reveals that several parties are making claims of ownership. For example, IBM state that they have a patent license, Microsoft state that they have patents pending and BEA "has no patent rights in the technology described in Business Process Execution Language for Web Services Version 1.1 specification dated 5/5/2003" [23]. Patents give the company some ownership of the technology and as such will ultimately result in financial gains if the technology is successful adopted. With this background, standards, like, BPEL, are negatively influenced by proprietary interests.

Proprietary pursuits in standards are also influenced by the available hardware and software infrastructure. If a company is to help in the advancement of a new technology they must have to hand the available infrastructure or, they must have the resources to source it. If enough companies are represented on the standard's committee it is possible to have a wide representation of environments. This would increase the interoperability of the standard once it is published. However, the reverse is also true; that is, if there is only one or two environments available the range of interoperability is reduced. For example, if a company like Microsoft for instance dominate a standard's committee then the Windows operating system might focus highly. This might mean that interoperability at an operating system level diminishes. This is another reason why proprietary interest in standards is detrimental. Standards that do not cross vendor platforms will also mean that the technology has a restricted reach.

There is an argument that says that vendors should not write standards as they lack the input of implementation experience [24]. A committee comprising of programmers instead vendor managers is likely to have a more detailed experience of the new technology undergoing standardization. More precise experience, from vendor-neutral contributors, would result in standards that do not have so much proprietary bias.

Proprietary interest in standards diminishes interoperability. Why does interoperability decrease as proprietor influence increases? We have revealed six factors for this: proprietary bias for their own products; financial considerations; limited narrow-base knowledge; in-house commercial strategies drive standards down one track and not the other; disputes concerning IPR stall roll-out; and infrastructure limitations bind standards to a limited configuration.

## 5. Solution

In this section we highlight the role that standards have in developing web services and propose that interoperable Web services are only possible with effective standards. We assert that standards that should shape interoperability. We will then come to conclusions that address the question of whether we should adhere to Web service standards or not. We will draw on these conclusions to devise a standards framework.

Standards will be at the core of successful, interoperable Web services [25]. At least we can propose that standards are essential for Web services [26] in that they become part of any definition. The process of defining and verifying standards in itself contributes to developing the software architecture it is trying to govern [27], [26]. When a person thinks of Web services they need to, implicitly or explicitly, receive and understand the message that they can have confidence in software that uses Web services. This would reverse the situation explained previously whereby Microsoft found that the lack of standards hindered the use of Web services. Using our framework of Web services standards would reinforce Web service architecture, standards and thus bolster business confidence.

So, what is the impact of well-designed standards for software-discovered and negotiated use of Web services (what we called *Scheme III*), in terms of the impact on themselves and on other entities? What bearing do standards have in the field of Web services? The first point to consider is the origin of standards. Who are the stakeholders and what influence do they have on the standards? We have seen that in some standards organizations there have been a majority of people on the committee from the same company. This must mean that the agenda of that company would influence that course of the standard-making process.

The second issue is about the dynamics of standards, both internally and externally. How do the people on the standard-making committees interact with each other and with other external influences? For example, each person on a committee comes with their own set of objectives. These objectives come into play during the negotiation stage. The external influences, such of proprietary interests, are harder to identify during the standard-making processes. The political bias of external influences will colour a standard as it develops.

The third influence on well-designed standards is whether there has been an inbuilt mechanism to alter the standard after it has been tested and used by several parties in live implementations. A mechanism should exist that takes feedback from these test-bed scenarios and feeds it back into the design of the standard. An effective standard should show the input of implementation experience [24].

Another influence that well-designed standards have is that the time needed to design a software application decreases. Why is this? Standards provide a framework in which to design software. For example, the standards focussing on Web service orchestration and choreography provide an essential part of the software architecture in that they say how services will interact with other services. Time needed to design Web services also decreases because organizations produce standards-compliant tools like WsdlValidator used to validate WSDL 2.0 (this tool can be found at the W3C website).

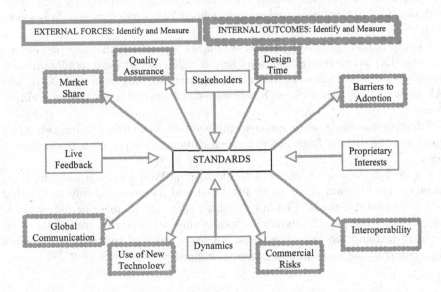

FIGURE 1. Framework for Developing Web Service Standards

Adherence to Web service standards lowers the risks for developers, for IT managers, service providers and service consumers alike. For developers there would be a Web service architecture to follow; for IT managers there should be a mechanism that tells the IT manager which infrastructure to follow for each contextual setup; service providers and consumers would have confidence in that Web services are built on tried and tested standards.

Well-designed standards will encourage use. Increased usage will stimulate the Web service marketplace. Vendors will have to comply with these standards if they want to keep and grow their market share. A vendor that can show that their product adheres to a standard will demonstrate a high degree of rigour.

Web service applications that conform with standards also inherit a quality assurance banner. A banner that when displayed tells prospective customers that this solution provider can demonstrate that they have followed an accepted course of action while developing their software. Quality assurance is a vital weapon in the marketplace.

Another effect that well-designed standards have is that they create a level playing field for software developers. The impact of this is bi-fold in that both the programmer and the IT manager gain credit; credit which stimulates business growth. The programmer knows that if they conform to the XML standard then a competitor at the other side of the world, using the same standard, does not have an advantage in terms of what can be done while staying in the bounds of XML.

The IT manager knows that they have at their disposal a software application that complies with XML for instance, across the world.

The software developed in these circumstances is not restricted by geographic boundaries. Global business based on well-defined Web service standards is a possibility.

Closely adhering to Web service standards will create an interoperable architecture that promotes transactions across different hardware configurations, different operating systems and different programming languages [28]. XML and SOAP are standards that are used by software developers to create interoperability systems.

Effective standards, while not ensuring invulnerable, interoperable web-based services, are the driving force in the implied campaign for seamless business processes.

Figure 1 depicts our framework for developing Web service standards. Each element in this diagram needs to be identified and measured as way to marshal any Web service standards. The outcomes, in blue, will increase or decrease accordingly. For example, the dynamics seen within a standard's committee need to be identified and any influence measured. As a result of taking measurements could mean that the makeup of a group is changed.

## 6. Conclusion

Web services interoperability needs standards. However, as this paper argues, at present there are too many overlapping standards, and they are not constraining enough. Furthermore, there is an excess of proprietary interest.

There are too many overlapping standards because there are too many standards organizations proposing too many standards. Where there is more than one standard for the same technical challenge, each standard in turn is weakened. The result is that, in effect, there is no standard for the challenge. Overlapping standards also mean that the design time for a piece of software is increased, as are the financial risks. Interoperability is decreased.

When standards are not constraining enough it means there is uncertainty about how to address a particular matter. Uncertainty means that two developers will bring their own interpretations of the subject. This again decreases interoperability.

Proprietary interest in standards brings unwarranted bias to the proceedings. This bias also results in a narrowing of the knowledge pool which is especially seen when one organization's strategy dominates the standard. When proprietary interest permeates a standard interoperability is decreased.

Our solution framework sets out elements that need to be identified and measured to ensure that interoperability, as well as the other benefits, is boosted.

We need Web service standards. But, as we have argued, developers need standards without overlap; for simpler software development and more efficient business processes, standards should be more constraining; for similar reasons proprietary interest must be lessened, ideally to a balance between support and gain. In this situation, Web service standards are worth investing in as long as we identify their contributory factors in order to strengthen the technical and commercial outcomes.

# References

[1] H. Zhuge, *China's E-Science Knowledge Grid Environment.* IEEE Computer-Intelligent, January/February 2004, 13–17.

[2] *Microsoft. .NET Live: Taking business to the next level,* Microsoft UK Pamphlet, 2004.

[3] T. Lahiri, and M. Woodman, *Web Service Architectures Need Constraining Standards: An Agenda for Developing Systems without Client-Side Software Adapters,* Proceedings of the IASTED International Conference on Software Engineering, Innsbruck, February 2006, 45–52.

[4] British Standards Institution, *What is a standard?* London, 2005. http://www.bsi-global.com/en/Standards-and-Publications/About-standards/What-is-a-standard/

[5] G. Bell, *A Time and a Place for Standards,* Queue, 2 (2004), No. 6, 66–74.

[6] WS-I. *WS-I: Web Services Interoperability Organization.* WS-I, 2006. http://www.ws-i.org/

[7] W3C. *World Wide Web Consortium.* 2006. http://www.w3.org/

[8] OASIS. *OASIS.* 2006. http://www.oasis-open.org/home/index.php

[9] Liberty Alliance, *Liberty Alliance Project,* 2006. http://www.projectliberty.org/index.php

[10] W. van der Aalst, *Don't go with the flow: Web services composition standards exposed.* IEEE Intelligent Systems. January–February 2003. http://is.tm.tue.nl/staff/wvdaalst/publications/p181.pdf

[11] D. Oberle, S. Lamparter, A. Eberhart, and S. Staab, *Semantic Management of Web Services,* Proceedings 3rd International Conference on Service-Oriented Computing, Amsterdam, 2005.

[12] D. Burdett, and N. Kavantzas, *WS Choreography Model Overview.* W3C, 2004. http://www.w3.org/TR/ws-chor-model/

[13] IBM. *Web Services Transactions specifications.* http://www-128.ibm.com/developerworks/library/specification/ws-tx/

[14] RosettaNet. *RosettaNet: What we do.* RosettaNet, 2006. http://portal.rosettanet.org/cms/sites/RosettaNet/About/What/index.html

[15] Microsoft. *UDDI,* 2003. http://www.ipade.mx/lib/Glosa/Consulta.asp?Letra=U

[16] S. MacRoibeaird, *Universal Description, Discovery & Integration (UDDI).* Sun Microsystems, 2002. http://wwws.sun.com/software/xml/developers/uddi/

[17] OASIS. *OASIS/ebXML Registry Services Specification v2.5,* 2003. http://www.oasis-open.org/committees/regrep/documents/2.5/specs/ebrs-2.5.pdf

[18] J. Albornoz, *Finding your way through Web service standards, Part 1: Will my Web service work with your client?* IBM. `http://www-106.ibm.com/developerworks/webservices/library/ws-stand1.html`

[19] F. Curbera, M. Duftler, R. Khalaf, W. Nagy, N. Mukhi, and S. Weerawarana, *Unraveling the Web services web: an introduction to SOAP, WSDL, and UDDI*, Internet Computing, IEEE, **6** (2002), No. 2, 86–93.

[20] M. Gudgin, M. Hadley, N. Mendelsohn, J.J. Moreau, and H.F. Nielsen, *SOAP Version 1.2 Part 1: Messaging Framework*. W3C. 2006. `http://www.w3.org/TR/soap12-part1/`

[21] E. Newcomer, *Understanding Web Services: XML, WSDL, SOAP, and UDDI*. Addison-Wesley, Boston, 2002.

[22] T. Bray. J. Paoli, C. M. Sperberg-McQueen, E. Maler, and F. Yergeau. *Extensible Markup Language (XML) 1.0 (Third Edition)*. W3C, 2004. `http://www.w3.org/TR/REC-xml/`

[23] OASIS. *OASIS Web Services Business Process Execution Language (WSBPEL) TC.* 2006. `http://www.oasis-open.org/committees/wsbpel/ipr.php`

[24] S. Vinoski, *WS-Nonexistent Standards*, IEEE Internet Computing, November–December, 2004, 94–96.

[25] D. Geer, *Taking Steps to Secure Web Services*, IEEE Computer, October 2003, 14–16.

[26] T. Pilioura, S. Tsalgatidou, and S. Hadjiefthymiades, *Scenarios of Using Web Services in M-Commerce*, ACM SIGecom Exchanges, **3**, No. 4, January 2003, 28–36.

[27] D. Fay, *An Architecture for Distributed Applications on the Internet: Overview of Microsoft's .NET Platform*. Proceedings of the International Parallel and Distributed Processing Symposium (IPDPS '03), 2003, 22–26.

[28] S. Baehni, P. T. Eugster, R. Guerraoui, and P. Altherr, *Pragmatic Type Interoperability*, Proceedings.23rd International Conference on Distributed Computing Systems, 404–411, May 2003.

Tosca Lahiri
Middlesex University e-Centre
School of Computing Science
The Burroughs, Hendon, London NW4 4BT
England
e-mail: `t.lahiri@mdx.ac.uk`

Mark Woodman
Middlesex University e-Centre
School of Computing Science
The Burroughs, Hendon, London NW4 4BT
England
e-mail: `m.woodman@mdx.ac.uk`

# Author Index

# Whitestein Series in Software Agent Technologies and Autonomic Computing

Edited by

**Marius Walliser, Stefan Brantschen, Monique Calisti and Stefan Schinkinger**

The Whitestein Series in Software Agent Technologies and Autonomic Computing reports new developments in agent-based software technologies and agent-oriented software engineering methodologies, with particular emphasis on applications in the area of autonomic computing and communications.
The spectrum of the series includes research monographs, high quality notes resulting from research and industrial projects, outstanding Ph.D. theses, and the proceedings of carefully selected conferences. The series is targeted at promoting advanced research

## Published titles:

■ **Cervenka, R. / Trencansky, I.,** both Whitestein Technologies, Bratislava, Slovakia

**The Agent Modeling Language - AML. A Comprehensive Approach to Modeling Multi-Agent Systems**

2007. 366 pages. Softcover.
ISBN 978-3-7643-8395-4

Multi-agent systems are already a focus of studies for more than 25 years. Despite substantial effort of an active research community, modeling of multi-agent systems still lacks complete and proper definition, general acceptance, and practical application. Due to the vast potential of these systems e.g. to improve the practice in software and to extent the applications that can feasibly be tackled, this book tries to provide a comprehensive modeling language - the Agent-Modeling Language (AML) - as an extension of UML 2.0, concentrating on multi-agent systems and applications.

■ **van Dinther, C.,** Karlsruhe, Germany

**Adaptive Bidding in Single-Sided Auctions Under Uncertainty. An Agent-based Approach in Market Engineering**

2006. 256 pages. Softcover.
ISBN 978-3-7643-8094-6

■ **Zimmermann, R.,** Erlangen, Germany

**Agent-based Supply Network Event Management**

2006. 340 pages. Softcover.
ISBN 978-3-7643-7486-0

■ **Unland, R.,** Essen, Germany / **Klusch, M.,** Saarbrücken, Germany / **Calisti, M.,** Zürich, Switzerland (eds.)

**Software Agent-based Applications, Platforms and Development Kits**

2005. 462 pages. Softcover.
ISBN 978-3-7643-7347-4

■ **Klügl, F.,** Würzburg, Germany / **Bazzan, A.,** Porto Alegre, Brazil / **Ossowski, S.,** Madrid, Spain (eds.)

**Applications of Agent Technology in Traffic and Transportation**

2005. 218 pages. Softcover.
ISBN 978-3-7643-7258-3

■ **Tamma, V.,** Liverpool, U.K. / **Cranefield, S.,** Dunedin, New Zealand / **Finin, T.W.,** Baltimore, U.S.A. / **Willmott, S.,** Barcelona, Spain (eds.)

**Ontologies for Agents: Theory and Experiences**

2005. 356 pages. Softcover.
ISBN 978-3-7643-7237-8

■ **Neagu, N.,** Zürich, Switzerland

**Constraint Satisfaction Techniques for Agent-Based Reasoning**

2005. 172 pages. Softcover.
ISBN 978-3-7643-7217-0

■ **van Aart, C.,** Waalwijk, The Netherlands

**Organizational Principles for Multi-Agent Architectures**

2005. 216 pages. Softcover.
ISBN 978-3-7643-7213-2

■ **Vázquez-Salceda, J.,** Utrech University, The Netherlands

**The Role of Norms and Electr Institutions in Multi-Agent Systems**

2004. 292 pages. Softcover.
ISBN 978-3-7643-7057-2

■ **Moreno, A.,** Tarragona, Spai **Nealon, J.L.,** Oxford, U.K. (eds.

**Applications of Software Age Technology in the Health Care Domain**

2003. 212 pages. Softcover.
ISBN 978-3-7643-2662-3

■ **Calisti, M.,** Zürich, Switzerlar

**An Agent-Based Approach for Coordinated Multi-Provider Service Provisioning**

2002. 292 pages. Softcover.
ISBN 978-3-7643-6922-4

■ **Günter, M.,** Zürich, Switzerla

**Customer-based IP Service Monitoring with Mobile Softwa Agents**

2002. 168 pages. Softcover.
ISBN 978-3-7643-6917-0